ACCLAIM FOR ALMA GUILLERMOPRIETO

AND

LOOKING FOR HISTORY

"Powerful and well-written. . . . Guillermoprieto digs far beneath the glib stereotypes wielded by outsiders to come up with a sensitive portrait of a region grappling with change. [Her] judgments are plausible, her reporting scrupulous and often courageous."
—*The New York Times Book Review*

"Guillermoprieto has become the most important journalist of this hemisphere. . . . [She] employs her reporting method with unparalleled skill."
—*The Sunday Star-Ledger*

"Powerful . . . a literary gem . . . wonderfully written dispatches that capture the richness and intensity of Latin America's reality. Those wanting a feel for the spirit of Latin America or what lies behind the headlines will hardly find more vivid accounts of the region's recent history." —*The Miami Herald*

"Informative and perceptive. . . . Guillermoprieto has a keen eye and an intimate knowledge of notoriously tangled political situations. . . . Her sharp analysis of the events that have shaped the politics of [Latin America], combined with her conversational style, bring home the reality of this troubled part of the world." —*BookPage*

"With astounding energy, [Guillermoprieto] braves the snarls of politics and the perils of mountains and jungle to hack her way to the heart of the matter and lay out the facts for her reader. . . . A truly instructive work."
—*Kirkus Reviews* (starred)

"Elegant. . . . [Guillermoprieto's] great skill lies in combining wide reading and sympathetic understanding of Latin American perceptions with a knack for the illuminatingly off-beat interview."　　—*The Economist*

"Brilliant. . . . She deserves a wide readership."
—Carlos Fuentes

ALMA GUILLERMOPRIETO

LOOKING FOR HISTORY

Alma Guillermoprieto writes for *The New York Review of Books* and *The New Yorker* and for several publications in Latin America. Born in Mexico, she has lived there and in Central America, the United States, Colombia, and Brazil. She is the author of *Samba* (which was nominated for a National Book Critics Circle Award) and *The Heart That Bleeds*. Named a MacArthur Fellow in 1995, she has also received an Alicia Patterson fellowship, Columbia University's Maria Moors Cabot Prize, and the Latin American Studies Association Media Award. She lives in Mexico City.

LOOKING
FOR
HISTORY

VINTAGE BOOKS

A Division of Random House, Inc.

New York

LOOKING FOR HISTORY

DISPATCHES FROM LATIN AMERICA

ALMA GUILLERMOPRIETO

FIRST VINTAGE BOOKS EDITION, MARCH 2002

The Library of Congress has cataloged the Pantheon edition as follows:
Guillermoprieto, Alma, 1949–
Looking for history : dispatches from Latin America / Alma Guillermoprieto.
p. cm.
ISBN 0-375-42094-0
1. Latin America—History—20th century. 2. Mexico—Politics and government—1988–
3. Cuba—Social conditions—1959– 4. Violence—Colombia—History—20th century.
5. Guevara, Ernesto, 1928–1967. 6. Perón, Eva, 1919–1952. 7. Vargas Llosa, Mario, 1936–
I. Title.
F1414.2 .G773 2001 972'.0009'04—dc21 00-062382

Vintage ISBN: 0-375-72582-2

Contents

INTRODUCTION

The seventeen essays in this collection are an attempt to render visible to U.S. readers some of the more hidden and enigmatic aspects of Latin American history and conflict. They are, with two exceptions, stories about recent political events in the region. And they are predominantly about the three Latin countries with which the United States has been or is about to become most intensely involved: Cuba, Colombia, and Mexico. They are not stories about that relationship, however, but about the countries themselves, written in the conviction that Latin America has its own independent life.

This may seem an obvious statement, but it has not often been the view of policy-makers in the United States or of the political actors on the Latin American stage. Latin American history in the latter half of the twentieth century took place against the backdrop of the Cold War, and it is the grotesque case that hardly any political decision was taken either in Latin America or toward it during that time in which the region's own needs or history were the primary consideration. Instead, the decisions were informed by fantasies, which all too often appeared in the guise of ruthless pragmatism: communism must be stopped; world revolution must be achieved at any cost. In either case, cataclysm and/or salvation were nearly always perceived to be just around the corner.

Cuba was, of course, the great staging ground both for the Cold War fantasy and for a transforming dream that inspired years of revolutionary fervor and counterinsurrectionary horrors throughout the rest of the hemisphere. For long decades a great fog of wishful thinking clothed what actually took place on the island: Cuba was the greatest threat to U.S. security, or, it was a near-utopia whose citizens enjoyed unparalleled prosperity and spiritual freedom. When I returned to the island after a long absence, in 1998, I was shocked to realize that the emperor was dressed in rags. The three stories about Cuba in this collection are an account of that return.

In the 1960s, no other country produced as many Cuba-inspired revolutionary movements as Colombia, and nowhere else did the guerrillas survive as long. Strangely, though, the ferment in Colombia never moved policy-makers in the United States to the acts of mighty wrath that they unleashed elsewhere on the continent. There were no massacres condoned or covered up by Washington as in El Salvador, no insidious CIA coup promotion as in Chile, no international grandstanding against the growing Communist threat. Left to its own devices, and at the mercy of its perilous geography, Colombia became instead the primary supply center for illegal drugs, for which a great many citizens of the United States appear to have an insatiable hunger.

Inevitably, perhaps, the clandestine guerrilla armies and the illegal drug traders of Colombia eventually found each other in the remote Andean valleys and Amazonian riverways of their country and there embraced. It was left to the Clinton administration to attempt war on this alliance, though it is by no means clear that the architects of the new interventionist policy are any more knowledgeable about this contradictory nation than any of their predecessors were. The articles about Colombia in this collection are an attempt to lay out some basic facts about such an unfamiliar place, and to untangle some of the threads of its tempestuous history.

Mexico, in Alan Riding's exact description, is the United States' distant neighbor. The links between the two nations are geographic and economic—Mexico is the United States' second-largest trading partner—and they are also, increasingly, political and cultural: the great migratory flow from south to north is transforming U.S. demographics even as it empties out the Mexican countryside. Yet the demise of the once all-powerful regime that ruled Mexico for more than seventy years remains a mysterious event north of the border, and the great Indian uprising in Chiapas of 1994, which took Mexico itself utterly by surprise, is clothed, once again, in the trappings of fantasy. The section of this book that deals with Mexico is a revision of several articles written over the last six years about these upheavals, beginning with a brief account of the event that shook the very foundations of the regime of the Partido Revolucionario Institucional, or PRI: the assassination in 1994 of its presidential candidate, Luis Donaldo Colosio. It ends with an account of the most recent presidential elections, in which, for the first time in seven decades, the PRI lost. At this writing the victor, Vicente Fox, is attempting to forge the difficult political alliances without which his administration will be seriously hobbled in its attempt to modernize the country's political system.

Interspersed with the essays on these three countries so important in their different ways to the United States, the reader will find essays that are reflections on the life and times of three prominent Latin Americans. The first two, Eva Perón and Ernesto Guevara, are themselves embodied fantasies, individuals whose existence transformed history and inspired faith as perhaps no others have done in the last fifty years.

The third portrait is of the Peruvian novelist Mario Vargas Llosa, a writer who attempted a political career and failed—perhaps because he did not possess that intangible star quality, that ability to generate fantasies, that so many Latin Americans hope to find in their leaders. He lost his fateful run for the presidency to Alberto Fujimori, and the twists and turns of that presidential campaign tell us a great deal about the problems of institutionalizing democracy in countries where most people are very poor and sorely tried, and where the political climate too often veers between almost apocalyptic hope and the bitterest disillusion.

The list of acknowledgments for a book such as this is of necessity very long. I have been able to write, awkwardly and incompletely, only a small part of what I learned from a great many generous people—friends, academics, politicians, observers, and, of course, the protagonists of these stories. In Cuba, particularly, I was overwhelmed by the generosity and hospitality of everyone I came in contact with, and by the painful and earnest fashion in which each person, regardless of political conviction, sought to make sense of his or her life and at the same time remain fair. It seems best for the moment to leave out their names.

In Mexico, the list of those who helped includes Gloria Muñoz, Liliana Nieto del Río, Gerardo Magallón, Herman Bellinghausen, Tim Golden, Carmen Legorreta, Conrado Márquez, Stephen Ferry, Andrés Aubry, Angélica Inda, Eduardo Luengo Creel, Teresa Jardí, Ciro Gómez Leyva, Gabriel Guerra, Carlos Monsiváis, *mayor* Rolando, Gonzalo Infante, Luis de la Barreda, Julia Preston, Percy and Nancy Wood, and Anne Reid. I owe even more to the wonderful generosity and friendship of the Espinosa family, Trina Kleist, Jacinta Ilescas Cruz, Gladys Boladeras, Damian Fraser, and Bertha (Pitila) Navarro.

Among those who helped in Colombia are Alirio Bustos, Daniel Martínez, *compañera* Norma, Aureliano Monsalve, Mauricio Romero, Jaime Abello Banfi, and, as always, Marcela Caldas, Bernardo Gutiérrez, Margarita Monsalve, Salomón Kalmanowitz, Ramón Jimeno, and Juanita León. I cherish their friendship and support.

All the articles in this collection, written over the last six years, were originally published in somewhat different form in *The New Yorker* and *The New York Review of Books,* some as essays or reportage and some as book reviews. It is wonderful to have the opportunity once again to thank beloved friends—Bob Gottlieb, Gloria Loomis, and John Bennet—for making this book possible, and for making it so much better than I ever hoped. I also owe deep thanks to David Remnick at *The New Yorker,* who has been so generous and welcoming; to the glorious fact checkers, one and all; and to the endlessly helpful, gracious, and overworked staff at the *The New York Review of Books.* Most of these essays were written at the behest of Robert Silvers, who at the *Review* pushed and trusted me in equal measure. His ferocious energy and commitment to the value of the written word will always be an inspiration.

Alma Guillermoprieto
September 2000

LOOKING
FOR
HISTORY

EVA PERÓN

LITTLE EVA

Was she really beautiful? What did she look like? It is possible to stare for hours at the photographs—never enough of them—in the recent crop of Evita books and find no answers. Soon we will know that she looked exactly like Madonna, but for the moment it is possible to say only that once she had become Evita her image was that of a different order of being—of a Virgin, perhaps, or a saint. A flickering apparition with attributes rather than features: the radiant impact of the gold-colored hair, something haunted about the eyes, the lingering sad ecstasy of the smile. The posters, the photographs, the blurred documentary footage all confirm it: she was not a person but an embodied gesture.

Not in the early photographs, though. Here she is, for example, in a picture reproduced in *Eva Perón*, a new biography by Alicia Dujovne Ortiz,[1] which shows her in the days before her hairdresser discovered that history needed Evita to be a blonde. It is mid-1944, and, thanks in large part to certain skillfully wielded influences, the provincial actress Eva Duarte, possessed of an unreconstructed working-class accent and an unfailingly gauche manner, has obtained her first feature role, in a movie called *Circus Cavalcade*. In the promo shot, brunet ringlets surround a pale, slightly thin-lipped face. The nose has a hint of the ski jump, but the eyes are large and their expression is pleasant. A big bow is strategically placed over what was a famously flat chest, but it

1. Published in English as *Eva Perón: A Biography* (New York: St. Martin's, 1997).

does nothing to disguise her terrible posture. She projected no sexuality, and there is nothing in the photograph to indicate that Eva Duarte's public personality might have been memorable either—an impression, or lack of one, confirmed by the kindest word that critics ever used to describe her acting: "discreet." There is nothing in the image, certainly, to suggest transcendence.

And yet the sense we have of Eva Duarte's destiny is so strong by now that it is almost impossible to believe that at the time the picture was taken she did not know, as we do, that this bland and to all appearances untalented girl, born illegitimate and on a ranch, was soon to become Evita. It would have been logical for anyone with more ordinary ambitions to think instead that 1944 was already the crowning year of her life: she had a movie role, a nice apartment filled with knickknacks, a modest degree of name recognition, and a new military lover—a very important one—with whom she was passionately, overwhelmingly involved.

Because the meeting between Eva Duarte, aspiring *radionovela* actress, and Juan Perón, putschist colonel, is the stuff of legend, it is impossible to be completely certain of anything about it, including the date and the circumstances of their first encounter. By most accounts, including Perón's, it took place on January 22, 1944, and the occasion was a benefit for earthquake victims, sponsored by a group of army colonels who had overthrown the civilian government six months earlier. Eva Duarte, who had recently gone for months without acting in any of the radio soaps that were the mainstay of Argentine broadcasting, and who had in the past endured typically sordid casting-couch arrangements in order to get work, was working now, thanks to her new friend Lieutenant Colonel Aníbal Imbert, who was in charge of the post and telegraph offices (and communications in general) for the new regime. Imbert had got her the starring role in a new radio series, based on the lives of famous women in history—Isadora Duncan, Elizabeth I, Mme Chiang Kai-shek—but it was Eva alone who then, drawn to the populist rhetoric of the new regime and always looking for an opportunity to stand out, maneuvered herself into the position of spokeswoman for the Radio Association of Argentina, and into events like the earthquake benefit.

In *Eva Perón*, Alicia Dujovne recounts the various versions of how that fateful evening Eva Duarte found herself being led to one of two empty seats on the platform, next to Imbert, who was waiting for his friend Juan Perón. (The most amusing story comes from the benefit's emcee, Roberto Galán, who claims that Eva stood beneath the stage, tugged on his pants leg, and said, "Galancito, darling, introduce me. I want to recite a poetry.") Dujovne sensibly speculates that instead it may have been Imbert himself—by that time heartily sick of Eva's anxious, clutching personality—who introduced her to Perón, at an earlier party. But in the brilliant novel *Santa Evita*,[2] Tomás Eloy Martínez recounts history as it should have been, and as it was told to him long ago in Madrid by an aging Juan Perón: Eva's heart belonged to Perón even before they met. It had become clear that the colonel, who was in charge of labor relations, was emerging as the real authority in the new regime. He looked magnificent in uniform. His smile was benevolent and virile. His radio speeches had thrilled her. ("I am only a humble soldier who has been granted the honor of protecting the working masses of Argentina.") She was twenty-four, he forty-eight. On the platform, sitting next to Imbert, she turned her great dark eyes on Perón as he walked to his seat.

"Colonel."

"What is it, my girl?"

"Thank you for existing."

She got his attention. Perón was ambitious but lazy, wily but aloof, and interested, as life would prove, in few things besides himself, politics in relation to himself, and his French poodles (and a fourteen-year-old mistress he took on after Eva's death, to whom he wrote fond letters about the French poodles). But Eva could force herself into his hitherto sterile emotional life because from their first meeting she offered herself up to Perón as his

2. New York: Knopf, 1996.

worshiper, and from that moment virtually until the instant of her death, eight years later, she did nothing in public or in private that was not in some way an act of devotion to him, an oblation of frankincense and myrrh. *"Mi vida por Perón!"* she cried a thousand times before the roaring crowds, and then she died. There are parallels that could be drawn between her life and the lives of other obsessively ambitious women who have forced their way out of poverty and to fame through the skillful, untiring manipulation of their own images—Madonna, let us say—but instead popular memory finds parallels between Evita's life and the lives of the saints, because she did it all for someone else.

In life, Evita was and wished to be only an instrument of Perón. (In death, she took on a life of her own, but we will come to that.) Toward the end, someone wrote an autobiography for her (she was barely literate), and it was called what she called Perón in all her speeches: *My Reason for Living.*[3] If anything, she was even more effusive about her husband in private. Joseph Page, in his excellent introduction to the English-language edition of a second text ghostwritten for Evita, this one as she was dying, called *In My Own Words,*[4] quotes a letter she wrote Perón: "Tonight I want to leave you this perfume above all else so that you will know I adore you and if it is possible today more than ever because when I was suffering I felt your affection and goodness so much that until the last moment of my life I will offer [misspelled] it to you body and soul, since you know I am hopelessly in love with my dear old man." By most accounts, Perón was sexually indifferent. Dujovne assumes, without telling us why, that Eva Duarte was actually frigid. Yet there is no doubting the passionate and romantic nature of Eva's commitment to her husband. By a lucky accident of history, her passion was fueled by precisely the same emotions that drove millions of Argentines to what Eva eventually baptized *la fe peronista*—the Peronist faith.

The facts of Evita's early life coincide nicely with those of the

3. *La razón de mi vida* (Buenos Aires: Ediciones Peuser, 1952).
4. New York: New Press, 1996.

poor she came to represent: she was, like so many others, born of a destitute woman who found it expedient, and possibly gratifying, to take a wealthy and powerful lover. (Juan Duarte was a landowner and small-town caudillo, or political boss, in a rural area about ninety miles west of Buenos Aires, and he was properly married. Juana Ibarguren was a woman he spent many nights with and was the mother of five of Duarte's children, of whom Eva María, born in 1919, was the youngest.) Like so many children born of these arrangements in a country where upper-class snobbery reaches extremes of refinement and viciousness, Eva was humiliated by her bastard status. (Juana Ibarguren and her children, who lived in a one-room house, were kept away from Juan Duarte's elegant funeral, but were allowed to say a quick farewell to the corpse at the wake.) Eva migrated on her own from the sticks to Buenos Aires at age fifteen, and, like so many of the expanding capital's other new residents, she looked for opportunity and found it lacking. She shared with her class a gnawing, all-encompassing resentment that was the precise counterpart of the seething contempt the ruling class cultivated for the plebes. Most important, neither she nor her fellow poor were inclined to be fatalistic. The Argentina that Eva Duarte grew up in was a nation of recent immigrants—Italian anarchist farmers, Spanish socialist shopkeepers, conservative German merchants—who had brought their politics with them when they migrated, and who firmly believed that they deserved the better life they were willing to work so hard for.

Perón—himself born out of wedlock, and pursuing upward mobility through an army career—was their catalyst. He was a cynical politician who systematically played off his followers against one another, often with tragic results, and his authoritarian approach to government probably grew out of his intense admiration for Franco and Mussolini. It may well be the case that he (and Eva) provided shelter for Nazis fleeing Europe after the Axis collapse, in exchange for a significant part of the Third Reich's treasure—Dujovne works hard to try to prove it in her biography—but generations of Argentines have remained impervious to these accusations, because of what Perón gave them: a political movement that legitimated and ennobled the working poor, and a decisive restructuring of the state which—by nationalizing key resources, establishing generous social-welfare programs, and institutionalizing a crony relationship between organized labor and the government—transformed Argentina from a sugar daddy for the rich into a sugar daddy for the poor. Perón was only one of several upstart colonels when Evita thanked him for existing, and his speeches did not then, or ever, reveal the kind of substantial political thinking that gets translated into lasting programs or gets used to interpret reality in other parts of the world, but he cannot simply be written off as a demagogue. He had a vision of a free Argentina: a nation that under his *verticalista* guidance would steer clear of both sides in the Cold War, and in which law and order would prevail, government would be responsive to the needs of its citizens, and workers would get the respect their efforts deserved. In that sense, he was revolutionary, and Eva Duarte, like millions of others, responded instantly to his appeal. As for his aloof, diffident personality (he liked to describe himself as "a herbivorous lion"), it, too, was a virtue, for it turned him into an empty vessel that Evita could fill with her faith.

Eva Duarte's role in history was determined within months of her first encounter with the colonel. One day she was a source of hilarity for upper-class women, who made a point of tuning in to her "Famous Women" broadcasts. ("What a daily pleasure, this nasal voice who played [Catherine of Russia] with rural tango accents!" one said.) The next, she had secured her movie role in *Circus Cavalcade,* because she was already the established mistress of Juan Perón, a man not known for passion, who had nevertheless rented an apartment in Eva's building so that he could be near her without violating the moral code. His new lover was not easy or pleasant to live with—she threw tantrums, demanded in public that he marry her, and soon displayed her contempt for all but his most slavishly devoted political associates—yet despite these defects she was the perfect woman for him, because she pushed him beyond his own apathy. Within weeks, Perón had taken the measure of her political genius, and he sent her out on the hustings. He looked on approvingly as she forged her new public persona. Dujovne, whose insightful biography is marred by the lack of sources for material that is often controversial, and by an irritating Argentine penchant for psychobabble, is invaluable when she is narrating Evita's act of self-creation.

The clothes changed first, in 1945. Dujovne cites a recollection of Francisco Jamandreu, designer to the stars:

> "Do not think of me the way you think of your other clients," Eva would tell him. "From now on, I will have a dual personality. On the one side, I am the actress to whom you can give poufs, lamé, feathers, sequins. On the other, I am what the Big Shot wants me to be, a political figure. On May 1, I must accompany him to a demonstration. People will gossip, it will be the first appearance of the Duarte-Perón couple. What will you create for the occasion?"

Jamandreu settled on a double-breasted houndstooth suit with a velvet collar, so elegant and practical that even Eva Duarte could be taken seriously while sheathed in it.

Then came the hair. The first photograph of Eva as a blonde appeared in a magazine on June 1 of that same year. Dujovne writes:

> Since hair dyes had not yet been perfected, the color's ambition was, in fact, not to appear natural. It was a theatrical and symbolic gold, a gold that imitated the effect of the golden halos and backgrounds of the religious paintings of the Middle Ages. . . . From then on, she would polish and refine her personality by gradually eliminating all excessive ornaments: first the banana earrings, then the flowered dresses.

She wore the new look when she was stumping for Perón during the following months, and probably during the third week of October 1945—a week that decided the colonel's destiny. The other colonels who had overthrown the civilian government with him were now enraged by, among other things, his increasing prominence, his populist tendencies, and his impertinent mistress. They put him under arrest on October 13. There was a significant degree of support for the move, and Eva herself was mauled that day by middle-class university students. But on October 17, Perón's working-class followers descended on Buenos Aires from every part of the country, in numbers that even the wily colonel could not have expected. Whether they were organized by Evita remains a matter of debate. (The evidence indicates that they were not, but this is a conclusion that Peronists and anti-Peronists alike consider a heresy.) What is certain is that Perón himself did little except sit quietly in a room of the military hospital where he was being kept prisoner, considering whether he should marry Eva and get out of politics altogether. In short order, though, his enemies decided that the only thing to do in the face of the tumult was to release him and call for elections. These Perón won handily, with the constant help of the woman who was now known as Eva Duarte de Perón, because shortly after his October triumph, El Conductor, as he was now called, had at last married her. In exchange for his vow, she gave up her acting career.

If this were a story about a man, no one would be asking what color suit he wore to the inauguration, but this is a story about a Latin woman of the 1940s who was obsessively interested in clothing, jewelry, and self-presentation, and was also uncannily perceptive about what the people she wanted to address looked for in her. "The poor like to see me beautiful: they don't want to be protected by a badly dressed old hag." The transformation of Eva Duarte was almost complete, but mistakes were still being made. After Perón took power, he dispatched the First Lady on a goodwill tour of Europe, and she sent a ripple of delighted horror through Paris society by appearing at a reception in her honor in a strapless gold-lamé evening outfit worthy of a cocotte. But she returned to Buenos Aires with a full and judicious wardrobe on order from Christian Dior, and eventually her confessor,

Father Hernán Benítez, prevailed on her to sacrifice all makeup except lipstick. As Dujovne points out, the effect of this act of contrition was to make her timelessly fashionable. Then the same hairdresser who had made her blond pulled her hair tightly back from her pale, broad forehead, wove a braid, and bound it in a shimmering knot at the nape of her neck. And, finally, Eva María Duarte de Perón adjusted her name. It is unusual in Latin America for a woman to be known only by her husband's name, but she wanted to be called Eva Perón, a Perón in her own right. She had pared herself down to the essentials, and she had become one of the most powerful women in Argentina and in the world.

Evita did not live on in memory because of the way she looked but because she looked beautiful, bejeweled, and radiant while consuming herself in a flame of devotion to her husband and the poor. The dramatic change in her appearance has historical significance, and Dujovne does a fine job of linking Evita's outward changes to the development of her personality, but all the author's laborious research cannot account for the essential transformation of Eva Perón: from a pushy, selfish twenty-six-year-old starlet (her age when Juan Perón first came to power) to a flagellant compelled to take on the suffering of an entire nation and make it her own. Was Evita really still Eva Duarte after she managed to give the slip to that telltale accent, and was she more sincere when she insinuated to a society lady that she would love the woman's diamond necklace as a present or when she gave her jewels away to the poor? Was the suffering mother of all Argentines the same as the ruthless politician? If she wasn't, then who died? (Some, of course, think she is still alive; the possibility of her reincarnation is a rumor that flares periodically through Argentina.) It is, at any rate, as difficult for those who believe that her spirit lives to describe her as it is for those who knew and loathed her in the flesh: She was grasping, shrewish, and so calculating that she orchestrated her acts of charity to distract attention from all the money she and her husband salted away in Switzerland. Or else she underwent a spiritual conversion when she met Perón that allowed her to channel the voice of the working masses. But it may be that she underwent a spiritual conversion and remained grasping, shrewish, et cetera. And also ignorant. If Perón had few ideas about how to use his country's wealth to generate real national prosperity, or how to create a true body politic, Eva, with her youth, her sixth-grade rural education, and her recent frivolous past, had none. She did what she could with the irresistible possibility that was granted her to do good, while living out a fantasy that dated back to the days when she left her hometown for the capital, impelled by the dream of becoming like her idol, Norma Shearer, in the role of Marie Antoinette.

The Peronist myth is that she and the poor identified with each other because Eva too had been poor. But one can wonder if it was perhaps that the poor identified with her rage and fed it, in turn, with their love, and whether it was the unbearable tension at the crux of these emotions that led her to die. Eva Perón died, in 1952, of uterine cancer, because she had refused to have an operation when the disease was first diagnosed, in 1950. She didn't have time, she said. She was too busy rallying recalcitrant politicians to support the Peronist reforms, lobbying Perón himself to push a women's-voting-rights act through Congress, and extolling Perón across the country in speeches whose flavor had not a little of the lachrymose *radionovela* actress she once was ("I come from the people; this red heart that bleeds and cries and covers itself with roses when it sings") but whose intensity was overwhelming.

All this she did in her spare time. Juan Perón, after taking office, slept calmly through his nights and lived an orderly existence, presiding over the government as it is a man's business to do. His wife worked through the evenings, slept little, and in the morning—tailored, perfumed, and decked out in diamonds—set out for the Labor Ministry, where she had a suite of offices but no official position. (Eva never would have a government job.) In the ministry's Great Hall, *los pobres* (*"mis pobres"*) were already waiting. The same scene was staged day after day: a line of supplicants, among them the lame, the halt, the destitute; a flock of anxious minions armed with notepads; and behind the vast desk, radiant and ever gracious, the Lady Eva. Did an old crone need dentures? Done. Did a timorous couple come to beg for wedding garments? *Hecho.* When the money ran out, she unfastened a diamond clip and handed it over. Perón had a horror of physical contact. Evita kissed lepers. She also took lice-infested urchins to the official residence for a rest cure and bathed them herself; started a union for domestic workers; and set up hospitals, children's homes, and a home for girls who traveled to the big city and found themselves penniless, as she once had.

Joseph Page writes that, even as Eva's health declined, the Eva Perón Foundation—a conduit set up by Evita for her multiple social works—grew into a "gigantic enterprise dominating virtually all public as well as private charitable activity and extending into the fields of education and health." Dujovne, noting that no charge of corruption against the foundation has ever been substantiated, imaginatively counters another charge: that its institutions—the provincial girls' home, for example, in which each floor was decorated in a different style (*provinciano,* fake English, faux Louis XV)—were merely lavish charity. The "fundamental idea that Evita hammered into the heads of the humiliated and the downtrodden" by practically forcing them to sleep in beds with embroidered sheets, Dujovne writes, was that they deserved such beds.

From the third year of Perón's first presidential term, Eva was dying, and death's proximity made her more vehement. All the fame and glory she had accumulated had done nothing to appease her fundamental resentment. She saw enemies everywhere. She acquired some newspapers and closed down others she couldn't control. She flew into rages in closed Senate sessions and saw to it that government officials who were anything less than obsequious lost their jobs. She fought hard to persuade her husband that the leaders of a conspiracy against him should be shot. (He refused.) In the ghostwritten *In My Own Words,* someone wrote words very like her own: "Those who speak of sweetness and of love forget that Christ said, 'I have come to bring fire over the earth and what I most want is that it burn!' " and "Fanaticism turns life into a permanent and heroic process of dying; but it is the only way that life can defeat death."

Perhaps she did consciously decide to die so that she might live. When her health broke down completely and she was forced to agree to an operation, it was too late. Even as she entered the last stages of the disease, though, she was changing. Perón was suddenly less important than the cause, and, despite having said so many times "I am nothing," she now desperately wanted the vice presidential slot on the ticket for Perón's reelection. Nevertheless, when a surging, beseeching multitude—probably the largest gathering in Argentina's history—asked that she join her husband on the ticket, at an electrifying public meeting on August 22, 1951, Perón vetoed her candidacy. He probably sensed that the woman he had always described as his invention was about to break free of his influence, and yet once more Eva obeyed him. Even though she had less than a year to live, it was far too late for her jealous husband to expunge her name. All Argentina knew her no longer as Eva Perón but as Evita only. It was one name, like a saint's, but in the diminutive, like that of someone fragile whom people hold dear. She was weakening visibly. She weighed eighty pounds.

Her last act of will involved yet another manipulation of her own body: in order to attend Perón's second inauguration when she was already too weak to stand, she had a plaster support made in which she was encased, upright, during the open car ride, the device covered by a long fur coat. (It may have included an arm prop, for she waved to the crowd the whole way.) On July 26, 1952, while tens of thousands of her distraught worshipers knelt and prayed that she might live, Evita died. She was thirty-three.

Three years later, the life gone from his movement, Juan Perón was overthrown. The herbivorous lion lacked the will to arm the workers with the machine guns and automatic pistols that Evita had bought from Prince Bernhard of the Netherlands for just such an occasion. Instead, Perón left quietly, bound for his long, comfortable exile in Franco's Spain.

The following is all true, supported by recorded fact and presented almost straightforwardly in *Santa Evita*, Tomás Eloy Martínez's fictional chronicle of Eva Perón's afterlife: A Spanish embalmer, commissioned by Perón even before Evita's death, transformed her corpse into a radiant effigy. (Ever conscious of her image, Evita on her deathbed requested a postmortem manicure, to change the color of her nail varnish from red to natural.) Peronists worshiped this figure until Perón was overthrown, in 1955, when right-wing military officers snatched the body away. And, according to the book, the embalmer had already made several copies of the body, which for the next fifteen years were part of a shell game played out in Argentina and in Europe. The generals who overthrew Perón found it unchristian to discard the real body, but they feared its power to stir multitudes against them, so, Martínez writes, the copies were deployed around Argentina until a safe, anonymous burial ground could be found for Evita's corpse. At one point, it was entrusted to an army major, and he put it in his armoire. One evening, he heard steps approaching in the dark and fired his gun lethally at the intruder. The victim turned out to be his pregnant wife. The chief of operations for the abduction of the corpse went mad with the body in his care. Every time he transferred Evita to a new hiding place, flowers and lighted candles appeared there. He watched over her so obsessively that he was finally removed to an insane asylum by his alarmed superiors, and in the late fifties they got the body to Italy and into a funeral plot in a Milanese cemetery, under an assumed name.

In 1971, Perón was living in Madrid with his new wife, Isabelita, a former cabaret dancer with an incongruous schoolmarmish air, and with her private sorcerer, José López Rega. As part of a peace overture to the deposed leader, whose movement continued to flourish in his homeland even as the very mention of his name was forbidden, the military returned to him Evita's bedraggled corpse. Isabelita combed its hair, the original embalmer restored it, and Perón put it in his attic. It appears to be true—at least, reliable sources claim that it is, and in *Santa Evita* Martínez makes

it impossible to believe that it could not have been—that López Rega then staged a ceremony in which Isabelita lay on top of the coffin while he tried to transmigrate the soul of the deceased Mrs. Perón into the living one.

In the end, Evita—so desperate not to be forgotten, so unaware of how impossible that would prove—didn't get the mausoleum she had wanted and had helped design, which was to be the size of Napoleon's tomb. (We know, however, that she got the equivalent: her operatic life was turned into the rock opera that is soon to be a major motion picture.) By the time of Perón's official return to Argentina from his Spanish exile, in 1973, he was ambivalent about Eva's fame, if not downright resentful of her, and wary of her Evitista followers, who had taken to chanting at mass rallies that if Evita lived she would be a guerrilla, and were about to go underground themselves. He did not bring the long-wandering body home with him.

The leftist Peronist guerrillas' archenemy would be the fiendish warlock López Rega, whom Perón appointed minister of social welfare, and who from that position set up the first of the organized death squads that would eventually undermine Argentina. Perón ruled with Isabelita occupying the vice presidency he had once denied Eva, and she succeeded him upon his death, in 1974. Isabelita immediately had Evita flown back from Spain so that Evita and Perón could lie in state side by side. But Perón had not wanted to be buried with Eva. (He never called her Evita.) He was placed in the Perón family crypt, where, in 1987, vandals broke open the tomb in order to saw off his hands.

Eva's still luminous corpse was taken to the Duarte family crypt, in Buenos Aires's fashionable Recoleta Cemetery. Having survived the array of indignities inflicted upon it, it has been allowed to lie in peace for nearly twenty years. Beyond Argentina, however, Evita's life has evidently just begun. It is not the same Eva Perón who coursed so tenaciously through her country's history that the world craves, but it is Evita all the same: heroic and fragile, grasping and motherly, parthenogenetic—like all real heroines—but in the service of a man, rebellious but condemned

by fate, angry but submissive to that fate. A shimmering figure that comes in and out of focus endlessly in order to allow us the hypnotic speculation that all true stars elicit: What did she really look like? Could she have looked like me?

—December 2, 1996

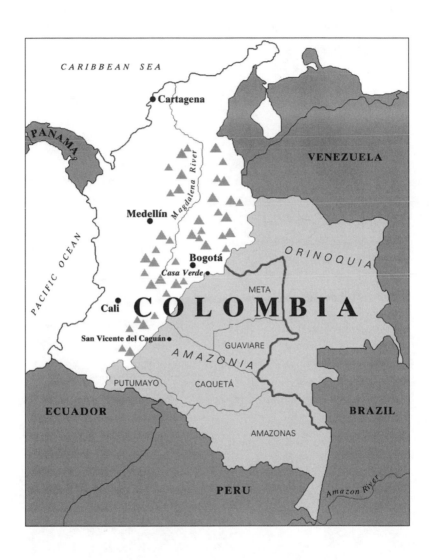

OUR NEW WAR IN COLOMBIA

The Clinton administration is proposing an escalation in United States foreign aid to Colombia so large that it will predictably alter the course of domestic politics and internal violence in that country. Colombia is already the third-largest recipient of U.S. foreign aid, after Israel and Egypt, having received $289 million in 1999. As the current aid bill now stands before Congress, the government of President Andrés Pastrana would receive $1.574 billion in direct economic assistance during the next three years. About one-fifth of the funds ($274 million) would be spent on assistance in economic development and general improvements in the country's legal and human rights situation. The rest of the money would arrive in Colombia in the form of military training funds and equipment.

This military help is being presented as indispensable to the fight against the cultivation of coca leaf in southern Colombia and the consequent export of cocaine to the United States. Most of the parties involved—the State Department officials who will shepherd the aid package through Congress, the gung-ho young men in the U.S. embassy in Bogotá who will get to supervise all the hardware, the Colombian army brass who are waiting for the assistance with the fervor of a cargo cult—claim, officially at least, that the funds are not intended for use in the war the Colombian state has been fighting for forty years against the world's most entrenched guerrillas. The question is how such use is to be avoided.

Colombia, which has a population of just under 40 million, is a country approximately the size of Central Europe. It is divided roughly into five regions: the lush Caribbean and Pacific coasts; the two-pronged Andean range, traversed by the Magdalena River Valley; the eastern grasslands, Orinoquia; and the jungle lowlands, Amazonia, that extend south to the Amazon River, where Colombia borders Brazil. Bogotá (population 6.4 million) and most of the prosperous cities, including Medellín, are perched in the mountains. Here the population is mostly white and mestizo. In the rich coastal plains and in the Magdalena River Valley, many people are black and mulatto. A small Indian population is scattered in native communities throughout the country.

Fewer than 2 million people live in the grasslands and the jungle, but between them these adjoining areas account for more than half the national territory—that is to say, an area roughly the size of France. There are almost no roads—dirt or otherwise—in this part of the country, and it is in fact such uncharted territory that maps from the national geographic institute still show the legend "Insufficient Relief Data" printed over large areas. Most of these two regions' inhabitants are recent arrivals: land-hungry peasants who carved out clearings for themselves over the last half-century or so. It is here, in the outermost regions of the *departamentos* of Putumayo, Caquetá, Meta, Guaviare, and Amazonas, that the coca-growing boom has taken place in the last decade.

The U.S. military funds, if approved, will be used for drug interdiction operations and for a special antinarcotics brigade, and also for Blackhawk helicopters, speedboats, and planes in which to transport the brigade's soldiers to the coca fields hidden in the jungle. Here troops will provide protection for police department fumigation teams, whose job it is to spray nontoxic herbicide on the illegal crops. Why should 2,000 or so highly trained and equipped soldiers be needed? Because in these parts of the country, the coca farmers are protected by an army of guerrillas, as many as 20,000 in total, who have been waging war on the Colombian state with increasing success. It is here, in the midst of this guerrilla territory, that the Colombian military has built headquarters for the new brigade, one battalion of which was trained last year with the help of U.S. military advisers. It is here that, against all the odds, the violent convergence of guerrillas and U.S. aid, U.S.-trained troops, and U.S. advisers is, according to the Clinton administration, not supposed to happen.

*

In August of 1986, I traveled with a Colombian writer and a local television team to the headquarters of the Fuerzas Armadas Revolucionarias de Colombia, or FARC, the largest, oldest, and richest guerrilla group in Colombia. At the time, it was only one of at least a dozen militant armed organizations. After some twenty years of fighting, a truce with the FARC had been declared by the government of Belisario Betancur, and our trip was one result. In response to the truce, the FARC had created a legal political party, the Unión Patriótica, and at its makeshift office in Bogotá a few small groups of journalists were able to negotiate expeditions to Casa Verde, the guerrilla headquarters in the *departamento* of Meta. I knew very little about the guerrillas or about Colombia at the time. It was surprising to discover, for example, that our destination was barely sixty miles from the capital as the crow flies. It was even more astonishing to learn that for years the army had been unable to dislodge the FARC from that nearby stronghold.

I understood why, though, as soon as we began our trip: we drove through the night from Bogotá over impossibly bumpy and steep roads to the town of Sumapaz, which sits on the slope of the Andes that opens southward into the jungle. From that point some members of our group were provided with splaybacked mounts, while those of us deemed hardiest by our guide—a guerrilla who happened to be a renegade priest—were invited to walk. At more than 10,000 feet above sea level, we trudged across the *páramo* of Sumapaz, a breathtaking expanse of icy swamp that seems to sit on the top of the world. Once, when a persistent freezing rain cleared, we were able to see the tips of snow-capped volcanoes more than one hundred miles away, and a double rainbow in a canyon at our feet. Around us we saw bizarre *frailejones,* which look like stubby, furry palms, and orchids and tree ferns, wild ducks and occasional herds of sheep. At night taciturn shepherds shared their tiny, freezing homesteads with us, and we lay wide-eyed in our sleeping bags through the night, praying for dawn to arrive so that we could recover a little warmth by moving through the icy drizzle. The *páramo* was inhabited, but there were no roads, no schools, no electricity, no sign at all that the state knew or cared about these citizens.

By the third day, mounts had been found for everyone, and the poor beasts struggled down canyons and across foaming rivers with us, then up again, then down, down, down into lush cloud forest. In a clearing we came upon a small community of polite, efficient youths in uniform, including many young women. Their barracks were well constructed. There was a campaign hospital and a spotless butcher shop, and what I recall as a rudimentary schoolhouse. A stream had been dammed and channeled to provide water for the common kitchen and the laundry area, and these gray waters were used, in turn, for latrines that can fairly be described as delightful, for they were raised on stilts above the running water, and were cozy and immaculate. I was taken upstream to another cabin perched above the riverflow, where I was left alone with a cauldron of hot water to bathe and change into clean clothes. And then at last my colleagues and I were taken into the presence of the leaders of the FARC, Jacobo Arenas and Manuel Marulanda.

The legendary Marulanda—more commonly known as "Tiro-fijo," or Sureshot—founded the FARC and remains to this day its military leader. Now seventy-two, he has the distinction of being the world's oldest living guerrilla. Jacobo Arenas, who died in 1990, was the cofounder and chief ideologue of the FARC, having joined forces in his early, Communist youth with the landless rebels and converted them to Marxism. At the time of our visit he was sixty-two years old.

One of the mysteries of the FARC's success, I decided after our first meeting, was how it had grown and endured despite the total absence of charismatic leaders. Jacobo Arenas was visually impenetrable, permanently wrapped as he was in a military cap, dark glasses (his eyesight was weak), and a thick woolen scarf that seemed to have lived with him for as long as the war had lasted. He was friendly (he offered immediately to play a game of Scrabble with us) and starved for conversation, but his own was hardly scintillating, even though he proudly described himself as an intellectual. Mostly, it seemed to us, he was obsessed with plots against him and his forces—bizarre plots involving CIA offers and infiltrators, government booty for his head, all-seeing antennae directed from great heights against Casa Verde, gifts of Chinese urns wired for sound. Given the realities of the Cold War and the CIA, his tales may well have been true, but the narrative was so fervid that a colleague and I could not shake off the impression of having been submerged in someone's delirium.

Marulanda was a different sort of character. He lived in his own little compound a short walk from the central headquarters, surrounded by an elite guard. Although we knew that he was in charge of military training and combat operations, he acted as if his main concerns were the chickens and the vegetable patch in his front yard. Stocky, almost irritatingly modest and of few words, he carried on one shoulder the white fringed towel worn by the rural people, the *campesinos.* Sometimes he used it to cover his head against the sun. Sometimes he took it off to swat a fly or two. He gave us a rather sketchier version of a discourse we had already had from Arenas (who pointed out a little too often that although Marulanda might be a *campesino,* he liked to read books).

In Colombia, Marulanda instructed us, the proletariat and the *campesinos* were allies in the struggle against imperialism and the unjust and oligarchic national state. The FARC fought for justice and equality. Although initially *campesinos* like Marulanda himself might have joined the fight only in order to defend their land, they were increasingly *concientizados,* and were now fully involved in the long, arduous struggle for socialism. When I tried to draw him out on his battle exploits, the conversation languished. "What about this scar?" I asked, pointing to a dent above one eyebrow. "I got that when my mother asked me to grind some cocoa beans and a screw in the cocoa mill flew off," he replied. Our group of visitors ended up spending much more time in Arenas's snug little cabin, where Arenas was happy to chat about old times and national politics—although it strikes me now that for someone with such frail access to communication and political information, he was remarkably uncurious about whatever news we might have had to offer.

In fairness to Arenas, he was concerned that his entire organization, from the leadership down, was so limited in its contacts with the world. He himself had not set foot in Bogotá for twenty years, he pointed out, and most of his troops had never done so. He knew the world was changing. And though he insisted that the truce and the fitful peace conversations the Betancur government had initiated did not deceive him, that the FARC expected only war and would never lay down its arms, perhaps he saw the creation of the Unión Patriótica—the legal party that would soon be contending in national elections—as a way of opening the FARC to the part of the country that was not rural.

Certainly, if the legal party had been allowed to survive, the FARC might at least have become aware of the enormous disconnect between the words with which it described Colombia and the way nonguerrilla Colombians perceived themselves. But a campaign of terror against the Unión Patriótica, and against the left in general, was unleashed simultaneously with Betancur's offer of peace. In 1988, when Colombians were first allowed to elect their own mayors, the Unión Patriótica participated, and won eighteen mayoralties out of about a thousand. Thirteen of these mayors were subsequently assassinated, often after having been forced to resign. No one has ever been charged with these murders, but it is widely assumed that members of the military, which has historically operated more or less independently of the chief executive, and sometimes at loggerheads with it, played a role.

In 1991, on the same day that a national convention charged with drafting a new constitution held its first session, the FARC headquarters where we had visited with Arenas and Marulanda was at long last bombed and overrun by the army—a valid military goal whose timing was evidently political. For all practical purposes, the Unión Patriótica was now dead, peace talks had been definitely suspended, and the FARC was on an all-out war footing again. By 1992, 3,500 UP militants and leaders of the legal party, including two presidential candidates, had been assassinated (although only a handful of those murders have ever been brought to trial). The guerrillas had lost nearly all of their urban, better-educated, politically minded leaders, and Arenas's paranoia had been brought to the seething point shortly before he died.

We left the FARC headquarters after only three days, rather stunned by the hardship we had been allowed to experience, which was only the palest reflection of the lifelong hardship endured by *campesinos* who may have decided that life with the guerrillas at least afforded some possibility—of revenge, of hope for the future, of camaraderie. And we were stunned too by the accounts of the bugged Chinese vases and by the cheerful discipline among the young men and women in the camp, as well as by the utter lack of political imagination we had found in Arenas and Marulanda, and the paradox of their great capacity to endure.

A conversation with Arenas stayed with me. I had wondered aloud what more the FARC troops could do, other than sit in their various camps—there were twenty-seven permanent military units, or *frentes,* at the time—staging occasional ambushes and worrying about the CIA. They had been doing this for the better part of twenty years, after all. When would the revolution finally get under way? "When the subjective and objective conditions ripen," Arenas answered imperturbably. But was this not, I persisted, rather like standing on a street corner in Bogotá on a Friday night, during rush hour and in the middle of the pouring rain, waiting for a taxi to come by? What if a taxi never came? What if conditions never ripened, what then? Arenas merely looked at me wryly.

The conversation has stayed with me because at this moment the FARC has sixty *frentes* of well-trained, well-armed, and well-

equipped young men and women operating throughout the country, engaging the Colombian military in combat, overrunning army
bases and police stations, taking prisoners, inflicting casualties,
bringing down helicopters, controlling and holding territory, and
holding the country hostage. Most guerrilla movements speak of
their infinite patience and act precipitately, but Jacobo Arenas's
FARC proved itself willing to bide its time. Watching recent television news reports in Bogotá, with their nightly quota of roadblocks, power pylon blowups, pitched battles a few dozen miles
from the city, and civilian casualties, it could seem as if the taxi
had arrived at last.

*

The motor that jump-started the guerrillas into a new phase also
energized the official Colombian economy in those same years;
this was, of course, cocaine. How and why cocaine became the illegal intoxicant of choice in the United States is a chronicle that
remains to be told. But the first American who suggested to a
Colombian cocaine hustler that he could find buyers for his product if the hustler could find a way to get it stateside ignited a fire
that has consumed tens of thousands of Colombian lives. A small
marijuana boom in the sixties preceded the cocaine explosion.[1]
Then the fashion in intoxicants switched to cocaine, which is
manufactured from the tealike coca leaf. Masticated or brewed,
coca has been consumed for centuries in the Andes as a cure for
colic, altitude sickness, and hangovers, and as a palliative for
hunger. Traditionally, it has been grown by Indian communities
who hold it sacred, and its sale—by the bushel in open-air markets or in boxed tea bags in city stores—is legal in Bolivia and
Peru. (Coca-Cola Company representatives still visit the Bolivian markets once a year to buy the key ingredient in their secret
formula.)

Colombia, which has a much smaller indigenous population

---

1. No one has described it better than Laura Restrepo in her thrilling and historically accurate novel *Leopard in the Sun* (New York: Crown, 1999).

than Bolivia or Peru, used to cultivate less coca, and for many years it grew what was considered an inferior product—meaning that the Colombian leaf produced a less potent alkaloid. But Colombia had a lackadaisical government, uncharted riverways, and a tradition of smuggling that dated back to colonial days. A small but flourishing illegal trade in marijuana, emeralds, and pre-Hispanic artifacts had kept smuggling techniques up to date, and by the early eighties non-Indian hustlers, many of them from the prosperous industrial city of Medellín, had consolidated their hold on the manufacture of cocaine from coca leaf, and on the export of refined cocaine to the United States. Among other things, these middlemen had figured out how to smuggle acetone and ether from the United States—precursor chemicals, as they are called, without which cocaine alkaloid cannot be extracted from the leaf.

By the end of the decade the illegal manufacture and export of cocaine had turned into a bonanza. Cocaine accounted for around 5 percent of the Colombian national product, according to calculations by Salomón Kalmanowitz, an economist who is currently on the board of the Banco de la República (the local equivalent of the Federal Reserve). "In arming the population, creating strong criminal incentives—crime pays really well!—fomenting corruption, financing both sides of the war, and destroying personal security," Kalmanowitz says, the boom had highly distorting and destructive effects on the national economy. But the fact is that Colombia had found what most developing countries lack, a cheap crop that can produce the levels of employment, return on investment, and national growth that only industrial goods normally provide. Construction soared, the service sector exploded, antiques dealers thrived, airline companies expanded their routes, artists made a more than decent living, and, beginning in 1992, many *campesinos* also felt less gnawed by hunger.

This last effect was a direct consequence of the "War on Drugs" decreed by President George Bush. In the late 1980s, the State Department and the Drug Enforcement Administration coordinated a successful antidrug campaign with the governments of

Bolivia and Peru: vast coca plantings were sprayed out of existence in both countries' Andean foothills; under U.S. guidance, Bolivian and Peruvian army planes began shooting down unauthorized aircraft entering their airspace. But demand for cocaine had grown, not eased, in the United States and around the world. Seeking safer territory for the unceasingly profitable trade, Colombian drug exporters began to sponsor coca plantings in their own uncharted jungles, and they financed a successful search for a variety of coca plant that would produce high levels of alkaloid in hot, lowland conditions. Seeking a better livelihood, peasants from all over the country flocked to the jungle *departamentos* of Meta, Putumayo, and Caquetá. And the FARC guerrillas were with them.

In a small town in Caquetá in January of the year 2000, I talked with a spokesman for the FARC, who explained the guerrillas' approach to the illegal drug trade this way: "For us, a *campesino* who plants coca is no different from one who plants cocoa," he said. "They both live off the land. We say that coca cultivation is no good, and we've established norms: they must plant two hectares of food crops for every hectare of coca. But what we can't do is deny the *campesinos* the right to grow this crop, because from the government on down, everybody in Colombia lives off coca."

What the guerrillas really can't do, apparently, is deny themselves the right to improve their own situation. Running even a small guerrilla army is expensive, after all, especially if all weapons and supplies must be acquired illegally and smuggled in. It did not take long for the FARC to notice that *campesinos* could use protection from the city types who paid them to grow coca, not to mention from government antidrug patrols.

During the same period that the Colombian traffickers were consolidating their supremacy in the world drug market, the guerrillas worked out a policy. "We don't look after coca fields, we don't grow coca, and we don't transport it," the official spokesman claimed. "But we do charge taxes, just as we do on everything else. Truckers [who drive through FARC territory] have to pay taxes. Shopkeepers [who operate in FARC territory] have to pay taxes. And the growers do too." The guerrillas, who see themselves as the legitimately established authority in areas they control militarily, levy taxes on both the sale and transport of coca (and recently also of opium paste from poppy fields in the highlands). In exchange, the *campesinos* expect them to guarantee that they all get paid, and paid equally, and that the money they receive is in some proportion to the product's market value. Estimates of the income derived by the FARC from this arrangement vary between $200 million and $600 million a year.

The transaction the FARC spokesman described—taxes in exchange for a protective armed presence—includes in his telling only two parties: growers and guerrillas. But it is hard to avoid the conclusion that a large and belligerent antigovernment organization can prove extremely useful to the drug lords as well. At the very least, there is a situation on the ground of peaceful coexistence between the guerrillas and the people who control the drug trade. Perhaps the guerrillas are telling the truth when they say there is no explicit agreement, and that the two sides never even come into contact. Another possibility is that the guerrillas don't merely look the other way when the little bimotor planes land on improvised airstrips in the jungle to pick up their cargo, or when motorboats bring in chemical engineers to tinker with extraction procedures in clandestine laboratories. Perhaps they unload some automatic rifles for themselves and the odd antiaircraft gun as well.

Whoever paid for the guns, there were enough for a force that has tripled, at least, since the bonanza in the jungle. The FARC's sixty military *frentes* are spread out through every region in the country, including the outskirts of Bogotá. In one or several of these, the guerrillas are holding the 500 soldiers and police officers they have taken captive since they began overrunning army bases and police stations in 1996. The word in the countryside is that one eats better in the guerrilla army than at home, and there is general agreement that the FARC controls or has strong influence in about a third of the one thousand or so municipal districts into which Colombia is divided—meaning that, at the very least, the organization has a say in who gets elected mayor in these districts and how municipal funds are spent.

*

The tacit agreement between drug traffickers and guerrillas in the southern half of the country is surprising only because in the northern part of Colombia the two sides are busy killing each other. Or at least it is fair to say that the various right-wing armed associations who fight the guerrillas—*paramilitares,* or *autodefensas*—depend on drug money for their machine guns and uniforms just as the FARC does.

The *paramilitares* first sprang up, like soldiers grown from dragons' teeth, in regions where the guerrillas made the mistake of kidnapping the wrong people. In the days before the FARC started taxing cocaine, they survived in large part off income derived from abducting, or threatening to abduct, ranchers and businessmen. Kidnapping as an illegal economic activity has a long history in Colombia. Many drug traffickers, for example, got their start-up capital through kidnapping and continued to use it as an additional source of income and power.[2]

It is the armed left, however, that has turned kidnapping into one of Colombia's widespread horrors. Colombia experts estimate that the FARC still derives as much as half its income from kidnappings. Another guerrilla group, the Ejército de Liberación Nacional, which kidnapped both a planeload of passengers and all the worshipers in a church in Cali last year, subsists almost entirely off extortion. In recent years the guerrillas have

2. The best account of a kidnap victim's terrorized life in captivity is to be found in Gabriel García Márquez's *News of a Kidnapping* (New York: Knopf, 1997), about the victims of the trafficker Pablo Escobar. Escobar, the most notorious of the Medellín traffickers, was killed in 1993 at the climax of a national manhunt. There is general agreement that his death, and the subsequent arrest of the leaders of a rival cartel in the city of Cali, led to a fragmentation of the drug trade, with no single leader aspiring since then to the kind of total control exercised by Escobar.

increased their efficiency in two ways. They "buy" kidnap victims from ordinary criminal organizations that do not have safe hiding places, as the guerrillas do in the wilderness, and they set up roadblocks on major highways, at which drivers' licenses are checked against a computer listing of all the bank accounts in the country.

At the beginning of the eighties, however, the guerrillas started kidnapping the relatives of drug traffickers, a drastic miscalculation. In response, the drug traffickers created and financed a group, called Muerte a los Secuestradores, or Death to the Kidnappers, which appears to have worked closely with the military to hit back at the guerrillas by murdering anyone suspected of associating or sympathizing with them. In 1981, in the mining town of Segovia, the FARC kidnapped the father of a small-time drug and emerald dealer called Fidel Castaño, a crime that would turn out to have fateful consequences.

According to the accounts of Fidel and his younger brother Carlos, the guerrillas—former friends of the family—demanded a ransom far beyond the Castaño family's ability to pay. The brothers offered what they could and were rejected. Fidel, in what Carlos would later describe as "a mistake," then wrote the kidnappers, stating that if the family came up with more funds "it would be exclusively to fight against you." According to a subsequent account by Fidel, his father, who had been held tied to a tree by a long rope for many days, slammed his head against the tree trunk until he dropped to the ground and there "was left to die" by the guerrillas, presumably of a heart attack. According to published accounts by Carlos, the father was killed by the guerrillas after the Castaños failed to come up with the ransom money.

The details matter a great deal to many people these days—not the least the FARC—because, according to a survivor I interviewed in 1989, in 1983 a group of men under orders from Fidel Castaño moved like a scythe through the riverside villages near Segovia where Castaño believed his father had been held, pulling babies out of their mothers' arms and shooting them, nailing a child to a plank, impaling a man on a bamboo pole, hacking a woman to pieces with a machete. By the time Castaño's men were finished, there were 22 dead. It was the first time since the brutal civil war known as La Violencia—from 1945 to 1965—that a massacre of such size had taken place in Colombia.

The massacre was the beginning of an assassination campaign that since then has left many thousand civilians dead in villages suspected of harboring guerrillas. Before his own death a few years ago, Fidel Castaño organized his hit men into a group called Autodefensas Campesinas de Córdoba y Urabá, or ACCU. His successor was his younger brother, Carlos, who turned the organization into a tightly disciplined combat group and formed an alliance with similar organizations throughout the country, calling it the Autodefensas Unidas de Colombia. In a recent television interview, Carlos Castaño claimed that his organization now has 11,200 troops. This figure is twice the usual estimate, but it is easy to believe the Autodefensas leaders when they say that they wish their numbers were growing a little more slowly, because, although there are more guerrillas and guerrilla sympathizers to exterminate with every passing day, controlling so many volunteers is tricky.

I had the opportunity recently to talk at length with a woman whom I will call Rosa, who is closely connected with the high command of the antiguerrilla ACCU. She was arrested not long ago, and she agreed that I could visit her at the detention center. (The office of the current Colombian prosecutor general, Alfonso Gómez Méndez, has aggressively pursued investigations of paramilitary crimes, and there are now six hundred people in jail, accused of collaborating in *autodefensa* massacres.) I find it troubling to describe Rosa or even refer to the circumstances of our meeting; people get killed all the time in prisons in Colombia, and she has a great many enemies. It seems reasonable to say, however, that she is now middle-aged, that she seemed vulnerable even as I tried to think of some reason why I should feel pity for her, and that although her life has always been "driven by the winds of violence," as she put it, her activities have been political, rather than military in the strict sense of the word.

Her family was well off by the standards of the provincial back-water she was brought up in, but her father, a devout Catholic, had strong sympathy for the labor movement. One of her first memories is of learning the songs of the Fifth Regiment of the Spanish Republican Army from activist priests who taught at her school. They told her about Dolores Ibarruri, "La Pasionaria," the Basque miner's daughter who during the Civil War exhorted the Republican troops to fight for liberty and face down death. Rosa was barely a teenager when she took to singing the Civil War hymns herself, to cheer on workers during strikes. At university, swept up in the radical fervor of the times, Rosa and her friends were soon helping *campesino* organizations coordinate invasions of privately owned ranches, set up roadblocks, and stockpile whatever weapons they could find for the coming revolution.

Although the FARC already existed, it was seen by many as old hat and insufficiently idealistic, and new guerrilla groups, and what used to be called "preparty formations," multiplied. The Ejército de Liberación Nacional, or ELN, as well as the Quintín Lame, an armed Indian rights group; the Partido Revolucionario de los Trabajadores; the M-19—all came into being. By the late seventies Rosa was closely identified with another of the groups to emerge from the university crucible, the Ejército Popular de Liberación, or EPL. The group was strong in the area of Córdoba, where in those days the population was fairly clearly divided between poor *campesinos* and the people with money who owned cattle ranches and farms where bananas and oil palms were grown.

How Rosa's destiny took her from the EPL to the heart of para-military power is, in her telling, a long, breathtaking, and not always reliable story, but she is only one of many defectors from the fanatic left to join the ranks of the murderous right. The *autodefensas* claim that fully one-third of their troops are former guerrillas, and even if one disputes the figures, there is no doubt-ing the general trend. Rosa's life, however, is unusual even in Colombia, where reality always seems to flow out of someone's dream, or nightmare.

The first thing that bothered Rosa about her leftist associates was what one might describe as their impact on the political ecology of the *departamento* of Córdoba. At the height of the revolutionary ferment, there were six different guerrilla organizations prowling around the hills in Rosa's region, each one demanding that the *campesinos* pay "taxes" to finance their coming liberation. "If a *campesino* had five cows, he had to give up one," Rosa says. "The guerrillas were eating up all the money from the NGOs [nongovernmental organizations]. They were hijacking mules. They were emptying out the community stores."

None of these organizations, however, was capable of defending the *campesinos* when the ranchers—including many drug traffickers turned aspiring landed gentry—began organizing assassination squads to deal with guerrilla collaborators. "Those people were terrible *masacradores*," Rosa says. "The rank and file were ranch guards, ranchers, drug traffickers, and everything you've heard about the [murders committed with] chainsaws, axes, and machetes is true." Although the guerrillas could not defeat the paramilitary squads, they did rather well when it came to turning on each other. One guerrilla group, the ELN, tried to dispute the EPL's local hegemony, Rosa recalls. "The ELN wanted to rule," she says. "And they killed whoever didn't obey."

One day the *campesinos* decided they'd had enough of multiple taxes and the conflicting, deadly demands on their political loyalties. The first one to rebel was a fisherman who turned on an ELN patrol that had approached him for money. In Rosa's description, the fisherman hacked a young man and a young woman guerrilla to death. "*Campesinos* don't know how to kill," Rosa observes dryly, having dwelt on the scene in some detail. "And when someone kills who doesn't know how to do it, he kills monstrously."

As for her own apostasy from the revolutionary cause, Rosa says it took place sometime after she was kidnapped in 1991 by one of the leaders of the antiguerrilla squads, the *paramilitares*. She had already decided by then that her commitment was to the *campesinos* and not the guerrillas, she says. Then came the kidnapping. She was abducted, she told me, after participating in a land invasion of a ranch owned by a well-known *paramilitar.* Her captors took her to a camp where "a fat man" was put in charge of torturing her to get information about the guerrillas. He broke off her teeth with pliers. (She paused in her narrative to show me that all her upper teeth had caps.) She was tied down while the fat man jumped on her stomach. She was forced to stand, bleeding, through the rest of the night, wondering when her execution would take place. At dawn, she was told to start walking. The bullet in the back she was expecting never came ("maybe because I never gave them the information they wanted, and they got tired of torturing me"). She kept walking and eventually found her way to her parents' house.

The lesson she appears to have drawn from this episode is not what one would expect. "After that time," Rosa explains, she and her kidnapper respected each other. "Me on this side, you on that one, we both agreed."

"It's funny how life is," she said, in conclusion to her narrative. "Because the guy who ordered the fat man to torture me and I are now pretty good friends." Presumably, this is because a few months after her abduction she crossed over to her enemy's side.

By then, Rosa says, a majority of the guerrilla group she was involved with, the EPL, had decided that a revolutionary war could not successfully be fought in Colombia, and had turned their weapons in, changing their organization's name, but not its initials, to Esperanza, Paz y Libertad (Hope, Peace, and Liberty). Peace was not forthcoming, however, because the FARC guerrillas soon appeared with their own guns and tried to establish control in the void they perceived had been created by the despised pacifists. The FARC began executing former EPL guerrillas. The survivors and their *campesino* supporters felt they had no option except to join forces with the right-wing paramilitary leaders who had tortured Rosa and murdered many of her comrades.

*

In the village of El Salado last February, in the *departamento* of Bolívar, where Rosa's friend Carlos Castaño operates, members of a paramilitary squad sang and danced in the church square while they tortured the villagers and slit their throats one by one. According to the local army commander, the deaths were the result of an armed confrontation between guerrillas and paramilitaries, but the prosecutor general's office, which is often at odds with the army on matters such as this, stated in no uncertain terms that the victims were civilians. Forty-four men and women, suspected by Castaño's people of guerrilla sympathies, were killed during the *autodefensas'* four-day rampage.

The latest Human Rights Watch report on Colombia presents in numbing detail dreadful accounts of dozens of similar mass murders, primarily involving Carlos Castaño's paramilitary troops. But from the point of view of those who have to approve the U.S. military assistance package, the most frightening aspect of the *autodefensas* may be their long, gleeful, and passionate association with the military. For years, detailed evidence has accumulated implicating senior army commanders, mid-level officers, and troops of connivance with, or even the planning and execution of, paramilitary massacres. "Together, evidence collected so far by Human Rights Watch links half of Colombia's eighteen brigade-level army units to paramilitary activity," the report states.

Very few military men have been demoted, much less brought to trial, for their role in mass murders, and perhaps this is also because, as public revulsion with the army's suspected role has grown, its participation has become more discreet. But perhaps it is because the executive and judicial branches of government remain incapable of controlling the rogue military establishment. In any event, intelligence sharing, the Human Rights Watch report states, remains the most pervasive and common method of collaboration between the Colombian military and the *autodefensas.* (The report also describes another form of cooperation, known as *legalización,* which is rooted in the Colombian army's tradition of demanding a high number of enemy casualties from officers ambitious for promotion. According to the report, paramilitaries will bring civilian corpses to army barracks and exchange them for weapons. The officers dress the corpses in camouflage and boots and claim that they were guerrillas killed in battle.)

A number of Colombian observers of the various wars in their country have pointed out that the aid package for Colombia now before the U.S. Congress is, at the very least, badly skewed. Most of the aid is supposed to be spent on the military; and it is supposed to be spent in the southern part of the country, where the guerrillas, and not the paramilitaries, will be the target. State Department officials who are lobbying for approval of the aid package have not ignored the paramilitary threat: they point to new human rights training programs for officers and troops as signs of progress, and occasionally they reproach the government of President Andrés Pastrana for its "passivity" in the face of the paramilitary attacks. But when the reproaches are combined with the proposed gift of stupendous amounts of hardware for the army, they tend to lose force.

The statements coming out of the Pentagon recently about the intended use of the aid money ("Everybody who's in the drug business—guerrillas, *autodefensas,* or drug traffickers—will be the focus of these operations"[3]) raise the strong possibility that this is really an antiguerrilla package disguised as an antidrug package. In Colombia, at any rate, it is taken as a given by all sides that the money is intended for anti-insurgency use. Partly, this may be because Colombians, who have spent twenty years paying a terrible price for the drug bonanza, cannot believe that anyone would be dumb enough to fight drugs with military assistance. And indeed, if the aid is really aimed at halting drug production, it has to be said that military wars waged on cocaine commerce do not have a good record of success. (It is easy to forget that the Clinton administration was not always so hawkish. Clinton's first chief of the White House Office of Drug Control Policy, Lee Brown,

3. Statement of Louis Caldera, U.S. secretary of the army, in Bogotá, reported in *El Tiempo,* January 22, 2000.

stopped using the term "drug war" when he took office. As I wrote after talking to him in Bogotá in 1993, this was because it seemed to Brown that it was dangerous to use the word "war" in reference to a native population—whether Colombians, or black inhabitants of the Bronx.)

In the particular case of the war decreed since the days of the Bush administration on the illegal commerce in cocaine, the balance sheet is dismal, although the large and thriving drug bureaucracy in the United States puts out reports every year citing ever-larger impoundments of cocaine and heroin. The figures are presented as evidence that (a) the war on drugs is being won, because seizures and arrests are increasing, and (b) the war on drugs is not being won fast enough, because seizures and arrests are increasing. Ever-larger budget allocations are necessary, according to this logic, to bring victory within sight.

At first glance, it is hard not to be impressed with the results of the war waged on drugs in Bolivia and Peru. In 1995, according to a recent report by the U.S. State Department, Bolivia had 48,600 hectares of coca under cultivation. In 1999 there were only 21,800. Even more dramatic are the figures for Peru, where production peaked at 115,300 hectares in 1995, and shrank four years later to barely 38,700. But if one takes the total combined figures for hectares of coca under cultivation in Colombia, Bolivia, and Peru in 1995, and again in 1999, the picture is somewhat different. In 1995 the estimated total was 214,800 hectares. In 1999 it was 183,000. In other words, there was no large decline in the total area under cultivation: coca cultivation expanded in Colombia to take up the slack in Bolivia and Peru. A cynic might even speculate that the 1999 decrease of 30,000 hectares is partly the result of some enhanced estimating. It would not be surprising if new, uncounted areas of cultivation have been opened on the other side of the Amazon, in the vast expanse of jungle that belongs to Brazil. It is in any case a reasonable wager that once serious drug interdiction programs get under way in Colombia, cultivation will shift to Brazil and Venezuela. As long as demand continues, that is.

Whether or not the military aid being proposed by the Clinton administration can be used successfully to fight drugs, what is true is that in Colombia a surprising number of people—perhaps a majority of those who shape public opinion—now see the aid package as the country's last best hope of ending the long, brutal confrontation with the FARC. They reach this conclusion at a time when the Pastrana government is engaging in the most serious and lengthy peace negotiations with the guerrillas in the history of this conflict. If the supporters of the aid package are right, U.S. might and money will be useful in defeating the guerrillas in the field or forcing them to take part in serious and practical peace talks. If the supporters of U.S. military aid are wrong, the FARC will retreat from its current armed clashes with government troops to more traditional forms of guerrilla warfare—ambushes, sabotage operations, urban terrorism, selective killings—which would enable it to survive indefinitely, and set the prospects for peace back for years.

—April 13, 2000

VIOLENCE WITHOUT END?

The war in Colombia between the army and an irregular paramilitary force, on one side, and various armed left-wing organizations on the other has claimed thousands of lives and sown terror in the countryside for decades. During the last couple of years, however, the guerrillas have sought to have a greater impact by interrupting daily life in the cities. In Bogotá, for example, a few days before the end of December, a group of Colombian friends considered their holiday options—a trip to the countryside or a long drive to the coast for a few days of sunshine—and decided that the choice would depend on the road conditions. The country's largest guerrilla organization, the Fuerzas Armadas Revolucionarias de Colombia, or FARC, had declared a holiday truce as a gesture of commitment to the peace talks that have been fitfully under way since President Andrés Pastrana took office in August of 1998. This meant, one friend said, that there would be no combat activity, and so the beach might not be a bad idea. But other members of the group were doubtful: the guerrillas had said that there would be no combat, but had they said anything about kidnappings?

Kidnappings are the worst danger for civilians who are traveling overland. At roadblocks set up by the guerrillas, which can last for hours, or even days, civilians will be allowed through only if a quick search through a computer database shows that their bank accounts are too small to qualify them as "kidnappable." Combined with the large number of targeted abductions, these "fishing expeditions," as they are known, have made Colombia the kidnap capital of the world: last year 2,945 abductions were reported to the police—eight a day. The guerrillas were responsible for most of them, all of which gave the friends' discussion a certain urgency. If the guerrillas had not included kidnappings in the cease-fire, a long trip was out of the question.

There had been no recent reports of guerrilla roadblocks, and the idea of a trip seemed plausible, until one member of the vacationing party remembered something. The rival guerrilla group to the FARC, the ELN, whose initials stand for Ejército de Liberación Nacional, derives its income almost exclusively from kidnappings and extortion. It is still holding fourteen passengers who were on a commercial plane that was carrying forty-six people when the guerrillas hijacked it a year ago. Founded in 1965, and led by the Spanish priest Manuel Pérez until his death in early 1998, the ELN is considered the most intransigent of the various armed left-wing associations that have prospered in Colombia during the last forty years. And indeed, the group of friends quickly realized, the ELN had not declared a truce for the holidays. All plans to spend the New Year somewhere other than Bogotá were immediately canceled.

Roadblocks and kidnappings that affect even the salaried middle class are only one aspect of the new fear in the cities. The ELN conducts campaigns—against the proposed privatization of the energy sector, against the export of the nation's oil wealth, against human rights violations—by blowing up oil pipelines and electric pylons. They have knocked down 270 pylons in less than a year: brownouts and power cuts have become routine in heavily populated and industrial areas like Medellín and its environs, and darkness threatens constantly in the capital. War refugees living in miserable conditions on the outskirts of the city probably number in the tens of thousands. For its part, the FARC is building up its clandestine structure in the capital; the *milicias Bolivarianas*—poor and angry youths in the shantytowns who have been recruited into the guerrillas' support network—are known to be growing.

The war's new setting is probably the most significant reason why the government of Andrés Pastrana sought peace talks with the guerrillas even before his inauguration, in August of 1998, and why those talks are now going on. Previous administrations attempted negotiations with the FARC, but those efforts always collapsed even as the war grew. The current effort is different from previous attempts because, as proof of the seriousness of its intentions, the government started off by making a great many concessions to the guerrillas. For the first time, and at the FARC's insistence, the meetings between the government and the insurgency are taking place inside Colombia, in a part of the country where the guerrillas have been active for many years, and from which all troops and police have been withdrawn. And for the first time, the two sides have agreed on a schedule and an agenda for their negotiations.

The talks could collapse again if the guerrillas decide that the foreign aid bill for Colombia now before the U.S. Congress is a mandate for more war. Or they could be sabotaged as previous ones have been, by the participants themselves or by their enemies, who are legion. But a new factor is that, after years of pretending that the war was happening in some other Colombia, many of its citizens among the middle class and the well-to-do, including university students and office workers—people like the frustrated vacationers at New Year's—have decided to make their voices heard.

In June of 1998 voters elected Andrés Pastrana, the candidate of the weak Conservative Party, which had not won an election since the maverick Belisario Betancur was elected president in 1982. Pastrana, who served a modestly successful term as mayor of Bogotá in 1988–1990, ran for president in 1994 and nearly won. Four years later his leading opponent was the experienced candidate of the Liberal Party, Horacio Serpa. Serpa, the leader of the social-democratic wing of his party, has a large and faithful national following, although his campaign was handicapped by his long, close association with former president Ernesto Samper, whose administration (1994–1998) was nearly brought down by drug-related corruption charges. If elected, both candidates promised, they would do whatever was necessary to bring the FARC to the negotiating table. In May, Serpa won the most votes, but not a clear majority, and a second electoral round was scheduled for June. A few days before the second vote a photograph was displayed across the top of the front pages of all the major Colombian dailies; it showed the peace adviser for Andrés Pastrana somewhere in the wilderness, deep in conversation with Manuel Marulanda—nicknamed "Sureshot"—the perennial and aging leader of the FARC guerrillas. Sureshot was wearing a Pastrana campaign watch. As Marulanda must have known when he allowed the photo-op, the meeting established Pastrana as the peace candidate. Five days later, on June 21, 1998, Pastrana was elected by a comfortable margin.

Pastrana has kept to his campaign promises, but progress in carrying them out has been erratic. As a candidate, Pastrana had announced that he would withdraw the army from a territory in which the FARC guerrillas would have free rein, so that peace talks could get under way. The joy that greeted the announcement of the talks was tempered in some circles by the realization that the demilitarized zone was in the heart of the coca-growing region of the Amazon jungle—where the FARC has been strong for years—and that this zone was rather large; 26,250 square miles, in fact, or about twice the size of El Salvador.

After Pastrana took power, months of tense prenegotiations with both the guerrillas and the army went by, as the fine points of just how much authority the state would cede were ironed out. At the same time, with Pastrana's encouragement, the United States got involved: the chief spokesman of the FARC, who goes by the pseudonym of Raúl Reyes, met secretly in Costa Rica with State Department officials. At last, on January 7, 1999, the "peace table" was installed with an oddly festive ceremony that featured jugglers, dancers, politicians of all stripes, and a host of famous entertainers—including a salsa group, Iván and his Bam Band, and a curvaceous pop star who showed up in skintight leather gear, with her mother by her side—but not Marulanda, who left

Pastrana to inaugurate the event sitting next to the guerrilla's empty chair. (Later, Marulanda said that he had learned of a plot to assassinate him at the inauguration.) Formal talks began two days later, but the FARC suspended them again almost immediately, on January 20, charging that the government had stood by while right-wing paramilitaries escalated their actions; they had killed nearly 100 civilians in the first three weeks of the year.[1]

At least, people said, the conservative Pastrana has been able to keep the recalcitrant army in line while the peace process stumbled along. But in May 1999, after Pastrana agreed to renew the demilitarization of the peace zone indefinitely so that talks could begin again, his defense minister resigned in protest, and seventeen army generals and two hundred colonels threatened to follow him.

On the other hand, the generals are still in place, the talks, though they have been suspended much more often than they have been in session, have never actually been broken off, and last January, after a full year of false starts, the two sides actually held working sessions.

It may be the first time that either party is feeling pressure from the civilian population. Colombians are notoriously anarchic—it is one of their great charms—but as the war has come to threaten so many aspects of normal life—going on vacation, turning on the lights, taking the kids to school—they have bestirred themselves. A grass-roots peace movement, probably the largest civic movement the country has seen, is taking an active part in the war and the attempts to end it. In addition to electing the president they thought could best guarantee an end to the war two years ago, voters had cast another ballot—a bright green card—during the previous municipal elections, to signify that they wanted peace. (Pastrana was elected with 6.1 million votes; Serpa got 5.6 million. The peace ballot got 10 million votes.)

In February of last year, a national march against kidnappings

1. For its part, the State Department suspended its meetings with the FARC after it assassinated three Indian rights activists from the United States in February 1999.

and disappearances was so successful that the organizers thought they would never be able to repeat it, but six months later a march for peace brought millions of Colombians out on the streets— 5 million, according to the most cautious estimates, out of a population of 48 million. The marchers, dressed in white, didn't take to the streets only in the cities: six hundred towns, small and large, also had demonstrations. (I was in New York City at the time, but I found out about the march when I ran into some Colombian friends who had little Colombian flags stenciled on their cheeks—they had been marching for peace down Fifth Avenue.) The demands of the marchers were addressed equally to the guerrillas, the right-wing paramilitary forces, and the government: uninterrupted peace talks, cease-fire now, and respect for civilians.

On the morning of December 31, 1999, I sat in a penthouse office in the heart of Bogotá with Camilo González, a pleasantly rumpled man who looks not unlike the Juan Valdez character of Colombian coffee ads. González, who is a man of many talents, was sitting in as a technical adviser for the Colombian Communications Ministry's Y2K watch. Before that he was minister of health, as a representative for the left in the administration of César Gaviria. These days, as coordinator of a movement called Citizens' Mandate for Peace, he is deeply involved with the marches and demonstrations against the war. When we talked, his mood seemed cheerful but cautious. He had unloaded the array of cell phones he carries about his person and spread them out on the table, and as we talked, he moved them around as if they were pieces on a chessboard.

I asked González how he saw the chances for peace, given that both the government and the insurgents seem deeply ambivalent, if not divided, about whether they want to make any concessions to the other side. One problem, he answered, is that although the military option is "strategically defeated" after years of confrontation, each of the warring parties believes that it can still make significant tactical advances. "They are suffering from a militarist illusion," he said, "in which the army believes that, given enough support, it can defeat the guerrillas, the FARC believes that it can continue its territorial expansion, and the paramilitaries believe that they can wrest control of the oil fields from the ELN guerrillas." (The ELN originally financed its actions with money from the oil companies that operate in the fields on the border with Venezuela: their leverage was the pipeline that they still periodically blow up.)

As the vote on aid in the U.S. Congress draws near, "everybody wants to show off their military capabilities," González said. "And so what is immediately ahead is an escalation of armed confrontation and at the same time an escalation of talks."

The big problem the peace movement faces now, González said as he played with the phones, is how to continue to engage the citizenry. After the euphoria of a huge demonstration, frustration can set in when it doesn't lead to immediate results. Still, he believed that the marches had already had an impact. The right-wing paramilitaries who are fighting the guerrillas had said that they would no longer recruit anyone under eighteen into their ranks; the ELN had hailed the peace movement's "authentic expression of popular sovereignty"; and even the FARC, in ignoring the movement so resolutely, had given an indication of how large a thorn in its side it is. (Soon, the peace movement would announce a letter-writing campaign, in which people are encouraged to write to the FARC leaders.)

As we chatted, the millennium festivities were already being prepared along Bogotá's main avenue, the Carrera Séptima, just outside. On Sundays and holidays the Séptima is usually turned into a bicycle path, which gets almost as crowded with bikers and skaters as it does with cars during rush hour. But today there would be a parade instead, of the peculiar, inventive, and informal kind Colombians love—more of a carnival, really. The weather for it was perfect; mild and sunny in this city of biblical downpours. Some people had expressed fear that the evening would turn into a drunken mess, but the street scene so far was mellow: all the city *barrios* were preparing floats and costumes with a millennial theme, and although it was early, dancers and musicians—jazz quintets, rock groups, salsa bands—were already putting on their makeup and warming up.

The most significant thing about the peace movement, González concluded, was that, even if it failed, it had given people a different way to see themselves. "After the marches we can say to ourselves that we're a peace-loving country, as opposed to our usual, self-flagellating 'We're a nation of violent, cheating crooks,' " he said. Perhaps he was reading too much into a movement that had barely started and could fizzle out any minute. But on this promising day, who could blame him?

Something of the same millennial spirit must have been present when the FARC negotiating team and Pastrana's peace commissioner, Víctor G. Ricardo, set off together in February for a leisurely tour of Europe. Ricardo, a pleasant-faced man of average build and average height, gives the impression of being both very intense and intensely unassuming. He is one of the president's inner circle, and it was he who appeared in the famous photo in the wilderness with the guerrilla leader Marulanda.

When we talked this January in the small, crowded corner office he occupies in Bogotá's lovely presidential house, Ricardo went on at length about the need for a spiritual transformation in Colombian society, which might have seemed like a ploy to avoid giving information, except that when one leafs through the three-volume official record of the peace process, it turns out that this is also what he says to the guerrillas. The peace effort at this point is all about building trust, Ricardo told me, and this effort was about to bear fruit, as talks finally seemed to start again in a promising way. The second stage would involve convincing the countries that consume cocaine to invest in Colombia so that the legal economy could grow. "It's a question of saying to the world, 'Look, Mr. World, we have a cocaine problem,' " he said. " 'But it is also true that you provide the market for it. Why don't you help us to solve something that is a problem for everyone?' " He denied that the talks were failing to produce results. "Very soon, sooner than you can imagine, you will see some very real results of the effort to build trust we have been working on," he told me.

And indeed, in the first week of February, Ricardo and all six members of the FARC's representatives at the peace talks boarded an Iberia flight (the commissioner had spent a frantic morning shopping for suits and ties for all of them) and flew to Madrid. Members of the Spanish, Norwegian, Danish, Swiss, and Italian governments had promised to receive the curious delegation, and for a month the FARC negotiators—who may or may not have traveled outside their native country before, and who have spent all their adult lives in the cocoon of isolation and paranoia that clandestinity generates—were shown versions of socialism, capitalism, and monarchy considerably different from the ones they learned about in their Marxist textbooks. They chatted with politicians, visited factories, talked to the workers, and had dinner with the CEOs. It was an extraordinary idea to have come up with and an almost impossible one to put into practice, and Ricardo emerged from the trip with an enhanced reputation.

*

No one expected the guerrillas' military activity to actually decline as a result of their European tour—it is taken for granted by observers and participants in the peace process that all sides will try to reinforce in the field their positions at the negotiating table. But no one expected them to try to assassinate Francisco Santos either. In this long war it is hard to judge whose ineptitude is greater. Last year someone—presumably on the right—ordered the death of Jaime Garzón, a fiercely funny and politically sophisticated man whose television "newscast," featuring uncanny impersonations of guerrillas, generals, politicians, and other characters, was a Sunday household ritual. Crowds lined the streets of Bogotá for his funeral. This year, credible evidence indicates that the FARC, which despises the peace movement, took out a contract on Francisco Santos, who started the free-form citizens' movement for peace of which Camilo González is also part.

In addition to being a scion of the family that owns the daily *El*

Tiempo—by far the largest newspaper in the country—Santos, thirty-eight, is also the paper's managing editor for news. But he devotes much of his time to the peace movement. In many ways, the movement grew out of the Fundación País Libre, the organization he founded that monitors kidnappings and helps victims and their relatives. Santos got the idea for País Libre in 1991, after he was kidnapped and held hostage for eight months by the drug trafficker Pablo Escobar.[2]

Last January, Francisco Santos was alerted by his various intelligence sources in Colombia that a plot to kill him was under way, financed by the FARC. He realized that he was being tailed constantly. His sources confirmed that the plot involved both the FARC commander of the area around Bogotá and a band of killers-for-hire that operates under orders from a network of criminals who are currently in jail. Early in March, Santos showed up at a restaurant half an hour after agreeing over the phone to meet a friend there. The owner of the restaurant, an acquaintance, said that suspicious-looking men had just come in asking for him. Convinced that the plot against him would continue, Santos decided to remove himself from the country.

Although Raúl Reyes, the FARC spokesman, immediately and energetically denied that his organization had anything to do with the murder plot, intelligence services insist that the guerrillas were responsible. This in itself might not mean much—one could even credit the spooks with pulling off a neat propaganda coup—but the declarations of Manuel Marulanda, "Sureshot," on one of the extremely rare occasions when he made himself available to reporters, still ring in the ears. He was asked last January whether it was true that he was unfriendly to the press. "It's not that," he answered. "The *jefes* of the press have a lot of debts, and we have to call them in. They distort everything, they are not correct in their dealings with us . . . so they have these little debts." What this all says about the guerrillas' real interest in, or understanding of,

---

2. Gabriel García Márquez's book-length account, *News of a Kidnapping* (New York: Knopf, 1997), is partly about Francisco Santos.

what is at stake in the peace negotiations is hard to say: they could be trying to sabotage them without appearing involved. On the other hand, they have been isolated for so long that they may not be able to measure the negative effects of their actions.

When I talked to Santos on the phone recently in his self-imposed exile, he was homesick and lonely. He is by nature chipper and hyperactive, but now that he is spending his days abroad, alone with the phone and the Internet, I had the impression that he felt as if he had been kidnapped again. He was perplexed about the state of affairs in his country. The peace movement has grown out of the conviction that Colombia's wars cannot be won with more wars, Santos said, but increasingly, since the FARC appears unresponsive to the general desire for peace, people like him feel that they have been put "between the sword and the wall." He feels that Pastrana requested the new American aid in order to brandish it as a threat against the FARC, but that the plan for spending the money is shaky. For example, he said, "if the aid gets approved, and Pastrana does not have a very concrete plan for dealing with all the civilians who will be affected [in the coca-growing area where the aid is supposed to be used, and where the FARC is strong], it will be a disaster," because the *campesinos* who grow coca are by and large supporters of the guerrillas, and there are a couple of hundred thousand of them, and in the past they have proved that they can be mobilized very effectively.

At this stage, Santos thinks, it will be devastating to Colombia if the U.S. aid package is not approved by Congress, because the Pastrana administration is so invested in the effort. But he would like to see most of the money used for social programs rather than military equipment, as the Massachusetts Democratic congressman William Delahunt has recently suggested. Whether that idea prospers or not, he concluded, is now up to the FARC.

Marulanda's comments on "little debts" and Santos's assassination plot do not sound as if the FARC were attempting to improve its handling of its image, but it is. Only a few days before announcing that the FARC intended to call in the "debts" of the press, Marulanda had allowed reporters to approach him and lob a few soft questions. The occasion was the inauguration of the headquarters for the talks in the demilitarized zone declared by Pastrana, but it also happened to be the day that Madeleine Albright was meeting with the president in the Caribbean resort city of Cartagena. The press interpreted Marulanda's apparition as a gesture of support for the peace process, but it was more likely designed to distract attention from the U.S. envoy.

For her part, Albright had a busy schedule in Cartagena, dancing with schoolchildren and dining with Gabriel García Márquez. This was her first trip to Colombia, and what she saw of it—one of the most beautiful fortress cities in the world, quaint streets, deluxe hotels—could easily have led her to conclude that the only thing wrong with Colombia is that it has a drug problem and a guerrilla problem, and that what one does with problems is fix them. But what Colombia has is an environment of violence in which, as the journalist Germán Castro Caycedo, who has interviewed many of its practitioners, pointed out to me,

> Manuel Marulanda joined the Liberal guerrillas [as a youth, in the early days of the Violencia] because his family were getting killed; the founder of the ELN, Fabio Vázquez Castaño, started that guerrilla group because *his* father was killed. And Carlos Castaño [no relation; the leader of the bloody antiguerrilla *autodefensas,* or paramilitaries] got into violence because his father was kidnapped and killed by the FARC!

None of these crimes was ever brought to court, and the list of children with murdered parents could go on forever, because, in Colombia, justice works poorly when it works at all. (A small portion of the aid package is allocated to improvements in the legal system.)

Colombia has what is often advertised as the oldest democracy in Latin America. Technically speaking, this is true, but the details have to be taken into account. Citizens were not allowed to elect their own mayors until barely twelve years ago. Popular elections for governors of the thirty-two *departamentos* took place beginning in 1992. Affiliation with either the Conservative or the Liberal Party was long a requirement for becoming a civil servant. The country was under a state of siege, or of emergency, for most of the last fifty years. The sons, grandsons, or nephews of presidents lay claim to the presidency with predictable regularity, as Andrés Pastrana did. Almost without exception, the principal newspapers, television stations, and magazines are owned by the leading political or business families, and until very recently the dominant tone in the most important newspapers and television stations was unfair, intolerant, and full of poisonous class prejudice.

*

The brutal twenty-year-long episode known as La Violencia was a civil war without battles; one in which peasants armed with peasant weapons—machetes, knives—carried out a long series of massacres against other peasants. It lasted from 1945 to 1964. In 1957, the Liberal and Conservative hierarchs who presided over the killings signed an accord that set the stage for much of what has followed: the two sides agreed that there would be presidential elections but that for the next sixteen years the two parties would alternate power.

That agreement was threatened in 1970, when the populist *caudillo,* General Gustavo Rojas Pinilla, ran an upstart candidacy against the Conservative Party nominee, Misael Pastrana, father of the current president. Although Pastrana claimed victory, many historians believe that a majority of the vote may well have gone to Rojas Pinilla. No independent body was ever allowed to count the ballots. Unfraudulent presidential elections have been the norm since 1974, but by that year there were as many as a dozen armed organizations roaming the country—including the M-19 guerrilla movement—which took its name from the date on which Rojas Pinilla was defeated, April 19, 1970—and the current survivors, the FARC and the ELN.

Assuming that escalating the war is the most expedient way of bringing it to an end, the question that comes to mind is just which of the many sides in warring Colombia the Clinton administration expects to benefit most from a billion-odd dollars' worth of weapons. The mere threat of that aid may already have proven useful enough. As the economist and historian Salomón Kalmanowitz—now on the board of the Colombian Central Bank— pointed out to me, "it has made the FARC more willing to internationalize the conflict and make it a political one, to bring in the European countries as participants and supervisors of the agreement—that is why the negotiators went on the European tour— and to allow the Red Cross and other nongovernmental organizations a greater role, in order to neutralize the U.S. presence."

The threat of U.S. aid, however, is not the same as the reality of the relatively small, and not beloved, Colombian military suddenly empowered with a billion-plus dollars. For it is they who will be the real beneficiaries of the aid package—President Pastrana, who requested the aid, will be gone from power in just two years. The gift of howitzers and heat sensors, helicopters and planes, assumes that the military establishment is capable of reforming itself from within, purging itself of the officers and soldiers who collaborate with the paramilitaries or with the drug traffickers, and elevating its combat spirit enough at last to take on the guerrillas and win. And it assumes that all of this can be accomplished in the coming two-year period when the military forces would be flooded with aid money. If these calculations are wrong, the consequences will make the present situation much worse.

In Colombia peace has always been achieved by use of force, leading to exclusions that lead to more violence. A great many Colombians who want an end to the war think that the military assistance package might help bring that end about; but on the basis of their past experience they seem to have no appetite for what the immediate consequences of an escalated war are likely to be. Indeed, as the peace ballot and the peace marches would indicate, what people want is not war at all, but a national reconciliation.

As midnight approached on December 31, 1999, "peace" was one of the frequent New Year's wishes of the group of friends who had failed to leave Bogotá on vacation. The city had turned out to be not such a bad alternative after all. It was midnight, the Séptima was pleasantly crowded with families and groups of friends, and no one at all seemed to be drunk. The parade had been a success: the jugglers juggled and the dancers danced and the musicians played, but the great hit had been a transvestite on stilts who had two giant balloons with painted nipples strapped across his chest, and outsize balloon genitalia tied on further down—all of which he stopped to wiggle merrily at the spectators whenever they cheered and called out to him, interrupting his storklike progress down the avenue.

Now it was midnight, and in the crowd, smiling men and women turned to perfect strangers and hugged them, wishing them peace and a happy new year. Fireworks bloomed in the sky to appreciative gasps. For now Bogotá felt safe; the holiday truce announced by the FARC would end in a few days.

—April 27, 2000

THE CHILDREN'S WAR

San Vicente del Caguán is a small town on the edge of the jungle that runs from the Andean foothills of Colombia down to the Amazon River basin. It has a sunstricken central square—a patch of dust and a few mango trees—with a graceless modern church on one end and a nondescript municipal building on the other, and around it a grid of narrow streets laid out in Spanish style. The layout is traditional, but San Vicente has the look and feel of the kind of frontier town where people have been lured overnight by the promise of money. There are loud cantinas; fleshy women in too much makeup under the glaring sun; block after block of storefronts selling boom boxes, high-heeled shoes, glitter eye shadow, and telephones shaped like hot dogs. More boom boxes and plastic jewelry are offered for sale along the narrow sidewalks. Mules, motorcycles, and roaring pickup trucks compete for space on the gutted road.

Beginning in the 1950s, the region was populated by poor *campesinos* from other, war-ridden parts of the country who cleared patches of land here and started a new life. Many hundreds pressed deep into the jungle and were never heard from again. The luckier ones survived to become modestly prosperous cattle ranchers. In the last ten years or so, however, a new wave of poorer and even more adventurous settlers arrived. They were looking to plant coca, the tealike shrub from which cocaine is processed, and, thanks to high prices for this illegal crop, the region's economy flourished. So did the finances of Colombia's oldest guerrilla group, the Fuerzas Armadas Revolucionarias de Colombia, known by its

Spanish acronym as the FARC. For years, the FARC had been involved with coca growers throughout the country, offering protection from government anticocaine patrols in exchange for a tax levied on the sale and transport of coca and cocaine paste. Thanks to the 1990s cocaine bonanza, San Vicente prospered, and so did the guerrillas. The most widely quoted estimate of how much protection money the FARC takes in each year from the coca business is $500 million. With these funds, the FARC has severely escalated its thirty-five-year war against the state, and brought the government of President Andrés Pastrana to the negotiating table.

In June of 1998, when he was still running for the presidency, Andrés Pastrana announced that if he was elected he would order military forces to withdraw from a portion of territory in the sub-Amazon region around San Vicente, in order to guarantee the FARC leadership safety so that the government's peace negotiations with the group could begin. The territory, referred to as the *zona de despeje,* or cleared zone, would include five municipal districts, each one with only a few hundred thousand inhabitants, but each with as much territory as a small European country. All told, the area in question added up to 26,250 square miles—twice the size of El Salvador. San Vicente, which sits on the edge of the cleared zone closest to Bogotá, would be the center for the talks. And the FARC guerrillas, who for all practical purposes already controlled the rolling countryside around it, would be allowed free rein in San Vicente. Six months later, in December 1998, the withdrawal of the military began.

With a handful of other passengers, I boarded a commercial flight from Bogotá in January to the undeclared capital of the *zona de despeje.* I wanted to request an interview with the leader and founder of the FARC, the aging Manuel Marulanda, whom I had met once before. In 1986, with a group of Colombian journalists, I made the arduous trip on horseback and on foot to the FARC's command center, deep in the canyons and rain forest of the Andean piedmont. Marulanda had received us then in his spartan compound, where he tended a vegetable patch and the war, surrounded by his private guard, which was composed principally of young women. Marulanda, a *campesino* from the Andes who had been fighting the government for twenty-two years by that time, was a stubborn and patient man, I thought then. And I was struck by his troops; a surprising number of them were girls, and although the FARC's leadership was graying, the guerrilla soldiers were remarkably young.

*

When I arrived in San Vicente, I headed for the FARC headquarters on the town square. A boy with a fuzz of hair above his upper lip opened the door to let me into an enormous, bare, and unkempt room, where a handful of kids were slumped on the floor and on gimpy plastic chairs, watching a Bruce Lee movie on a television set that had been placed on an upended crate. There were machine guns—FALs and AK-47s for the most part—propped against the wall, but the boy who opened the door carried his rifle on his shoulder. The girls had obviously been shopping on the main street, and I wondered where they had gotten the money for mascara and nail polish.

To jog Marulanda's memory about my long-ago visit, I had brought a picture I took of him then, smiling into the camera. The commander-in-chief of the FARC does not, as a rule, give interviews, and as it turned out, I would be no exception this time around, but the photograph was useful nevertheless. I knew that journalists could spend days waiting for any contact with the high command, but *compañera* Nora, a trim, agreeable woman in charge of the FARC's liaison with the public, and the only adult in sight, examined the picture and immediately wrote down my interview request. A courier was leaving in a few minutes for the camp outside town where the FARC commanders live, she said obligingly, and I could send the photograph with him, along with a note. Soon the guerrillas in the room also noticed the picture. They nudged one another and took silent reconnoiters around my chair until at last one of the girls—small, chubby, droll-looking—took it from me and held it up close. Her expression was dreamy. "You love him a lot too, don't you?" she said.

There were no signs of a personality cult on the walls. In fact, there were no posters, no slogans, no banners—hardly anything at all. In the small office where Nora received visitors, there was a creaky desk, a fan, a couple of chairs, and a lone photograph of Marulanda in conversation with Víctor G. Ricardo, Pastrana's peace commissioner. A second framed picture could only have come from the former Soviet Union: it was a full-length pastel-tinted lithograph of Lenin, in which Vladimir Ilyich was portrayed with unusually small hands and feet, standing on a mound of flowers and gazing upward—looking for all the world like the Virgin Mary ascending. A third photograph, a blurry snapshot of the FARC's deceased ideologue Jacobo Arenas, graced the entrance hall. There were in conversation no references to Marulanda's teachings or to his superior wisdom, and yet the more I talked with the round little girl who loved him so much—I'll call her Claudia—I wondered what kept her going if it wasn't a kind of absolute faith.

Her family was from the region, I soon found out. She had taken to bumping up against me and squeezing me every time she found me chatting with Nora in the little office, with a persistence I was beginning to find alarming until I thought to ask how old she was. "Seventeen," she answered. And how long had it been since she'd seen her mother? "Four . . . no, five years," she said. She had left home to join the guerrillas when she was twelve. Later, I listened while she told her best friend—also seventeen and as lively and doll-eyed as Claudia—how on a recent day, in a moment of daring, she had taken a taxi to her hometown, which is outside the demilitarized zone. The access roads to the zone are patrolled by the army and also by members of a paramilitary detachment that operates in the neighborhood. But Claudia felt sure she would pass unnoticed because she had grown up so much since she'd left home, and because she was wearing civilian clothes.

"I just thought I'd like to say hello to my mom, you know?" she told her friend. "But when I got to the last checkpoint I saw one of the soldiers staring at me and I thought, son-of-a-bitch! I didn't take off my bracelets! All the soldiers know that we guerrillas like to wear these little black elastic bands—they're expensive! One thousand five hundred pesos [about seventy-five U.S. cents] just for one, and if I take them off now, he'll suspect something. I said to the taxi driver, 'Turn around, take me back to San Vicente right now!' and the taxi driver kept saying, 'You're a guerrilla, aren't you? I've seen you before.' 'No I'm not,' I said. 'Take me home now!' I was scared."

About 30 percent of the guerrillas' troops are estimated to be female. Nora, who is thirty-three, told me how she too had joined the guerrillas as an adolescent eighteen years ago. "It was something I wanted to do since I was little," she said. She came from the highlands, or so I guessed from her sharp Andean features and her accent, and when she was ten a guerrilla column with women fighters passed through her village. Nora says that she saw the brisk young women, in uniform and carrying guns, and thought they were the most powerful and glamorous creatures she had ever seen. When she turned fifteen, she persuaded her parents that she had to join them. I wondered if she had missed her family, and if she hadn't found the life unbearably hard at first. "Not really," she said. "There were so many of us children. It wasn't like our mother had time to baby us." And as for the hardship, "maybe if I'd been some middle-class momma's girl"—she glanced up at me and corrected herself—"maybe if I hadn't been of *campesino* origins, I would have suffered. But I was so used to hard work that what I had to go through felt easy."

Perhaps only a Colombian *campesino* could survive the hardships imposed on the FARC troops, but it didn't seem to me that Claudia, sturdy and young as she was, found her life easy. Life for the guerrillas has changed, in any case, since Nora's days as a foot soldier, as a result of the FARC's decision to shift away from traditional guerrilla ambushes and hit-and-run operations. Since August of 1996, when the FARC overran a government military base for the first time and took sixty soldiers prisoner, the guerrillas have been waging something very like real war against the Colombian state. Attacks on police stations in small towns and military bases in the countryside are now the norm. The element of surprise is key to the attacks, and from what I could understand, Claudia might have been part of one of the FARC's two mobile columns, whose specialty is marching cross-country at such speed that they have attacked and retreated before the military intelligence services can even detect their movements.

I gathered this about Claudia's posting one morning when I failed to drink most of a glass of soda pop. "Me, I would never do that," Claudia said. "If you were with the guerrillas, you'd learn to drink up. Otherwise you're on campaign someday, and it's broiling hot, and there's nothing to drink and you remember that last little gulp of ice-cold soda you left behind the last time you went through a town and you really regret it. I swear to God you can feel the bubbles on your tongue!" Her best friend joined in. "And what about those cross-country marches?" she said. "Nine hours with no rest stops, and you're not allowed to carry water because it'll weigh you down, and you're humping all that goddamned equipment on your back and the load is killing you and you think you're going to pass out from thirst . . . son-of-a-bitch! It's hard!"

The absence of any decoration or sense of order at the FARC headquarters seemed logical after talking to Nora and Claudia. Ten years ago, when the army bombed the FARC central command, Casa Verde—this was where I had interviewed Marulanda, in the Andean foothills less than a hundred miles from Bogotá—the guerrillas lost their only permanent base. Only the leadership had lived in Casa Verde year after year, in any event, and not the troops, who are currently estimated to number between 14,000 and 20,000. Nora told me that she had a steady *compañero* for many years—until he was killed—which is more stability than most of the guerrillas seem to achieve. But it did not strike her as odd that their relationship should have been lived out in a series of shacks and plastic tents, and that the only fragments of their life together she could hold on to were what she could carry on her back: she had been homeless her entire adult life.

I asked Nora what the FARC's policy was with regard to romance, and she reeled off a dizzying number of birth-control devices, including condoms, that are distributed to all the girls. The guerrillas are free to take up with anyone they choose inside the organization, she said, but I wondered how little Claudia, as starved for attention and physical affection as she so evidently was, made her choices. And what if, despite the IUDs, pills, patches, diaphragms, condoms, and jellies, she got pregnant? Nora herself had a fourteen-year-old daughter, she answered proudly. Like all guerrilla children, she had been sent away to her grandparents shortly after she was born. Nora kept in touch with her as best she could. I told Nora that I found it difficult to understand why anyone would choose the life she had, and she gave me the same answer, almost word for word, that I had heard from the guerrillas in Casa Verde so many years ago, and that I would hear often enough in San Vicente. "It is because there is so much injustice in Colombia, and one has to struggle against it."

There is considerable evidence that not all the FARC troops, particularly the boys, are volunteers. Runaways have said that they joined because the guerrillas threatened to punish their families if they didn't and, in other cases, that their families offered them to the FARC when they couldn't pay the taxes that had been levied on their produce—whether it was coca or some other crop. In any case, it makes sense, from the FARC's point of view, to recruit the very young; they are malleable and strong enough to survive the punishing physical demands that are routinely made of them. And although there has been some outcry recently, in Colombia and abroad, about the FARC's adolescent army, and although the guerrillas are now anxious to polish their international image, Manuel Marulanda himself quashed any discussion of increasing the guerrillas' recruitment age to eighteen.

Last January, in the course of one of his extremely rare public appearances, he declared, first, that the FARC would soon be calling in some of the "little debts" the press has with the organization, and, second, that fifteen would remain the recruitment age, "because we have a norm that says we recruit from age fifteen up." After all, forcible conscription of adolescents, particularly in the countryside, was until a few years ago how the government army found its combat troops.

*

On the evening that I arrived in San Vicente, I found myself sitting in a crowded, noisy restaurant, drinking *guanábana* juice with one of the FARC's principal spokesmen, discussing the guerrillas' approach to human rights. I wanted to know about kidnappings, since Colombia now has the highest kidnap rate in the world—eight a day in 1999—and, together with a rival guerrilla group, the National Liberation Army, or ELN, the FARC is responsible for most of them. Money raised from protecting coca growers, money from kidnappings, and extortion money paid to ward off the threat of kidnappings are the main source of financing for the war. The guerrillas, who see themselves as the legitimate authority in areas they control militarily, regard the ransom and extortion money as income tax. Now that approval in the U.S. Senate of a $1 billion military aid package seems imminent, the rate of kidnappings appears to be soaring as the guerrillas prepare for a brutal escalation of what is already a brutal war.

To give the FARC spokesman due credit, he did not obfuscate or fudge or gloss over what I had expected to be an explosive topic, except at the very beginning. "Don't call them kidnappings," he told me. "We call them *retenciones*." (Rosa, a woman I later talked to who is closely connected to the high command of the Autodefensas Unidas de Colombia—the right-wing paramilitary troops who wage war principally against the civilian supporters of the guerrillas in rural areas—made a comparable objection when I asked her about the paramilitaries' policy of mass murder of civilians: "Don't call them massacres," she said. "We call them multiple military objectives.") "Kidnappings are a violation of human rights," the FARC spokesman went on to explain. "*Retenciones* aren't. When people don't pay taxes to the government, they are put in jail.[1] Since we don't have jails, we take our prisoners away somewhere. A lot of people pay without any problem. They come to us and say, 'How can we work this out?' Others send in their money without our even asking for it."

A portly gentleman who was one of the small group sitting at our table listened quietly to this explanation. It had been startling to find him at FARC headquarters, for he was a prominent Latin American politician. Visitors from all over the world have made publicized journeys to San Vicente in recent months—the travelers from the United States include the chairman emeritus of America Online and the president of the New York Stock Exchange[2]—but the politician was here on a very private visit. He would be identified only as "someone with long experience in Latin American peace processes," and he was here because his government, like others among the more powerful countries in the region, was deeply concerned that the peace talks in San Vicente should progress. As far as he could see, if the U.S. military aid package were approved, the talks would founder, the war would escalate into a bloody stalemate, and regional politics would feel the impact. But how were the talks proceeding?

After a year of stalling, the government delegates and the FARC negotiators sat down together at last in January and hammered out a schedule and an agenda for their talks. The headquarters for the dialogue—a prefab compound in a small village an hour away from San Vicente—was officially inaugurated. At the scheduled sessions, procedural questions are discussed and views are exchanged on what both sides have agreed will be the central topics of the talks: the economy, "humanitarian agreements" regarding the conduct of the war, and political reform. So

1. There is, in fact, no legal provision in Colombia for jailing citizens who fail to pay their taxes. Tax fraud, however, is punishable with jail, but in practice the sentence is rarely applied.
2. Both men accepted an invitation from the Pastrana government to meet with the guerrilla leadership and put in a good word for peace and the free market.

far, fifteen months after the talks were officially inaugurated, a real negotiation has yet to begin. It is easy for warring parties, under pressure from their constituencies and the international community, to establish a ritual encounter in peace negotiations, celebrate that encounter on a regular basis, and call it progress—this is usually referred to as a "peace process," as opposed to peace talks—and there are signs that this is what is happening in San Vicente. At the current rate, years could go by before any agreement affecting the actual conduct of the war is reached, and even this would depend on certain conditions: that the successor to President Andrés Pastrana, who will be elected two years from now, will have a mandate to proceed with the talks; that the guerrillas will also decide to continue talking despite the escalation of the war against them that the U.S. military aid package will bring, if approved; and that the army will remain neutral.

This last condition is particularly difficult. Last May, seventeen army generals and two hundred colonels threatened to resign over the issue of the *zona de despeje*, of which San Vicente is the unofficial capital. They were outraged about the size of the territory that had been granted to the guerrillas and, most particularly, about the limit set on how long the army will be kept outside the zone; that time expires in June, but it is indefinitely renewable.

Toward the end of last year there was a strong rumor that a large contingent of the paramilitaries' best-trained men had gathered just outside the zone, ready to invade. When I talked to Rosa, the woman with close links to the paramilitary high command, she would neither confirm nor deny that this rumor was true. But she did say that if the FARC were to be granted legitimacy—a more or less unavoidable condition for any peace treaty—she foresaw that a great many officers, primarily captains and colonels, would defect into the paramilitary force. The largest paramilitary force, the Autodefensas Unidas de Colombia, led by a man called Carlos Castaño, is said to number around 6,000. It is known to have close ties to the army field commanders who have been fighting the guerrillas—with atrocious violations of human rights—for years. At this stage, support for Castaño is still either tacit or clandestine among the officer corps. No one knows how many officers might be involved, but the numbers are said to be high.

It can be argued that better training and equipment, and the improved morale that would come from better results in the field, would make it possible for the army to reform itself from within. This is the view of the U.S. embassy, among others, and of a reform-minded Colombian major general I talked to, who pointed out that a portion of the U.S. aid package—$1.5 million—is earmarked for human rights training for the troops. A larger question is what the social and political costs would be of canceling negotiations and pushing for an exclusively military solution to the war.

Alfredo Rangel, a military analyst who last year published a widely quoted book about the war and its various areas of stalemate, makes a point of reminding interviewers that the FARC has significant support in the regions where it operates. Rangel points out that the last time there was a major campaign against coca cultivation—in the area more or less comprised by the *zona de despeje*—the FARC mobilized 100,000 *campesinos;* for nearly three months, they blocked all the access roads to the area. Nationwide, the guerrillas have some form of influence in about six hundred municipal districts—more than half the total in Colombia. And if one judges by their military effectiveness, Rangel notes, the FARC's ability to launch surprise attacks repeatedly, and in different parts of the country, is in itself politically significant. "In each case, a single warning by the civilian population would be enough to alert the army," he says. "And it doesn't happen."

Defeating the FARC in the field necessarily implies taking on some part of the rural population, but Rangel is among those who think that the U.S. Senate should approve the aid package for Colombia. The hope, Rangel says, "is not that the army will annihilate the guerrillas, but that the guerrillas will come to accept a peace formula under pressure from the improved military effectiveness of the army, as a result of the U.S. aid package." (This is, of course, not what the aid money is designed to accomplish. On paper, at least, it is supposed to help Colombia fight the cultivation of coca and the export of cocaine to the United States.)

The makeup of the FARC rank and file is another delicate issue: what is the cost, in morale and popular support, of bombing adolescents? Manuel Marulanda may well have had this particular point in mind when he insisted that the FARC will not increase the age for conscription into the guerrillas.

In view of the costs of escalating the war, the only thing worse than a stagnant, ritualized peace process is no peace process at all. As long as the talks go on, the guerrilla commanders who are involved in them are at last exposed to people, arguments, and problems that they never have had to deal with before. For the first time, the guerrillas are coexisting with the citizens of a small town, and even having to get along with its mayor, a bluff politico called Omar García.

One sweltering day, as I crossed San Vicente's central plaza, I heard what sounded like a terrible commotion coming out of the town hall. It was only the mayor speaking into the dreadful sound system, and everyone listening to him was calm, but García was saying some remarkable things. He took power in January of 1998 as the elected candidate of the Liberal Party, even though the FARC had called for an electoral boycott and San Vicente was then a focus of the war.

Six months later the mayor heard on the news that peace talks would be held and that his town would most likely be the headquarters for the guerrillas. He was never granted the meeting he requested with President Pastrana, but he was told that under the terms of the *zona de despeje* agreement, the autonomy of all the mayors in the area would be respected. Since then, he has been trying to make that agreement stick.

On this morning García was addressing a meeting of the one hundred or so leaders of the community action boards in his district. Some had the knobby-jointed, undernourished look of country people; some looked like accountants. On the platform with García were the municipal department heads and also "Mauricio," the FARC liaison with the local community.[3] Mauricio, a husky man in his mid-thirties with a florid complexion, who is in person affable and almost puppylike, had stationed one or two armed guerrillas at each of the hall's entrances. He himself was wearing a camouflage uniform and carrying a machine gun as he faced the audience. Having spent the previous afternoon with him, I suspected that Mauricio was not actually trying to intimidate San Vicente's elected officials. He was simply approaching the town hall as he would a hillside: give me one man at the foot of the tree with the view, and two more to guard the retreat.

Nevertheless, it seemed brave of the mayor to talk as he did. "I'm not here to say one thing in public and another in private," he said, looking at Mauricio. "We have a police force, and according to the agreement half of the members are appointed by us and half by the FARC. But who has authority over them? The municipality does, because if it doesn't, then what we have is yet another private armed group. And the evidence is that the FARC is using the police force as a recruitment center into its ranks. This can't be." The mayor was drenched in sweat, the audience was silent, and Mauricio's face was very red.

*

Apologetically, Nora announced one morning that Manuel Marulanda would not be receiving me, but that I was invited instead to a press conference by the chief spokesman of the FARC, a former Communist Party member who goes by the pseudonym of Raúl Reyes. There were four of us at the conference: a local TV producer-cameraman-soundman and his reporter, myself, and our taxi driver. We had driven for a couple of hours through cattle country at breakneck speed, finally coming to a halt at the top of a windswept hill where Reyes, a small, graying man who has something of a priestlike air, emerged from the foliage. The television producer asked the taxi driver to crouch out of camera

3. All guerrilla names, including Manuel Marulanda's, are pseudonyms. It would appear that only guerrilla commanders are given last names.

range and hold up two microphones from other news organizations in front of Reyes, to give the event more of the atmosphere of
a news conference. Reyes read a brief communiqué announcing
that a ten-day cease-fire—which had been called by the FARC as a
gesture of goodwill toward the talks—would not be prolonged, as
so many had hoped it would be. Then he answered a few of my
questions.

I asked him how he saw the grass-roots peace movement that
mobilized millions of people in marches and demonstrations all
over Colombia last year. "The great majority of the people in
Colombia want peace," he said. "So those people [the organizers
of the peace movement] didn't do anything special. It doesn't
have the slightest importance: the FARC could call for a demonstration at any moment, and millions of Colombians would come
out for it."

I thought of the guerrilla boys and girls I had seen shopping
for tennis shoes and barrettes in the streets of San Vicente, of the
tense relationship—but a relationship nevertheless—between the
FARC and the local mayor, of the guerrillas' contacts with U.S.
businessmen and Latin American politicians, and I asked Reyes if
he felt that the FARC had changed in any way as a result of the
experience of sharing social and political space with the inhabitants of San Vicente. "Absolutely not at all," he answered. "The
FARC has had a presence in these five municipal districts for a
long time. The only change is that now we can approach the *pueblo*
in the towns and give them a relief, but that kind of work has
always gone on in the countryside. Nothing is different."

That evening I had dinner in a *fonda* down the block from the
one frequented by the guerrilla leadership, and watched the
commander of the paramilitaries, Carlos Castaño, give his first
televised interview. The restaurant was full of ranchers in dusty,
pointy boots and cowboy hats. Some were with their families and
some sat by themselves or in groups, playing cards. They had been
paying no attention to the television screen—there is one in every
restaurant and store in San Vicente, and it is always on—until the

newscaster announced that the Castaño interview was coming on. One of the ranchers turned the volume way up, and everyone turned their chairs to face the screen. Over the past ten years Castaño has been directly responsible for the murder of thousands, perhaps tens of thousands, of Colombians living in the countryside, whom his spies fingered as sympathizers or supporters of the guerrillas. His crimes and his links with the army field commanders have been repeatedly denounced by Human Rights Watch and Colombian human rights organizations, and he is a figure of terror and revulsion to many, but clearly not to the cattle ranchers, forced for years to pay "taxes" to the FARC.

In the three-part interview, Castaño talked about how his father had been killed by the FARC, and how, despite the fact that he too obtains funds for his war against the guerrillas by levying taxes on the cocaine trade, he is in favor of coca-eradication programs, and how, when his men kidnapped Piedad Córdoba, a black activist senator from the Liberal Party, "the *negra* had a good time." (Castaño's troops rarely release their victims, but kill them instead. Córdoba later told me what Castaño had said to her in captivity: that the international outcry her abduction had provoked was forcing him to release her.) The leader of the paramilitaries kept his back turned to the camera throughout, but his voice ebbed and flowed expressively, and in moments of indignation the emphasis he put on every word made his meaty shoulders quiver. Compared with the stolid Raúl Reyes, Castaño was by far the better communicator. This also seemed to be the impression of the ranchers, who had not even looked up when Reyes appeared on the news, and who were now hanging on Castaño's every word. After his segment ended, they turned the volume back down and, without comment, went back to their tables.

Castaño has since given a second interview, in which he showed his face to the camera, wore a suit, acted like a politician, and made a tacit bid for recognition of his *autodefensas* as a belligerent organization on a par with the FARC. As the historian Gonzalo Sánchez once explained, one problem with the persistence of violence in Colombia is that there are never two but many sides involved in each conflict, and that when the government begins negotiations with one party, all the other parties demand the same treatment too. Perhaps Castaño's *autodefensas* will be incorporated in some fashion into peace negotiations, as the guerrillas of the ELN are apparently about to be. Leaving behind the various blood hatreds and ideological firing lines between ranchers and guerrillas, the paramilitaries, the Liberal Party, the Conservatives, and the army—in San Vicente, and in hundreds of other small towns like it—will take time even if the talks succeed.

On my last morning in San Vicente, I stopped by the FARC headquarters to say goodbye and found the atmosphere unusually relaxed. Nora was trudging about as always in her standard guerrilla-issue Wellington boots and carrying her machine gun. But she had just washed her hair and let it down, and at one point she put aside her weapon and had a long, neighborly, and clearly enjoyable chat with a middle-aged civilian woman. The large room where the guerrillas congregate smelled of pine soap and looked clean, and along the wall a row of knapsacks was stacked up neatly. A dozen boys in civilian dress, even younger-looking than the ones I was used to seeing in uniform, sat or lay on other knapsacks on the floor. They were watching television, as usual, but they were seeing a new kind of programming: guerrilla salsa music videos. A tall, long-haired young man in camouflage sang about freedom, the homeland, butterflies in the jungle, and ecology to a tropical soundtrack, while behind him other young men and women, in uniform and carrying weapons, danced and sang backup. (A beautiful black boy used his rocket-propelled grenade launcher as partner.) I asked one of the guerrilla girls who came bustling by what I was seeing. "They're FARC videos," she explained with a den-motherish air. "I put those on because these aren't guerrillas like us, but recruits, and they shouldn't just be watching *telenovelas* all the time."

At the *fonda* just next door I ordered *guanábana* juice and stared at the television, on which something called *Xena: Warrior Princess* was showing. Xena is beautiful and chaste. She is strong and fights on the side of the weak and against the exploiters and evil usurpers of power. She lives in some unidentified time before cars, machine guns, or body-concealing clothes were invented. Two waitresses, as young as the guerrillas next door, were glued to the program. And then I realized that the guerrillas were too. The FARC videos were still playing just on the other side of the wall, but the kids were taking turns sneaking out of the headquarters to stand at the doorway of the *fonda,* watching Xena.

—May 11, 2000

POSTSCRIPT

On June 29, 2000, Congress voted to approve $1.3 billion in aid to Colombia. Most of the money will go toward military training and the purchase of fifty helicopters for army use. Slightly less than 10 percent has been earmarked for improvements in human rights and in the justice system. The bill also sets the limit on the number of American military personnel who can be in Colombia at any one time at 500. At the height of U.S. military involvement in El Salvador, the total number of military advisers was never more than 150. At this writing, the peace talks, which have been stagnating for months, appear on the verge of collapse.

ERNESTO "CHE" GUEVARA

THE HARSH ANGEL

So many incinerated lives: the would-be guerrillas who starved to death in northern Argentina, the young men drowned in vats of excrement in Brazil, the eviscerated martyrs of Guatemala, the sociology student in Argentina whose severed hands were delivered in a jar to her mother—the children of Che. The slogans that defined those furious and hopeful times—"Two, Three, Many Vietnams!" and "The First Duty of a Revolutionary Is to Make the Revolution"—were Che's slogans. They sound foolish and empty now, but because it was Ernesto (Che) Guevara, the guerrilla hero, who pronounced them, they were heard and followed around the world. The range of his influence spans almost the entire latter half of the twentieth century.

He was the century's first Latin American: an astonishing fact, given that hundreds of millions of people in the hemisphere are joined by the same language, the same Iberian culture, the same religion, the same monstrously deformed class system, the same traditions of violence and rancor. Despite those essential bonds, Latin America's twenty-one nations lived in determined isolation and a common mistrust until Che came along and, through his acts, proclaimed himself a citizen of them all. He was an artist of scorn, heaping it on the sanctimonious, the officiously bureaucratic, the unimaginatively conformist, who whispered eagerly that the way things were was the best way that could be arranged. He was a living banner, determined to renounce all the temptations of power and to change the world by example. And he was a fanatic, consumed by restlessness and a frighteningly abstract hatred, who in the end recognized only one moral value as supreme: the willingness to be slaughtered for a cause.

Another astonishing fact is that so many members of my generation, who were just coming of age at the time of his death, wanted to be like him, and to obey him, even while we knew so little about him. It was only after he was hunted down by Bolivian army forces, on October 8, 1967, and the unforgettable picture of his corpse—emaciated torso, tousled hair, and liquid, vacant eyes—was displayed on the front pages of newspapers around the world that Che became familiar to young people. It was in death that he became known. Three biographies have come out this year. Two of them—*Che Guevara: A Revolutionary Life* by Jon Lee Anderson,[1] and *Compañero: The Life and Death of Che Guevara* by Jorge Castañeda[2]—are groundbreaking: they take on the difficult task of demolishing the Che legend, as it was created and nurtured over the decades by the Cuban regime he had helped found. The third, *Guevara, Also Known as Che* by Paco Ignacio Taibo II,[3] hews too closely to the official myth. Taibo, best known outside Mexico as the author of a number of inventive detective novels, is an engaging and lively writer, but his hagiography is intended only for the true believer.

Anderson's book is an epic end run around the guardians of the Che legend. A journalist who has made a career writing about wars and guerrillas, Anderson lived in Cuba for three years in order to do this project, and he persuaded Che's second wife, Aleida March, to let him read Che's private diaries. He also seems to have talked to everyone else still alive who ever knew Guevara, and one of the things that such dogged reporting has enabled him to do is to tell us, in wonderful new detail, about the hero as a youth.

Ernesto Guevara de la Serna was born in Argentina in 1928, the son of an intellectually curious, high-strung mother and a debo-

1. New York: Grove, 1997.
2. New York: Knopf, 1997.
3. New York: St. Martin's, 1997.

nair, womanizing father who ran through his wife's fortune and never quite managed to get any of his own business schemes off the ground. The couple fought constantly, and the father slept sometimes on the living-room sofa, sometimes in another house. At the age of two, Ernestito, the firstborn and favorite of the Guevaras' children (they had five), developed asthma, and for long stretches throughout his childhood he was bedridden. Spurred on by his mother, Celia, he became a precocious and methodical reader and a stoic patient. As with Teddy Roosevelt, physical hardship and endurance became a habit, and Ernesto seems never to have succumbed to the invalid's temptation to engage in complaint and self-indulgence.

In adolescence, and at least partly as a response to his handicap, Ernesto emerged as a full-fledged macho, having his way with the family maids (once literally behind the back of his favorite and very straitlaced aunt, who was then sitting primly at the dining-room table); refusing at the age of fifteen to attend a protest demonstration because he did not have a revolver; making it a point of pride never to bathe. (His upper-middle-class schoolmates remember his nickname, Chancho, or Pig, not so much because it was ugly as because he was so proud of it.) Before his machismo destroyed him, it served him well: it tempered his will and spurred him to become an athlete—one who, despite the crippling asthma, always made a point of outracing, outkicking, and outhiking his less exigent peers. (Machismo also gave him style: in the midst of his physical exploits, he would stop and suck on his inhaler for a few moments, or give himself a quick adrenaline injection through his clothes, and then return to the field.)

At twenty-two, when he was studying medicine in Buenos Aires, he discovered that the life of a wanderer suited him. Interrupting his studies, he left home and motorbiked alone through northern Argentina. The following year, he and his best friend embarked on an eight-month hitchhiking adventure: it took them through northern Argentina again and then on to Chile, Peru, Colombia, Venezuela, and, finally, the United States. He was already a disciplined diarist, and a few years later, when he was no longer signing himself "Pig" but, rather, "Che," he took his notes from that trip and turned them into a book. It was translated into English in 1995 and became a brisk seller for the British publishing house Verso, under the title *The Motorcycle Diaries*.[4]

The diarist is an idealistic young medical student who has chosen his profession as a way of doing good in the world but otherwise does not think much about politics. The living conditions of the people he travels among shock him, but he is just as susceptible to the wonder of Machu Picchu. He comes across as high-spirited—jumping into a cold lake to retrieve a downed duck—endlessly curious, amusing, and very likable: "Allergic as I am to the cold, swimming . . . made me suffer like a bedouin. Just as well that roast duck, seasoned as usual by our hunger, is an exquisite dish."

By his own account, this jolly and enthusiastic young man was buried forever at the expedition's close. The last section of *The Motorcycle Diaries* is eerie. In a dreamlike, utterly different voice, he recounts a meeting with a mysterious prophet, who tells him that revolution will come to Latin America, and that it will destroy those who cannot join it. After recounting this conversation, Guevara writes:

> I knew that when the great guiding spirit cleaves humanity into two antagonistic halves, I will be with the people. . . . Howling like a man possessed, [I] will assail the barricades and trenches, will stain my weapon with blood and, consumed with rage, will slaughter any enemy I lay hands on.

We will probably never know when Guevara tacked this final entry onto the original, beguiling text, or what circumstances provoked it. We do know that his discovery of the revolutionary faith transformed him, as a writer, into a hopeless termagant. And we know something more remarkable: that the words he wrote were not simply a young man's posturing, for from the time of his

---

4. Published in the United States as *The Motorcycle Diaries: A Journey Around South America* (New York: Norton, 1995).

final departure from Argentina the following year, 1953, to the moment of his death, in 1967, the asthmatic, footloose, irreverent diarist sought to become the iron-willed avenger of his prophecy. Another idealistic and enterprising young man, upon being confronted with the poverty, racism, and injustice that Guevara sees and records in *The Motorcycle Diaries,* might have strengthened his commitment to medicine, or thought of ways to give Latin America's poor the weapon of literacy. For reasons that even the most ambitious biographer can only speculate on—rage against his father, love of humanity—Guevara decided instead to spend his life creating Che, the harsh angel.

Guevara remained a pilgrim for another three years, waiting for a cause to find him. During that time, he floated northward again, read Marx and Lenin, and decided that he was a Marxist. In Bolivia in 1953, he was a skeptical witness of Víctor Paz Estenssoro's populist revolution, whose limited—but hardly insignificant—achievements included the liberation of the Indian peasantry from virtual fiefdom and the establishment of universal suffrage. For his part, Guevara never considered any alternatives to violence and radicalism, and perhaps it is true that in the Latin America of those years it required more self-delusion to be a moderate reformer than to be a utopian revolutionary. At any rate, a nine-month stay in Guatemala was cut short by the 1954 coup against the reformist government of Jacobo Arbenz—a coup sponsored by the Central Intelligence Agency. This monumentally stupid event not only set Guatemala on the road to decades of bloodshed but confirmed Che's conviction that in politics only those willing to shed blood make a difference.

In late 1954, Guevara arrived in Mexico, and he spent two years there that would have been listless and inconsequential but for two events. He made an unhappy marriage to a Peruvian radical he had first met in Guatemala, Hilda Gadea, and he had a child with her. (Guevara and women is a nasty subject. Anderson, ever attentive to his subject's sex life, quotes from Guevara's unpublished diary on the courtship: "Hilda declared her love in epistolary and practical form. I was with a lot of asthma, if not I might have fucked her. . . . The little letter she left me upon leaving is very good, too bad she is so ugly.") And he met Fidel Castro, who arrived in Mexico in 1955, fresh from a two-year imprisonment in Cuba following his disastrous assault on the Moncada army barracks.

There is no record of Ernesto Guevara's ever before, or subsequently, expressing unrestrained admiration for a fellow being. Fidel, with his natural bonhomie, energy, and boundless faith in his own leadership, was the exception. The chemistry was mutual: Fidel trusted him, relied on him, and, on the evidence, loved him more than any of his other comrades, with the possible exception of Celia Sánchez (Fidel's closest companion until her death, in 1980). Guevara's relationship to love, whether it involved his parents, his comrades, or his women, was uneasy, but his love of Fidel was wholehearted and transforming, because it opened the path to the life he was seeking. Within hours of their first meeting, Guevara signed on as a medic for Fidel's harebrained plan to land an expedition on the eastern end of Cuba and start an insurrection against the dictator Fulgencio Batista.

In November of 1956, the creaky yacht *Granma* set sail from Veracruz, bound for Cuba and glory. By then, the Argentine Guevara, who, like all his countrymen, interjected the word *che*— roughly, "man," or "you"—at least once in every sentence (as in "Hey, *che,* is that the way to clean a rifle, *che?*"), had been rebaptized. He would be, forevermore, *el Che*—the Argentine. It was a term that underlined not only the affection and respect his comrades felt for him but also their intense awareness of his differentness, his permanent standing as a foreigner in the revolution he had adopted as his own.

He was keenly aware of his outsider status as he sailed for Cuba. Other portents must have been harder for him to see. There was his medical training, for example, which had drilled into him the universality of the principle of the scientific cure (that is, that penicillin, say, will get rid of pneumonia in both a French peasant and a Mexican socialite). A central flaw in his thinking for the rest of his life was to assume that what he learned about guerrilla warfare in the process of overthrowing Batista amounted to a prescription—a necessary remedy for every form of social disease. Another flaw was that he was inescapably committed to a certain definition of virility and to the code of conduct it implied: a macho definition, not unusual among Latin Americans of his generation. As a result, he found it unbearably humiliating ever to lose face, back down, admit defeat. He could not see that Sancho Panza might be as heroic as Quixote. And he was as blind to nuances of character as he was tone-deaf: for all the painful insights into his own nature that he reveals in his diaries, and for all his astute observations in them on landscape, warfare, and political dynamics, there are no credible portraits of his fellow-men. There are only revolutionaries, who are full of virtue, and counterrevolutionaries, who are worthless.

The next chapter in Che's life coincides with one of the century's most startling military triumphs. Having landed as disastrously as was to be expected on Cuba's shores, Che, Fidel Castro, Fidel's brother Raúl Castro, and a handful of others survived Batista's ferocious assault and went on to forge the beginnings of a revolutionary army in the Sierra Maestra. By 1958, Che's military intuition and daring, his organizational skills, and his outstanding personal bravery had won him the undisputed title of Comandante and a leading role in the revolution. Sharing his life with Cubans, who have always held ablutions and nattiness to be almost supreme virtues, Guevara still refused to bathe, or even tie his shoelaces, but now that he was Che, his odorous aura was part of a mystique. He was roughing it in the great outdoors, planning strategy with Fidel, sharing his camp cot with a stunning *mulata,* risking his life and proving his manhood on a daily basis. His days, as he narrates them in *Reminiscences of the Cuban Revolutionary War*[5] (again, reworked pages from his diary turned into a book), read blissfully like an adventure out of *Boys' Life.* And yet it is at this point, according to Anderson, that Che wrote in his unpublished diary:

5. New York: Monthly Review Press, 1972.

A little combat broke out in which we retreated very quickly. The position was bad and they were encircling us, but we put up little resistance. Personally I noted something I had never felt before: the need to live. That had better be corrected in the next opportunity.

Happiness and the desire for it—"the need to live"—were, in a revolutionary, symptoms of weakness.

Che's life following the revolution's triumph was a slow accretion of wreckage, and it is in the narration of this collapse that *Compañero,* Jorge Castañeda's beautiful and passionate biography, is most lucid. We turn the pages hoping that the trouble will end soon, that Guevara may be spared, or spare himself, if not from failure, then from ludicrous defeat; if not from hideous physical suffering, then from death; if not from death, then from ignominy. But Castañeda is as unflinching as his hero: he has searched CIA records and the recollections of Guevara's closest comrades in order to prise away layers of after-the-fact justifications and embellishments of the Che legend. In the process, he makes Ernesto Guevara understandable at last, and his predicament deeply moving.

Castañeda's Che is a man who could not bear the natural ambivalence of the world, and found relief from it (and, curiously, from the torment of asthma) only in the unequivocal rigors of battle and radicalism. Appointed first to the National Agrarian Reform Institute and then to head the Central Bank in Fidel's revolutionary regime, he was, like so many other battle heroes, before and after him, flummoxed by the day-to-day realities of governance. Why should Cuba have a monetary policy that sought to placate imperialism? Why was it necessary to compensate exploiters and oppressors for their sugarcane haciendas instead of merely expropriating the land for *el pueblo?* Why corrupt workers by offering them more money to work harder? Che nearly killed himself accumulating "volunteer work hours" of his own, cutting cane and stacking sacks of sugar after the grueling hours he put in at his desk, in order to prove that moral incentives could beat lucre as a stimulus to productivity. He may have begun to suspect toward the end of his stay in Cuba that other mortals liked to put their free time to a different use. He certainly believed that the Revolution's leadership was tacking dangerously toward pragmatism. "The New Man"—a new type of human being that the Revolution was to manufacture—was not being turned out swiftly enough.

Che was unable to deal with his disapproval of the course that Fidel was taking and his simultaneous love for the man; with his disillusionment with the Soviet Union and the self-satisfaction of the burgeoning Cuban bureaucracy; with the palace intrigues of the new regime (particularly those of Fidel's brother Raúl); and, probably, with the gnawing awareness of his own failings as a peacetime revolutionary. It seems reasonable to interpret his decision to leave Cuba as Casteñeda does—as the result of his need to get away from so much internal conflict. (In the course of explaining this decision, Castañeda provides an extraordinary account of the ins and outs of Cuban state policy, Cuban-Soviet relations, and Castro's dealings with the United States.) Che was leaving behind a second wife, six children, his comrades, his years of happiness, and the revolution he had helped give birth to; none of these were enough to convince him that he belonged.

Guevara's original intention was to return to his homeland and start a guerrilla movement there. A 1965 expedition to the Congo, where various armed factions were still wrestling for power long after the overthrow and murder of Patrice Lumumba, and his last stand in Bolivia, Castañeda writes, followed improbably from Fidel's anxious efforts to keep Che away from Argentina, where he was sure to be detected and murdered by Latin America's most efficient security forces. Castro seems to have felt that the Congo would be a safer place, and the question of whether it was a more intelligent choice doesn't seem to have been addressed either by him or by the man he was trying to protect. (In Cairo, Jon Lee Anderson notes, Gamal Abdel Nasser warned Che not to get militarily involved in Africa, because there he would be "like Tarzan, a white man among blacks, leading and protecting them.")

As things turned out, the Congo episode was a farce, so absurd that Cuban authorities kept secret Che's rueful draft for a book on it—until recently, that is, when one of his new biographers, Taibo, was able to study the original manuscript. Guevara was abandoned from the beginning by Congolese military leaders, such as Laurent Kabila, who had initially welcomed his offer of help. He was plagued by dysentery and was subject to fits of uncontrollable anger, and emerged from seven months in the jungle forty pounds lighter, sick, and severely depressed. If he had ever considered a decision to cut bait and return to Cuba, that option was canceled weeks before the Congo expedition's rout: on October 5, 1965, Fidel Castro, pressed on all sides to explain Che's disappearance from Cuba and unable to recognize that the African adventure was about to collapse, decided to make public Che's farewell letter to him: "I will say once again that the only way that Cuba can be held responsible for my actions is in its example. If my time should come under other skies, my last thought will be for this people, and especially for you."

Guevara was sitting in a miserable campsite on the shores of Lake Tanganyika, bored, frustrated, and in mourning for his mother, when he was told that Fidel had publicized the letter. The news hit him like an explosion. "Shit-eaters!" he said, pacing back and forth in the mud. "They are imbeciles, idiots."

Guevara's final trek began at this moment, because once his farewell to Fidel was made public, as Castañeda writes, "his bridges were effectively burned. Given his temperament, there was now no way he could return to Cuba, even temporarily. The idea of a public deception was unacceptable to him: once he had said he was leaving, he could not go back." He could not bear to lose face.

A few months later, having taken full and bitter stock of his situation, he made the decision to set up a guerrilla base—intended as a training camp, really—in southern Bolivia, near the border with Argentina. From there, he convinced himself, he would ultimately be able to spark the revolutionary flame in Argentina and, from there, throughout the world.

He knew, of course, that his death would fan that flame. One wonders if he had any sense in the final awful weeks of how badly things would end, not just for him but for everyone involved in the ubiquitous attempts at armed radical revolution that followed upon his death. I am thinking now of Guatemala, which, more than any other country in the hemisphere besides Cuba, formed Guevara's view of the world and was a testing ground for his ideas about class warfare and the struggle for liberation, and which paid the price. And I am thinking of the Guatemalans I knew, like the poet Alaíde Foppa, a feminist editor, art historian, and critic, who was a great friend of my mother's. Alaíde had lived in exile in Mexico with her husband, Alfonso Solórzano, since the 1954 coup against Arbenz. They had five children, including Mario, who returned to Guatemala in the late seventies to found an opposition newspaper. The youngest, Juan Pablo, joined a Guatemalan guerrilla organization. The group's founders, who had trained in Cuba and been directly encouraged by Che, shared his faith that a small group of steel-willed men could win the people's support and overthrow an unjust regime, no matter how large or well trained the enemy's army might be, or what foreign powers might decide to intervene. In 1979, Juan Pablo was captured by the military and killed. In Mexico City two weeks later, his despondent father died when he walked into oncoming traffic.

Just before Christmas of the following year, 1980, I arrived in Mexico from Central America, expecting to spend Christmas Eve with my mother at Alaíde's house. That did not happen, however, because when I walked into my mother's apartment I found her holding the phone, silent with shock. Alaíde, following her son's death, had apparently made the decision to match his sacrifice: she traveled to Guatemala City on a courier mission for the guerrillas, and there, the caller on the phone had just told my mother, she was almost instantly detected and "disappeared" by the security forces. According to information gleaned by her relatives, she was kept alive and tortured for months. Her corpse has never been found.

And then Mario was killed. I had last seen him the previous year. We had had dinner in Mexico City, and he had listened joyfully to my account of the Sandinistas' overthrow of Anastasio Somoza in Nicaragua—a spectacularly unforeseen event, which I had covered as a reporter, and which had revitalized flagging guerrilla forces everywhere. I had no idea that within weeks of my meeting with Mario he himself would go underground, joining the guerrillas' urban infrastructure in the Guatemalan capital. He learned in clandestinity of his mother's disappearance, and then he too was betrayed. Someone revealed the location of his safe house to the army (probably under torture, which true revolutionaries, unlike other human beings, were supposed to resist to the end, but rarely could), and Mario was ambushed and killed. This occurred during a period of weeks when the military regime unleashed a campaign of systematic massacre directed against Mayan *campesinos* who had joined the guerrilla group that Mario belonged to. Because the *campesinos* were poorly trained and poorly armed, and the army troops were not, and because support for the guerrillas was only substantial, not overwhelming, thousands of impoverished men and women paid with their lives for their revolutionary beliefs. It was only last year, after twenty years of brutal struggle, that peace was signed in Guatemala.

Alaíde and Mario appear in my memory whenever I try to make sense of those fervid times. I remember my mother too, who, having been forced at last out of her distrust of politics, stood timidly in a crowd in front of the Guatemalan embassy and whispered slogans against the dictatorship (she hated crowds and slogans, and did not know how to shout), because something had to be done even though there was nothing left to do. Alaíde was exceptional only in that she was sixty-seven when she responded to the call issued in Havana by Fidel on the day he told Cubans that Ernesto Guevara was dead. "Be like Che!" Fidel cried, and the exhortation gave purpose to an entire generation that desperately needed a way of being in the modern world, a way to act that could fill life with meaning and transcendence. But, in the end, Che, who, unlike Fidel, was quite uncurious about how the real world worked—why people supported or failed to support a cause, how General Motors turned out cars, what accounted for the Mexican ruling party's longevity—could offer only one course of action, and this was his tragedy, and that of Alaíde and her children: the only way to be like Che was to die like him, and all those deaths were not enough to create the perfect world that Che wanted.

I think of Che, starving and thirsty in Bolivia, hardly able to walk because of weakness and asthma, and lost, wandering in circles with a handful of comrades through the scrubby Bolivian highlands while the army and its CIA advisers drew their noose tighter. (Perhaps, Castañeda speculates, he and his hopeless cause had been abandoned at this stage by the support network in Cuba.) His companions on this dismal trek were men who had signed on, out of devotion to him, for what was evidently a suicide mission, but he would deprive them of what meager rations there were as punishment for the smallest act of indiscipline, and call them trash. Che, who loved animals, wrote in his diary that he had stabbed his skinny mare in a fit of rage and frustration. One can see from his account how diminished and stilted were the emotions he dared allow himself three months before he was killed, and how very stubborn he was:

> I am a human wreck and the episode with the little mare proves that at moments I have lost control; this will be rectified but the situation must weigh evenly on all of us, and whoever doesn't feel capable of bearing the load must say so. This is one of those moments in which large decisions must be made: this type of struggle gives us the opportunity to become revolutionaries, the highest rank in the human species, but it also allows us to graduate as men. Those who are incapable of achieving either of these two stages should say so and abandon the struggle.

Guevara was born in Latin America's hour of the hero. So many of our leaders have been so corrupt, and the range of allowed and possible public activity has been so narrow, and injustice has cried out so piercingly to the heavens, that only a hero could answer the call, and only a heroic mode of life could seem worthy. Guevara stood out against the inflamed horizon of his time, alone and unique.

There is, however, a problem with the heroic figure (as the Cubans, who kept Che's diaries and documents secret all this while, perceived), and that is that the hero can have no faults, and is answerable, as Che was, only to his own exalted sense of honor. This picture of the hero is still satisfying to large numbers of Latin Americans who are not in a position to exact an accounting from their leaders but do, on the other hand, demand that their leaders act grandly and provoke fervor and states of rapture, as the dead Che now does. But the living Che was not the perfect hero for his time and place: he demanded that others follow his impossible example, and never understood how to combine what he wanted with what was achievable. It remains forever a matter of debate whether Che's life and example speeded the advent of the present era, in which there are no perfect causes, and where men like him are more than ever out of place.

—October 6, 1997

A   V I S I T   T O   H A V A N A

J*anuary 23, 1998:* The pope is in Havana, and at the last moment I have flown to Cuba to see for myself what such an event might look like. Hundreds of other nonreligious foreigners like myself, I gather, have been drawn here by the same hungry curiosity: we wish to see Fidel at the open-air altar that has been set up in the Plaza de la Revolución, flanked by the images of Che and José Martí, kneeling as John Paul II celebrates mass. The papal visit is expected to change many things, but much has already changed, and after fifteen years' absence from Cuba, I find it difficult to adjust to the startling new reality already evident at the airport, busy with tourists and pilgrims even at this late hour. At the luggage belt a man in uniform offers his services as a porter. Customs agents do not bother to inspect my luggage, which I have kept carefully free of any literature that might be considered suspicious. Taxis with meters wait at curbside. They expect to be paid in dollars, whose possession was cause for severe punishment only five years ago.

In the comfortable, spare hotel room that comes with my budget papal tour package, I switch on the television to CNN and catch bits of the pope's homily during the morning's mass in Camagüey. His Spanish is fluent, but because of his speech difficulties, which are supposed to be a consequence of Parkinson's disease, one has to pay close attention in order to understand the words. On this occasion he is discussing the tasks and problems of the young, and there is little that he has not said before. On another channel the Cuban evening news is broadcasting other fragments of the day's events: Fidel Castro, in an elegant dark suit, is seen looking alternately at the pope and at the floor of a beautiful portal in the National University. The pope is shuffling painfully across the entryway, and Fidel Castro is taking tiny steps to match his pace. His hands are clasped as if in prayer, and the look in his eyes seems reverential. Later, I will be told by someone whom I assume to be reliable that the emotion visible in the face of this militant atheist is avowedly genuine: How, Fidel has commented, could he have failed to be stirred by the presence in Cuba of this particular pope, given that he spent years in his childhood and adolescence attending mass and praying for the Holy Father every day at Catholic schools? In the Cuban leader's eyes, he has declared on other occasions, John Paul II is one of the most powerful men in the world because, unlike political world leaders, he does not have to make alliances with or offer concessions to anyone. One assumes that when he says this Fidel is wistfully including himself among the ranks of the uncomfortable concession makers, and that it is when he compares the pope's freedom with his own long servitude to the geriatric leaders of the Soviet Union that his admiration increases. In addition, Fidel's most sincere respect is probably reserved for those who demonstrate physical courage, and this is a virtue of which the pope gives evidence with every crippled step. And more—my informant says that a great friend of Fidel's has quoted him as saying, more or less, the following: The pope is an unpretentious man who receives one in private, without interpreters or aides, and listens courteously, unlike so many heads of some dipshit states (*paisitos de mierda*) who come here and feel they can give themselves all sorts of airs.

It can be argued that Fidel owes his life to the Church, or, more specifically, to Archbishop Enrique Pérez Serantes of the city of Santiago: in 1953, when dictator Fulgencio Batista's troops were hunting down, torturing, and killing participants in Fidel's disastrous attack on the Moncada barracks, the bishop led a campaign to protect the lives and physical integrity of the captured rebels. Fidel himself had fled with two others into the Sierra Maestra hills following the failed assault. To his eternal chagrin, an army search party found the exhausted three while they were sound asleep. They were not shot on the spot because the commanding officer turned out to be a man of uncommon scruple, who shouted to his men as they were preparing to fire, "You don't kill ideas!" At around that same hour, a group of five other freshly captured rebels farther down the road to Santiago were about to be executed by a different group of soldiers, but just as the firing squad was taking aim, they were spotted by Monsignor Pérez Serantes, who had been driving up and down the country road searching for the rebels and calling out to them.

The priest gathered up his skirts and ran toward the prisoners, yelling "Don't kill them!" to the soldiers. A short while later, Fidel and his two captured comrades appeared on the same road, bound for Santiago, where their captor would have to turn the three over to a notoriously bloodthirsty superior. Although the bishop demanded that the prisoners be surrendered to him instead, for safekeeping (Fidel, for the record, protested that he was surrendering to no one), they were nevertheless delivered to the butchers at the Moncada army barracks. Yet the fact that their arrest had been witnessed by the archbishop must certainly have contributed to Castro's later safety in prison.

The episode is narrated in detail in Tad Szulc's *Fidel: A Critical Portrait,*[1] but when Frei Betto, a Brazilian Dominican friar who is a great admirer of the Cuban Revolution, asked him about it in 1985, in the course of a series of interviews, Fidel determinedly avoided discussing the archbishop's role in protecting the rights of the Moncada prisoners. Among those who know him, Fidel has a reputation for generosity when it comes to recognizing political debts and favors—but he is also someone who rewrites history at his convenience, and when Frei Betto asked him about the archbishop, Fidel was much more interested in demonstrating that it was the hopelessly reactionary character of the Catholic Church in Cuba that forced him to formulate his repressive policies against

1. New York: Morrow, 1986, p. 278.

it. A brave, if conservative, priest who acted in accordance with his humanitarian beliefs did not fit the discourse of the moment. The interviews with the Brazilian friar were collected under the title *Fidel Castro y la religión: Conversaciones con Frei Betto*[2] and published simultaneously in book form in Mexico and Cuba by Siglo XXI Editores in 1986, and their clear intention is to show the Cuban leader at his nondogmatic best—a delicate task. Nevertheless, *Conversations* is an enlightening and even engaging book on many counts: Frei Betto, a cheery and seemingly guileless man, feels passionately about food, and as a result we learn not only that Fidel is also a cook, but that he is the kind of cook who argues about whether the mixture of ground vegetables and meat used to clarify beef stock (the "raft") should include an egg white mixed with its shell or without it. We learn that in his private office Fidel has a large portrait of his comrade and revolutionary hero Camilo Cienfuegos, done in pastel colors (but not one of Che). We learn that the private, informal Fidel cannot help expressing almost everything, including emotions, in terms of numbers and fractions and percentages, just as he does in his speeches. (And in his private correspondence: Szulc quotes from the letters he wrote while in solitary confinement following the Moncada assault. "I have now spent three thousand hours completely alone, . . ." he records, and, to another friend, "I am convinced one could make happy all [of Cuba's] inhabitants. I would be disposed to bring upon myself the hatred and ill-will of a thousand or two men, among them some relatives, half of my friends, two thirds of my colleagues, and four fifths of my former college companions! . . ."

Mostly, we see how Fidel, among whose emblematic slogans is "Turn Defeat into Victory!" is also skilled at making a virtue of necessity. The conversations with Frei Betto are, it would appear, intended for many kinds of readers, but addressed to one in particular, John Paul II. When Karol Wojtyla assumed the throne of

---

2. Published in English as *Fidel and the Revolution: Castro Talks on Revolution and Religion with Frei Betto* (New York: Simon & Schuster, 1987).

Saint Peter, his views on communism were known within the socialist world, but so were his distaste for modern capitalism and his view that the United States' economic embargo of Cuba was wrong. Fidel appears to have made some inquiries among his East European contacts about just who this new pope was, and within months of John Paul's election, in February of 1979, he invited him to use Cuba as a refueling point on his return from a visit to Mexico.

The Cuban Church was also eager for a visit that would strengthen its hand against the government. In 1989, the collapse of socialism interfered with a visit whose date had already been set, and subsequently a harsh criticism of the regime by the Cuban bishops chilled relations again for another few years. Yet the fact remained that only the pope could publicly embarrass the Miami-based organizations of Cuban exiles who, together with Jesse Helms, are the embargo's only significant lobbyists. Despite the pope's skillful maneuvering to replace the left-wing hierarchy in the Latin American Catholic Church with bishops and cardinals who shared his own conservative views; despite the disastrous encounter between the pope and Fidel's Sandinista allies in Nicaragua in 1981; despite the pope's role in bringing down the Communist regime in Poland; and despite the fact that until 1991 Catholics were openly mocked, kept out of the ruling party, and denied the smallest privileges the regime had within its power to offer, Fidel held true to his initial insight that the most powerful weapon against the thirty-year embargo against his country—or "blockade," as it is invariably referred to in Cuba— would be a visit by the pope. When the pope rebuffed his initial improvised invitation in 1979, Fidel sulked for a bit, but by 1985 he was campaigning for a visit again, through diplomatic channels as well as indirect ones, like the published interviews with Frei Betto. In these interviews he also appears to be convincing himself, almost before our eyes, that John Paul II and he are, *au fond,* compatible. In subsequent interviews and speeches Fidel would represent Karol Wojtyla as an enlightened Polish patriot, a courageous fighter, a great athlete, a man of deep faith, and a world leader whose social concerns are virtually identical to those of the Cuban Revolution, much as the successive bureaucratic leaders of the Soviet Union that Castro had to deal with always appeared as selfless and loyal revolutionaries. Here, with Frei Betto, Fidel is just feeling his way:

> In these days I am trying to gather material. I've not only got already almost all the books by [revolutionary theologians Leonardo] Boff and [Gustavo] Gutiérrez, but with great interest I've also asked for and obtained copies of all the Pope's speeches in his last tour through Latin America. . . . I'm convinced that in these visits the Pope must have understood the difference that exists between the abundance of material goods and extravagant spending that can be observed in wealthy and developed Europe . . . but also the dreadful poverty, the massive misery that . . . he found in Latin America's cities and fields. . . . And I confess to you, the Pope's concerns regarding this topic pleased me.

Later in the conversation he adds, "It must be acknowledged that the Pope is a remarkable politician." Twelve years after the interviews with Frei Betto, Fidel has managed at last to establish conditions and offer guarantees sufficient to persuade Pope John Paul II, a sick and possibly dying man, and a very remarkable politician indeed, that a trip to Cuba will satisfy both sides' aspirations. There is a difference, though, between the two: the Church has made no concessions. In order to visit Cuba, John Paul has not softened his stand on any issue—from abortion, so widely practiced here, to the demand that open-air masses be permitted and broadcast live. And for him, it is a risk-free excursion. No one within the Vatican or among the faithful will condemn him for traveling to a Communist state—look what a similar trip produced in Poland!

Fidel Castro, who is also rumored to be very ill, has made many concessions. Following up on the offer he dangled before Frei Betto, the Cuban Communist Party modified its statutes in

1991 to admit confessed Catholics. Harassment of all religions has ceased (although this is not to be confused with freedom; Catholics are still not allowed to teach schoolchildren, for example). And the pope's masses are indeed being broadcast live. Fidel has everything to lose: his own faithful, who learned their atheism at his knee, may well feel betrayed and disaffected. As for Catholics in Cuba, who knows their number, or what they are capable of, or what sympathies they may inspire once they are allowed in the open?

*

January 24: At sunrise, I awake wondering what the man from the strip-mined flatlands of Poland might make of the sparkling din in the air: thousands of different bird calls—whoops and whistles and twitters and cheeps—come from the mango trees and *almendros* that surround the hotel as well as the nuncio's residence not far away, where the pope is staying. Havana is one of the most beautiful cities in the world, with an exhalation of ferns and flowers twisting their way around the crumbling pastel columns of porticos that shelter even modest houses from the sun, their charm made only more poignant by the fact that they look as if they could be brought down by blowing hard on them. The mango trees are in full, lush bloom, the air is cool, and a dense mist hides the ocean from view. The pope is acutely sensitive to physical beauty: during his visit to the Dominican Republic years ago I watched him, still in his prime and brimming with the excitement of being who he was at that particular moment, coo with delight as he was shown around Santo Domingo's glorious sixteenth-century cathedral.

His five-day experience of Havana is to be limited both by his frailty and by his itinerary: every morning he is whisked to the airport and to a different provincial city, and every afternoon he is whisked back in time for a meal, rest, and then a meeting that begins after dark.

Nevertheless, from the back of the compact version of the Popemobile he is using here, he can see Cubans pedaling or walking to

work or standing in line for a bus when he rides out to the airport in the early morning. He will see that they are carefully
combed and neatly dressed in simple outfits of tacky synthetic
stuff, or in cotton T-shirts and shorts, all impeccably ironed and
worn with something ornamental—even if only a necklace of
plastic beads or a few rings made of tin alloy or bands of copper,
or a scrap of hemmed material folded and tucked into a shirt
pocket. He will see that they are orderly, cheerful, happy to see the
pope, and wherever he goes, they will wave and call out a greeting
to him.

It is too bad that he will not get close enough to know that they
are freshly bathed, if only with a bucketful of water, and that if
they have soap they will smell of it, and that if they don't they will
have perfumed themselves with a little *agua de violetas* or with a
few drops of lemon juice dabbed on their hair. The pope, like
sightless people or the deaf, will have learned by now to use other
senses to determine the character and mood of the people he travels among, and although it might seem that huge outdoor events
offer little chance for knowledge, his most intense communication
with those people evidently takes place in the course of the daily
outdoor masses. The uninhibited good nature with which Cubans
at mass banter with the Pope and improvise little conga refrains
for him (they do the same thing with the characters on the screen
in movie houses) has already amused him in his first two masses in
Santa Clara and Camagüey.

Today I am meeting relatives of a Cuban I knew in Mexico,
to take a walk around Old Havana and watch the day's mass
on television in a coffee shop or bar. During my last visit, which
took place at the height of Cuba's Soviet-sponsored prosperity, in
1983, it was possible to walk for miles without finding a place
to buy anything to eat or drink, and one was reduced to knocking
on a door and asking for a glass of water when desperate. But
now there are little coffee and pizza stands everywhere in Havana,
and the occasional peddlers with pushcarts offer everything from
lemon ices to fresh hot rolls as they wander among the city's col-

lapsing mansions and devastated apartment buildings. We aim to be fancier today, though, and splurge at one of the new dollars-only hotels.

In the Cathedral Plaza of Old Havana my friend's parents and I stand and stare. They live and work in Havana but have not been here in a couple of years—they have been too busy, they say—and we are all having a hard time taking in the changes. The plaza is and always has been small—in memory, about the size of a large stage set—intimate, unpretentious, delicate in its proportion and execution, the coral limestone used for the construction of its enclosing palaces giving the whole a lacy, tropical flourish. In the ruinous state in which I last saw this space (the Revolution did not then attach much importance to the monuments of colonialism), it was heart-stopping—a symbol both of the Cuba that had been denied and of the Cuba that existed, and of the power of beauty to endure. In 1982, UNESCO declared Old Havana a World Heritage Site, and began restoration, which continues today under the supervision of the Cuban government.

The government now attaches great importance to the monuments of the colonial era because, following the collapse of the Soviet Union and the end of its subsidy of the Cuban economy, tourism has become the primary source of foreign currency, over-taking sugar by a long stretch. Refurbished, polished, cleaned, and freshly painted, the Cathedral Plaza is now so pretty it sets the teeth slightly on edge. Droves of tourists—Italian and Mexican and Canadian and German—march through the plaza and are ushered by their tour guides into an *artesanías* store, where local crafts of truly startling ugliness are displayed on painted wood pedestals.

At a table in a restaurant set behind the lovely columns of the former Palacio de los Marqueses de Aguas Claras, a trio is offer-ing to sing for a group of Germans. It is early in the morn-ing for this kind of thing, but the Germans look as if they may have been here since the night before. And the young musicians look like the kind of skilled, highly disciplined professionals a national network of music schools still churns out by the hundreds, and for whom a stint as strolling serenaders in a tourist trap is now a prime job opportunity. Here and there, other hopefuls shake maracas and wave straw hats at the foreigners as they stroll through this elaborate stage set. Cubans still live in Old Havana, of course—a short walk reveals the chaotic, steamy, impoverished dwellings shown in the film *Strawberry and Chocolate*—but the whole point of the plaza is to pretend that they don't.

As my new friends and I stroll past a shiny Benetton boutique and chic bars and restaurants and even a chic thread-and-button store on a corner, I can see them avert their eyes from the numerous prostitutes working the cobbled streets, resplendent in their Lycra bodysuits or minimal shorts and halter tops. My friends, I soon realize, believe deeply in the Revolution, and during the hours we are to spend together, they will always interpret the disasters everywhere in view in as favorable a light as possible. Prostitution is not such a large problem, they say. In much the same way that revolutionaries used to deny that the *gusanos*—the Cuban exile community—were a significant issue, they add that only some young girls "with no principles" are creating a bad image for everyone else. "For example, in our families there isn't a single prostitute," the wife says. We enter an enchanting bakery, painted lime-yellow and blue and cooled by ceiling fans, and stare at the baked goods on display. My friends have insisted that the treats for sale in Old Havana aren't just for tourists but for Cubans as well. "See?" they say, pointing to a Cuban family at the counter, quietly buying a few sweet rolls.

But they themselves are buying nothing, although the bread seems cheap: twenty U.S. cents for a dinner roll. We work the price out in pesos: at twenty-three to the dollar, a roll costs 4.60 pesos. Each of my friends, it turns out, holds a middle-level managerial position in a state enterprise, and each earns 275 pesos a month. "That is why everyone is in *la lucha*"—in the struggle, or the hustle—they admit at last. "There are plenty of things to buy now, but you have to pay for them in dollars, and Cuban salaries are paid in pesos." Since for the moment they have not found a way to join *la lucha,* they cannot afford to buy bread.

The issue of *Granma* I acquire from a vendor in front of the cathedral is eight pages thick, tabloid-size. There is such a severe paper shortage in Havana these days that toilet paper is nonexistent, and, for lack of anything to buy in bookstores or anything to buy books with, better-off Cubans, having already sold or bartered their best furniture, their cutlery, their paintings, their picture frames, the statues on their family crypt, their jewelry, and their garden ornaments, have now taken to delivering the contents of their bookshelves to the used-book dealers who operate stalls in front of the former Palacio de los Capitanes Generales. The toilet paper problem and the *Granma* problem are not unrelated; in poor countries, squares of newsprint are a common substitute for toilet paper, but in Cuba the skinny—and scarce—issues of *Granma* are not enough to fill the need, and so I wonder if the stacks of Marxist literature that are said to go for a song these days are being put to good use—I dare not ask my friends. In any event, the coverage of the papal visit in the current issue of *Granma* makes interesting reading, for beyond the live broadcasts, it is the only information about the visit to which most Cubans have access. In today's *Granma*, for example, they learn that the world media "classifies the meeting between Fidel and Pope John Paul II as 'historic,' " that a congressman in El Salvador "classified the visit as transcendental," and that the Jamaican daily *The Observer* "writes that the visit . . . is an example of rejection towards the U.S. embargo policies." The front page describes at length yesterday's meeting between the pope and representatives of Cuban culture—among them, movie directors whose works have been censored and intellectuals who have learned to keep their opinions about Fidel Castro closely to themselves. Without quoting him directly (or any other Church hierarch by name), *Granma* tells us that the pope "underlined that in Cuba one can speak of a fertile cultural dialogue, which is the guarantee for more harmonic growth and an increase in the initiatives and creativity among the members of a civil society." A further article describes with some sense of color the enthusiastic reception given to the pope by the youth of Camagüey. If memory serves, there is no significant difference between these stories and those describing earlier state visits by, say, Michael Manley or Pham Van Dong.

At the newly refurbished Hotel Ambos Mundos (the words "where Hemingway used to stay" are invariably attached to its name), we sit at the bar and watch the end of this day's mass. It is being broadcast live from Santiago, the eastern city that prides itself on its militant nationalistic spirit, and where Fidel's 1953 assault on the Moncada barracks kindled the armed rebellion that would bring him to power in 1959. It is easy to forget that the Cuban nation is not yet a century old, but in Santiago the long fight for independence from Spain and freedom from United States dominion, and the central importance of the Sierra Maestra in the Fidelista revolution, are never forgotten. The pope's Cuban advisers have no doubt suggested that Santiago is the perfect place to address the question of patriotism and the nation during his homily.

The crucial words of the day, in fact, are not spoken by John Paul or even by the cardinal of Havana, Jaime Ortega, who as a young priest spent some time in the notorious work camps where in the mid-1960s Jehovah's Witnesses, homosexuals, militant Catholics, and even unruly youths such as the now-hallowed singer Pablo Milanés were sent to have their thinking corrected. The statement that will echo the longest—and that may well be the first statement critical of the Revolution to be distributed by a state-controlled medium in the last thirty years or so—comes in the course of a salutation to the pope by the bishop of Santiago, Pedro Meurice, who now holds the same position as the lifesaving bishop Pérez Serantes of so long ago. The heart of Meurice's impassioned declaration, much quoted since then, comes when he talks of a "growing number of Cubans who have confused the fatherland with a single party, the nation with the historical process we have lived through during the last few decades, and culture with an ideology."

Friends familiar with Catholic policy say that the Vatican probably decided from the first that the pope, in his role as head of state, should not be the one to refer specifically to the problems of the Catholic Church in Cuba, and that Cardinal Ortega should also remain above the fray, leaving Meurice to vent the feelings of the priests and other Catholics during his official salutation to the pope. Foreign journalists read into Meurice's speech the Vatican's statement of defiance, but a complementary interpretation is possible: together with the fact that the pope chose to bring up the issue of political prisoners—there are hundreds of them—only at a meeting he knew would not be televised, it could stand as evidence of the diligence with which the Church is seeking to avoid a counterproductive confrontation with Fidel, his party, or his faithful during this trip. This is not to say that the Church ignored the impact Meurice's words were likely to have. He is known as a firebrand, and Santiago, the fiery town, is said to be the place where anti-Castro sentiment is running strongest. It is here that the first loud chants of *"Libertad! Libertad!"* will be heard during the mass.

Friends who were there will tell me later that significant numbers of Fidelista Cubans walked out during Meurice's speech, that significant numbers of Catholics cheered wildly, and that in general in the plaza the feeling was that something enormous and irrevocable had taken place. But in the streets of downtown Havana, Meurice's words have had no immediate impact that I can see. The hotel bar opens out onto the street, and as we sit in front of the TV set, Cubans stroll by and stop to watch the screen. A mass is an unfamiliar event for most of them. Unless it is the pope himself, they have little sense of who is at the microphone (or up at bat, or on stage, as they would probably say, since a public gathering to them would suggest the national sport or a dance concert but not the liturgy). Meurice is unknown beyond Santiago. Cardinal Ortega is not recognized when he walks down the street—to my knowledge, he has never appeared on television before the papal visit, nor has he been quoted in a newspaper. After years of the revolutionary meetings called *actos,* people have learned to stand for hours without listening very hard, and that is how they stand today in front of the television, commenting on how tired the pope looks, how cute he is, how old he is, how very nice it is that he has come to visit Cuba, before moving on to other subjects or continuing their walks. And so we too watch this historic moment, not listening to Meurice's speech because we are busy ordering beers, and because I am hypnotized by the deliberately offensive way in which the waiter treats my friends, who are not only Cuban but black—evidently middle-class, evidently respectable, but black nevertheless, and evidently dollarless. But it may be that racism isn't involved. It may be that there is something indefinable about my friends—the chunky, socialist cut of his worn shirt, perhaps, or a kind of discipline, or a kind of primness—that tags them as Party loyalists, and it may be the case in downtown Havana, where hustlers and dealmakers are in charge, that the last of the true believers, with their tiresome principles and their dignity and their intolerance and their dogmas, are despised.

My friends appear to devote enormous energy to figuring out the immediate future—where to get dollars, how to get a spare part for their rickety Soviet Lada—and to figuring out ways not to think of the long-term future. Their lives changed in 1990, and during the remaining days I will spend on the island, as I talk to more Cubans about the bitter days of hunger, brutal physical hardship, and uncertainty they endured between 1990 and 1994, I come to feel that the demise of the Soviet Union must have been an event as inconceivable and shattering as the arrival of the Spaniards on Mexico's shores was for the Aztecs. And I can see why one would want to avoid thinking about the future, because, no matter what happens, the future looks terrible for people like my friends—men and women between the ages of forty and sixty who were brought up by the Revolution and given a new life through it.

The husband comes from a dirt-poor family that migrated from the countryside to the slums of Havana, and thanks to the Revolution he is now fluent in two useless languages—Russian and Bulgarian—and holds a degree in a useless discipline—Marxist economics. Mistakes were made in the past, he tells me—like the work camps, the repression of the Catholic Church, the view that young men with long hair were an evil virus that could bring the Revolution down—but they have been rectified. Now that the worst of the *período especial* is over—this is what the government calls the free fall the country went into in 1990—Cuba is finding its way again. Look at how much has been done to restore Havana, he says, several times. A big foreign consortium has signed a contract to restore the old city, "and leave it just as it was." Just as it was before the Revolution, that is to say.

But so many things are already on their way to being just as they were: prostitution and racism, and corrosive poverty that is eating away even at the regime's proudest achievements. One afternoon during this trip I will go with my friend to the Hermanos Ameijeiras Hospital to pick up a relative who has just had a knee operation: this patient has been released into the sweltering chaos of the hospital gates, where people on stretchers wait for hours for a gasping public service jitney to collect those living more or less in the same direction and take them home. She is lucky to be getting a private ride, but I'm not sure how well she'll do when she gets home. The anesthesia from the operation has not yet worn off: when it does, she will have to learn to put up with pain, because, other than the warning that she cannot take aspirin, the surgeons have given her nothing. There are no painkillers for minor surgery at Havana's largest and most modern hospital.

It is hard to imagine that thirty-five years' worth of Soviet subsidies ended in this. When I ask friends where all the money went (between $50 billion and $75 billion is the most moderate estimate, a figure that includes low-interest loans, direct subsidies, and subsidized prices for Cuban products) they come up with a rather short list: the army and all its equipment, from uniforms to missiles; the island's now-outdated electric power system; the nuclear plant that was supposed to free Cuba from its dependence on foreign oil, and which was left two-thirds finished; the highway system; some monstrous buildings—mainly designed as residences for "foreign technicians," as the socialist-bloc advisers were known, but also some schools and hospitals—and the biomedical industry, which may yet bring in significant foreign income.

By comparison with the Dominican Republic, say, Cuba is hopelessly behind on computerization, infrastructure of all sorts, even modest industries like canneries or match factories, and—now that the exhortatory slogans have changed from "Ten million tons of sugar!" to "Two million tourists in the year 2000!"—tourist accommodations. On the other hand, very few poor Dominicans can aspire to the education received by a poor Cuban (all but a few Cubans are poor; virtually all Cubans have a diploma from a tolerably competent high school), and not all that many Dominicans have the kind of discipline, the *espíritu de sacrificio,* or the sense of having played a relevant, heroic, and inspiring role in the history of the twentieth century that serves as spiritual fuel for Cubans like my friends.

"We just have to get the economy working again, under these new conditions," says the husband, "and then everything will be all right." Proudly, he tells me that if I wish to make an international phone call I can do so at the Hotel Habana Libre, where he drops me off. It turns out that I can indeed buy an electronic card there for $10, insert it into a working phone, and get an instant connection to virtually any city in the world, thanks to a Mexican company that has contracted to modernize Cuba's ancient phone system. Perhaps the fact that my friends would have to pool their entire monthly wages to buy one of these cards and talk with their daughter in Mexico for about ten minutes is only important in the short term. Perhaps it is inevitable that tourists will want to buy human bodies along with their beers and maracas. Perhaps the fact that in the crumbling two-room apartment where my friends live they only have running water every other day is trivial. They certainly seem to think so.

After taking an almost intolerably crowded bus that reeks of diesel back to my hotel (this is easily said, but it involved a one-hour wait, which the Cubans standing in line with me endured with veritable Christian patience and good humor), I find that I lack the energy to venture out again. Instead, I turn on the Cuban television station and watch a terrible movie and a documentary that seems to have been filmed in real time and with a single middle-range lens, about a new road that has been built in an outlying part of the island. The camera appears to have been mounted in the cabin of a truck, and it keeps its gaze determinedly on the new road ahead; when the narrator describes the many awesome twists and turns it takes, we take those turns with him, eyes on the asphalt. In addition to the narrator's voice, we hear only some feeble background music. Hardly a human being appears on screen. The Cuban film industry once produced exciting and original fiction films and documentaries as a matter of course, but the talent pool seems to have gone stagnant. Programming ends with a broadcast of a performance by the Ballet Nacional de Cuba. I am already dozing when I realize that the grimacing figure staggering about in a tutu is none other than Alicia Alonso. According to *The Encyclopedia of Dance and Ballet,*[3] she was born in 1917.

*

January 25: Sunrise again, and I have been walking briskly through the cool, expectant dawn, headed for the Plaza de la Revolución, where today's mass, the central act we have all been waiting for, will take place. The pilgrims and foreign priests at the hotel left for the plaza in chartered buses hours ago, and I am afraid that I have already missed something, that a river of people has already flowed into the plaza and left me behind. In a characteristic tactical masterstroke, Fidel has gone on television a few days earlier to exhort everyone—Catholics and Fidelistas—to show up at the plaza today, and to greet the pope warmly, and to refrain from any sign of disrespect, such as whistling at bits of the homily they might not like or shouting revolutionary slogans. Even when set against John Paul II, Fidel is no mean politician:

3. New York: Putnam, 1977.

after this broadcast appeal, the large contingent of Cuban exiles who are making their pilgrimage to the Plaza will look foolish, or worse, if they try to turn the mass into a political rally. And no one will be able to say whether the crowds in the plaza are the pope's or Fidel's. No one will be able to claim that the *acto* was an act of defiance against the regime. In effect, Fidel has offered his faithful on loan to the pope for the day, like the splendid host he is reputed to be.

But it seems that his faithful are staying away. There are people out on the streets, certainly, but very few of them are going in my direction (even though the ever-vigilant neighborhood Comités de Defensa de la Revolución have been reminding people that they are expected at the event). It is only in the vicinity of the plaza, where the loudspeakers broadcasting an *animador's*—emcee's— enthusiastic chanting can already be heard, that the odd cluster of people I see here and there, carrying missals or rosaries and little plastic flags in the Vatican's yellow and white colors, start to form into a crowd. These are the pope's faithful.

It is not quite 7 A.M. when I reach the Plaza de la Revolución, and it is already more than half full of people who have obviously been here for hours, looking as if they are about to levitate from sheer joy. Hymns are being sung with the kind of full-throated enthusiasm I remember was voiced for the Revolution back in the seventies. The crowd, I conclude, is overwhelmingly Catholic and not, as Fidelistas claim about Catholics, overwhelmingly elderly, although it is, as is also alleged, predominantly white. A bizarre visual displacement has taken place: on the front of the National Library, where large portraits of Marx, Lenin, or the like usually hang, there is a gigantic mural of the Sacred Heart of Jesus. A slogan underneath it reads JESUS CHRIST, IN YOU I TRUST. The emotional epicenter of the plaza is no longer the podium that is always set up for revolutionary *actos* at the foot of a horrid statue of José Martí erected by Batista, but a graceful white canopy set at right angles to it, which shelters the altar where the mass will take place.

Because the altar is not set very high, it will be almost hidden from view by 9 A.M., when the plaza has filled and the mass is about to begin. Police barriers divide the crowd in half and define a pathway along which the Virgin of Charity, Patroness of Santiago and indeed of Cuba, is now carried in procession to the altar. Unexpectedly, the Popemobile is suddenly visible along this pathway too, and there are screams and a flurry of enthusiasm as the crowd catches sight of John Paul II. It is still early and the skies are gray; no one can be suffering from heatstroke or dehydration, but the Red Cross volunteers posted throughout the plaza are kept busy ferrying people on stretchers to the first-aid tents—elderly women, mostly, who may have fainted from sheer emotion. Has Fidel arrived? Where is he? I ask over and over again. No one seems to know, or care.

And now it is the Mass, set to beautiful Cuban music specially composed for this occasion. The *clave de son*—the distinct Afro-Cuban one-two-three, one-two, beat clicked out with wooden sticks as a convocation to the dance—fills the sound system. Everywhere, people are waving yellow-and-white flags. They sing along, tentatively and then more forcefully, guided by booklets that have been handed out. "He who sows love harvests love," they sing. I come from a long Mexican anticlerical tradition, but these sentiments are a refreshing change from the intransigent chants of the Revolution ("Whoever pops his head up, hit him hard, Fidel!"). Throughout the mass, crowds continue to enter the plaza. Oddly, though, throngs are also leaving it. One possible explanation is that these are the non-Catholics who have come here out of curiosity or because Fidel said they should, and who, having seen enough, depart.

I leave too, because no one can tell me if Fidel is here and I cannot bear to miss the spectacle I have come all this way to witness. In search of a television, I wander around a poor neighborhood behind the plaza until I hear the mass blaring from a television set. The sound comes from the front room of a tiny house whose front porch holds a couple of rusty bicycles and a decrepit lawn chair. Inside is more dilapidated furniture, the television, and a pleasant-looking woman who is peeling garlic in a creaky aluminum rocker in front of the set and who immediately offers me her seat. She brings me a glass of cool water, and then a tiny cup of sweet, dark coffee, keeping up a running commentary all the while on the mass. The pope is handing Bibles to a group of Church activists, including an elderly woman whom he draws to him for an embrace. "See that!" my hostess exclaims. "That little old lady must feel like we do when we get our Party card!" Her mood changes when the camera cuts away to the row of chairs immediately in front of the altar to show, at last, the sight I have been waiting for: Fidel Castro, attending mass in the Plaza de la Revolución. Behind the altar, facing where he sits, is the mural of the Sacred Heart of Jesus. I remark that this is a sight I never expected to see. "And neither did I," my hostess says, not smiling. "Neither did I."

My hostess is a lifelong Party militant in her mid-thirties. She and her eight-year-old son sleep in one of the two bedrooms in the little house. The other is occupied by her former husband, who in the seven years since the couple divorced has been unable to get the officials in charge of these things to authorize new living quarters for him. There will be meat for Sunday dinner today because a friend has brought her a cut of pork, but even though the food situation has improved greatly and she says she no longer goes hungry, as she did during the lean 1990–1994 years, the shelves in her kitchen are nearly bare. She offers me a present—a commemorative issue of *Granma* on the anniversary of Che's death.

Later she will insist on giving me a farewell present as well—a color photograph of Fidel—before walking with me to the main avenue, from which we can see the Sacred Heart of Jesus. The day she came upon the mural as she was walking to work will remain in her memory forever, she says. "I remember all the years that we would evaluate our coworkers in our work centers, and we had *compañeras* who were hardworking, and skillful, and punctual, and loyal, and comradely, and when it came time to evaluate them for promotion or grant them the right to new living quarters, we would always say no, because they were Catholic. And now here is this mural in the place where we usually put our heroes. Was this what we held back our Catholic *compañeras* for?" she asks in a sudden outburst. "I accept what I am told to accept, because I am loyal. But I do not understand."

I wonder what Fidel makes of this strange new position he finds himself in. I wonder if his admiration for John Paul II is increasing as he watches him play a crowd with a skill few men other than Fidel himself have ever shown. The pope's most important sermon addresses the question of the embargo and the evils of neoliberalism, "which subordinates the human person to blind market forces and conditions the development of peoples to those forces." The interesting thing is that the crowd I take to be overwhelmingly Catholic, and therefore, perhaps, conservative, cheers and claps with rising enthusiasm during this impassioned denunciation. "Do you think people are supposed to clap during Mass?" my hostess wonders, and at that point the pope interrupts his discourse, jokingly, to address that very question. "The pope likes it when you applaud," he says, each word an effort. "Because when you do so, he can rest a little bit." The camera shows us that Fidel is laughing with the crowd.

Although the pope is speaking more clearly than he has throughout the trip, his voice is nearly gone, his facial muscles are so deteriorated that a smile is almost impossible, and still he manages to convey irony, humor, and a bantering tenderness in his improvised remarks that have the crowd in a frenzy of delight. When the cheering stops, he continues with the prepared text. "At times unsustainable economic programs are imposed on nations as a condition for further assistance," he reads, and by now my hostess is with the crowd in its enthusiasm. "Did you hear that!" she yells. "That man is going to be a Party militant by the time he leaves this island!"

In the plaza the roaring approval goes on for so long that the pope holds up a hand. "Thou art a very active audience," he admonishes, again with that bantering intimacy. "But now we must continue." He holds the pause a beat. "It's only one more page."

And now, while the orchestra plays a lilting Creole melody, it's time for the kiss of peace, the moment in modern Catholic ritual when people turn to each other and embrace while wishing each other peace. The screen shows members of the Communist Party Central Committee exchanging hugs with nuns, cardinals wishing peace to Fidel. One of the young priests serving as acolytes for this liturgy is in tears. The mass is over.

Something extraordinary has taken place. Later, I will ask a wise and wily priest just what it was that occurred. "None of us knows," he answers. "And the first thing we have to do now, all of us, is sit down and reflect on what we saw. One thing is certain: it has been proved that all Cubans—Cubans from the island and Cubans from Miami, nonbelievers and Catholics—can gather joyfully and in peace, for a good cause. And if this happened once, it can happen again, with the right conditions."

I comment on the general perception that Fidel was entranced by the pope, and on my perception that the pope was not necessarily entranced back. "The pope is entranced by no one," the priest says dryly. "The pope is entranced by his God."

Perhaps, I suggest, this is because his need was nowhere as great as Fidel's. After all, what could Cuba offer the pope in exchange for the Vatican's stand against the blockade? Rather sharply, I am told that for the pope there was never any question of an exchange. "The pope has a different sense of time, he is Polish, and he likes to point out that for two hundred years Poland did not exist as a nation, until at long last, because there were always Poles who took care to keep alive the language and the culture and the idea of the fatherland, Poland reemerged among the world of nations. And so the pope says," says the priest, "that if we cannot know if our acts will have consequences a hundred years from now, or two, or five hundred, all one can do is what one feels is right at any given moment, without expecting results."

This is not the way a seventy-one-year-old man fighting for the survival of the regime he created can afford to count the years. There is no way of knowing what shape the change that is coming to Cuba will take or how fast it will go. Fidelistas, having absorbed the lessons of glasnost rather differently from those of us who watched it taking place far from the island of Cuba, are afraid that opening up their country to the world, as the pope exhorted them to, will bring unruliness and disaster. And yet the consequences of the world opening up to Cuba, as the pope also demanded, and as all Cubans on the island want—an end to the blockade, and to their country's diplomatic isolation, in other words—may result in far speedier and more uncontrollable change. The officially enshrined ideals of selflessness and sacrifice have been undermined more thoroughly by tourism and the corruption and cynicism provoked by the hunt for dollars than anyone would like to admit.

On the other hand, tourism generates its own liberation. It is impossible today to monitor the potentially subversive activities of every happy beachgoer. Nor will Fidel again dare ever to jail or expel a priest. Now that more than 100 political prisoners have been released, a subsequent increase in the regime's many forms of political repression could unleash a worldwide rejection by tourists that would bring the economy to its knees in no time. Thousands of Cubans risked their lives crossing the strait between their island and Florida on rafts made from inner tubes—and many died in the effort. Those who chose to stay behind lived through the 1990–1994 crisis with stoicism, but no one expects that the reaction to a new time of hunger would be so peaceful. It could even be argued that, economically crippled and internationally isolated as it is, restricted to tactical maneuvers and unable to formulate any initiatives that are not, in fact, concessions, revolutionary Cuba, Fidel's dream of a perfect Cuba, is already a dream of the past.

Curiously, although the Fidelistas may be full of fear and apprehension, Fidel himself is busily opening the floodgates to the new times, as the pope's visit demonstrated. The only question is how aware he is of what he is doing, and how many allies he has among the aged comrades who have run the country according to his dictates for nearly four decades. His brother and appointed successor,

Raúl, gave a numbingly dreary speech two days after the pope's departure that made no allusion to the visit and was remarkable only in the consistency with which it hewed to the old formulas. Within the Party ranks, a social-democratic tendency is clearly visible, although there is no way of knowing at this point whether the ostensible reformers in the "new" generation, middle-aged Party leaders like Ricardo Alarcón and Carlos Lage, represent that trend. Nor can one predict whether the currently harassed or imprisoned members of the anti-Communist opposition, some of whom identify themselves as social and Christian democrats, will prove any match for the well-off Miami-based conservatives who are anxious to incorporate themselves into the political scene and the economy once Fidel is gone. And how will Fidel leave? Lately, he has been heard saying things like "no man is immortal," but has he considered the possibility that he may not be allowed to die on the job?

For the moment, it is the pope who is making his departure this misty Sunday evening, Fidel once again standing reverently at his side. Once again, John Paul II is making a little joke. "When I came out of the Cathedral this afternoon, after all these days of heat, it was raining," he begins. "I asked myself, Why? Why rain? Can it be that it is a sign that the Cuban skies are weeping because the pope is leaving?" Fidel watches him with an open-mouthed smile, one great showman rejoicing in another's brinkmanship performance. "No!" the pope thunders. "That would be a very superficial hermeneutics!" and the shadow of a sly smile flickers across his face. Fidel is laughing, and John Paul goes on to say, in Latin, that rains are a sign of hope and good fortune.

—March 26, 1998

LOVE AND MISERY IN CUBA

For many of the long years that the Revolution has been in power in Cuba, much of it was off-limits to the potentially unfriendly gaze. Not only were all sorts of facts and procedures kept secret; all foreigners were barred from access to large portions of Cuba's territory, and even Cubans were told where they could travel and therefore where they could look. The reason stated for so much secrecy was the imperative of the Cold War, but another reason was not given, and perhaps those who established the limits never formulated it clearly to themselves—it was simply understood that the way the Revolution was seen was critical to its survival. Its failures were hardly a secret, but it was important that they not be visible.

So it comes as a double shock to arrive in Cuba as a tourist and see so much of it open to one's foreign stare, and to see also how brutal in many cases the new stare of the foreign visitor is. On a tour bus the modest and articulate woman who is our guide attempts to explain the currency system, but she is interrupted by a hefty middle-aged Mexican of some means who has been looking frankly at her body. "You're very good-looking, *cubanita*," he says. "I like your hair." She thanks him less than graciously for the compliment, but he is unfazed. He makes a few comments about the pitiful state of the economy, and a short while later interrupts again. "Where can we see some table-dancing?" he wants to know.

Airports and airplanes, natural collection points for foreigners, are in other parts of the world centers of regimented behavior: no smoking, fasten your seat belts, step up to the counter. At the brand-new international departures lounge in Havana, these rules don't hold: hundreds of young men on charter tours—Mexican, Italian, and Spanish, on this occasion—sprawl on the floor, spill beer on the just-polished marble and throw the cans at each other, boast openly about their diminished supply of condoms after an Easter weekend sex holiday in sunny Havana, and blow cigar smoke in the face of the women at the check-in counter.

In the old days guerrilla apprentices from Brazil and Uruguay and El Salvador came here and treated each brick laid by the Revolution with reverence, and nevertheless were kept within strict boundaries during their stay. With an ordinary tourist visa provided with any charter tour package, however, the new type of foreigner can rent a car or buy a domestic plane ticket and travel just about anywhere he pleases in Cuba. On a decrepit plane that miraculously survives its daily run from Havana to Santiago and back, two Italians join the other tourists and Cubans who have already fastened their seat belts. They are late, it would seem, because they are less than coherent, or more than a little drunk. Convulsed with giggles, they make their way up the aisle, and then one of them decides that the jokey thing to do is to sit himself heavily in the lap of another traveler—a Cuban. "I'm sorry," the Italian slurs in deliberate English. He does not look at all repentant, and his friend is howling with laughter. Gently, the stewardess tugs the offender away from his victim and pushes him toward an empty seat.

To say that Cuba has opened itself up to tourism in this context has connotations that are unfortunately true: the island has become an established part of the world sex tour circuit. Of all the ways the Revolution could have looked for emergency money following the collapse of the Soviet Union, none was less predictable than this, and not only because the eradication of prostitution was one of Cuban socialism's proudest achievements—in the rhetoric, at least. Personified by Fidel Castro, the Revolution has craved nothing so much as respect, but prostitutes, who have given up the right to choose by whom they are possessed, are generally not respected. They can be stared at by anyone, as if the stare itself were the equivalent of sexual commerce. Indeed, in Latin cultures the way a man looks at a woman—or at another man, for that matter—can be cause for conflict. A penetrating stare in the wrong direction may lead a man to feel that he needs to defend his honor. And yet in Cuba the brazen stare has replaced the old obsession with the respectful gaze.

Although there does not appear to be any official reference to the phenomenon in any government speech to date, the decision to tolerate, and even encourage, prostitution appears to have been deliberate. After all, once it was decided that only tourism could provide the emergency currency needed to keep the country afloat, how could Havana hope to compete with the likes of Martinique, Santo Domingo, Curaçao, or Cancún? Not on the basis of its shabby hotels, limited food supply, and terrible flight connections, certainly.

Five dollars, the young Mexicans standing with me at the departure line boast at the end of their sexual holiday, was enough to buy "a spectacular *mulata*" for the evening. They are happy. So was the businessman who checked into my hotel on the same day I arrived. I had come to see what had changed in Cuba in the wake of John Paul II's January visit—how the euphoria of those days had carried over into everyday life during the Easter holidays. Soon I was trying to solve the problems of my room—a fog of mosquitoes, the fact that if the windows were kept closed nothing could be seen of the outdoors, because for incomprehensible reasons the glazing had been varnished black—but the businessman had other concerns. Less than an hour after our joint arrival, I stepped into the hotel elevator and ran into him again. He had changed into tropical gear, and was now in the company of a woman who could, indeed, only be described as spectacular: lithe, with skin the color of bitter chocolate, and dressed only in high heels and an electric-blue body stocking.

Later that evening I saw him escorting the electric-blue woman and another marvelously beautiful woman into a taxi. The following morning he appeared at breakfast and rose to greet a different woman altogether. That evening he had changed partners again. The last time I saw him, the woman in the body stocking was back. He looked throughout earnest and busy, like someone with many important appointments to fit into an already crowded schedule.

At Twenty-third and Línea, Havana's central crossroads, young girls gathered from early in the morning in front of the Habana Libre hotel, dressed and painted for display. Passing them, I tried to convince myself that they were over sixteen. I was on the way to a weekly conference for foreign journalists that is held nearby, and I was struck by the fact that there seemed to be no attempt to zone prostitution, to restrict it to certain types of hotels or certain neighborhoods or otherwise hide it from view.

The press conference, attended by some fifty journalists, was different. There, nothing could be shown, no information could be revealed. To give the press officials credit, they seemed utterly relaxed about the fact that I was there as a reporter without the right kind of visa, and that, as I told them, I planned to look at what had become of the dissidents who were released from jail in February, following an appeal by the pope. They were willing to let me look, but providing straightforward answers to the questions put to them by the gathered press corps was a different matter.

Was it true that a certain aged Colombian guerrilla leader had died not in Colombia last February, as was initially stated, but in a hospital in Havana, as a guerrilla defector was now claiming? The answer, compounded of careful evasions, was not even an explicit denial. Was it true that an important promoter of U.S. investment on the island had been denied a visa? Again, the circumlocutions made nothing clear. The session ended without a sentence of real information being exchanged. The day's issue of *Granma,* the official newspaper, was again a model of obfuscation. None of the topics raised in the press conference were covered in the day's stories.

It is hard to understand just who is being protected by this censorship. True revolutionaries have presumably had time throughout these nearly forty years to develop an immunity to counter-revolutionary versions of the truth. The regime may have thought that it should protect from foreign influences the poor Cubans it described as "lumpen" and "scum" because they refused to accept revolutionary austerity. But as it happens, this is the group of people now most heavily engaged in prostitution and related black-market activities. They are, therefore, the very Cubans who are most in contact with the new type of foreigners, and who have the greatest access to the foreigners' contrasting versions of reality. Because they are also likely to be the significant breadwinners in some of the poorest Cuban households, their influence is probably great. And because these households are so poor, the effect of their commerce with foreigners is likely to be subversive. Under these circumstances the distinction between what the government does not wish to see and what it does not want others to look at seems, at the very least, arbitrary.

Perhaps it is nothing more than fear of the foreign gaze that is behind Cuba's perceived need to fill its jails with dissidents. Many who were in past years allowed to voice their unfavorable opinion of the socialist regime and wander the streets unsupervised were hustled into prison once they shared these opinions with a foreign journalist. Elisardo Sánchez, for example, founder of the Cuban Commission for Human Rights and National Reconciliation, spent two and a half years in prison after talking to Julia Preston, then a reporter with the *Washington Post.* Sánchez claimed that the relatives of prisoners who were executed in a notorious military trial in 1989 were not allowed to take the bodies home for burial. That the government brief against Sánchez virtually admitted this fact did not affect Sánchez's four-year sentence. José Angel Carrasco, founder of a movement whose acronym, AMOR, reveals a certain wistful romanticism rather than any violent impulse to take up arms against Fidel Castro, was sentenced to seven years after he gave an interview to *Le Monde*'s Bertrand de la Grange. (De la Grange was subsequently beaten and arrested before he left the island.)

One of the most striking cases is that of Dessi Mendoza Rivero, a doctor in Santiago, capital of Oriente province, who founded the College of Independent Physicians in 1994. Over the next three years he was called in regularly to the local State Security offices for questioning and scolding, and often spent a night in jail for good measure, but it was not until June of last year that he was arrested and charged with the crime of "enemy propaganda." The previous month he had held a few phone conversations with an assortment of foreign correspondents based in Havana. His statements were, if anything, moderate and cautious. Despite the best efforts of the government health authorities, he said, an epidemic of dengue fever was devastating his city. The first outbreak of the epidemic had been detected in January, and by May, Dr. Mendoza's estimate was that between fifteen and thirty people had died. In addition, he thought that thousands of *santiagueros* had already been affected by the virus, which can turn lethal if the patient has suffered from dengue before or is undernourished or otherwise immune-deficient.

Dengue is generally transmitted by mosquitoes, and Dr. Mendoza may have been concerned that visitors to a scheduled trade fair in Santiago could be exposed to the virus. It may have been the government's concern that potential dollar-carrying visitors could be exposed to Dr. Mendoza's information and cancel their trip. Or it may have been that, once again, the Cuban regime's intense horror of a dissenting or irreverent gaze set off a reflex chain of actions and convinced the judge who presided over the trial that what Dessi Mendoza deserved for his *infidencia* was eight years in prison. This despite the fact that information on the epidemic that was essentially in agreement with Dr. Mendoza's figures was published by the official Santiago newspaper, *Sierra Maestra,* one month after his arrest.

Dissenters are invisible in Cuba, and inaudible. They have no access to the airwaves or the official press, and are not allowed to hold public meetings without permission, which in effect means that dissenters have never once held any public meeting—so it seems inevitable that those who feel the need to protest should end up talking to foreign reporters.

When I sought out people who had been released from jail following the pope's petition on their behalf, I asked them repeatedly if they were not afraid that talking to me might get them into trouble again. Their answer was generally a pro forma statement in defense of freedom of speech—which was certainly sincere, and even heroic, in view of their histories. But it also struck me that there was something helpless about their situation when they were faced with an inquisitive foreigner. It was not so much that they made a decision to speak to me, but that they desperately needed to talk to anyone at all: they were lonely. They had stories to tell and opinions to give, and although neighbors might be friendly and friends might be supportive, any political conversation in Cuba is haunted by the terms of discussion enshrined long ago by the regime: *Dentro de la Revolución, todo. Fuera de la Revolución, nada.* Within the Revolution, everything; outside it, nothing—a radical restriction whose borders are impossibly vague. How much can you say, how closely can you look—even if the dissident before you is your best friend and you basically agree with the concrete points he or she is making—before you find that you have all unawares crossed over to the enemy side? Seeing becomes a fraught activity, and talking about what one observes can lead to ruinous disillusionment, or jail.

For the released prisoners, enforced silence seems a particularly cruel restriction, because people who have spent time in jail necessarily have terrible things they need to tell. I heard a story from a man who had served three and a half years of his seven-year sentence (again, for "enemy propaganda") before the pope put his name on a list. He spent the months between the time of his arrest and final sentencing at the detention center run directly by State Security, the Villa Marista. He lost twenty-six pounds during those weeks, confined with four other prisoners to a cell whose only access to the outside world was a slot on the cell door. When a prisoner was taken from his cell and through the hallway, the slots were shut, which meant that no one was able to know who his fellow prisoners were.

The hallway was wide enough for only one person, and when a prisoner was let out of a cell for whatever reason, he had to march ahead of the guard, and was told to do so quickly and with his eyes to the floor, while the guard marched so closely behind him that the man I interviewed said he could still not forget the sensation of the guard's legs brushing his own at every step, forcing him forward. During these two months, he said, he was allowed out only once for an hour of sun and exercise, alone, on a patio, and this was the week before his transfer to the general prison at Combinado del Este. At the new prison he shared an overcrowded cell with men who, by and large, had been convicted of violent crimes, and were repeat offenders.

Prisoners serving harsh sentences at Combinado del Este are kept in galleys with forty to sixty other convicts, and, according to various sources, are fed so poorly that prison doctors classify their stage of undernourishment as either "moderate," "severe," or "critical." The prisoners are allowed one two-hour visit by two family members every two months, and during these visits they can receive as much food as their relatives can carry (no canned goods, or items that require cooking). But many prisoners don't have good relations with their relatives, or else have relatives who are poor and live so far away that they cannot make the visits on a regular basis. The hunger they suffer is at the heart of the story that the man I talked to felt most compelled to tell, even though his wife gently tried to steer him away from the subject during our conversation.

This man is white. The cot above his in the overcrowded cell was vacated one day, and he began using this space to store the relatively bountiful supplies that his family lugged to prison every two months. Across from this cot was another, occupied by a young black man. My storyteller for some reason was specific about the youth's race, although he couldn't recall his crime, or didn't feel that it was relevant. One night, the man who slept in the cot above the young black man's (they were stacked in layers of four) discovered him stealing a small jar of preserves that belonged to the storyteller. As punishment, the young black man was severely beaten by the other prisoners. (I did not ask the storyteller what part he had in this.) The young man was taken away to the infirmary, and one month later he was dead. "Not as a result of the beating, you understand, but because he was so hungry. He died of hunger," my storyteller insisted. And then he repeated several times, in a tight voice, that what he could not get over was the fact that the young man was the same age as his son.

This man was released from prison after John Paul II's visit, and he is now awaiting an exit permit so that he can go abroad. (I do not mention his name or his other circumstances, not at his request, but out of my own fear that being quoted in an interview might send him back to prison rather than into exile.) According to a statement released by the Cuban government, 75 prisoners had already been freed before the pope presented his list of 302 political detainees, and 70 "will not be liberated under any circumstances whatsoever."

According to the Cuban Commission for Human Rights and National Reconciliation, 115 prisoners, out of the pope's list of 302, were released in the days following his visit. But matters are not so simple. Gerardo Sánchez, brother of Elisardo Sánchez and president of the commission, has looked at the records available for these dissenters and found something interesting: a great many of them had already served either half or two-thirds of their prison sentences, which is the point at which first and second offenders, respectively, are eligible for parole. Several knowledgeable Cubans confirmed to me that there was nothing unusual in this. As a matter of course, they said, political prisoners are detained long past their parole date, until some important person—Danielle Mitterrand, the pope—comes to visit and speaks to Fidel on their behalf. No real amnesty is involved.[1]

Given the conditions under which the members of the Commission for Human Rights have to work, it is remarkable that they can collect or verify any information at all. As a former political

1. Fidel himself would have fared poorly under this system. Captured in August 1953 following his assault on the Moncada army barracks, and sentenced to fifteen years in prison, he was freed by Batista less than two years later, following an amnesty campaign in Cuba on behalf of the Moncada prisoners.

prisoner himself, Elisardo Sánchez is not allowed to have a computer or a fax in the house he shares with his brother and several other members of the Sánchez family. Many other commission members or supporters don't have phones. Many relatives of men and women in jail who might like to give their names to a human rights organization probably don't know that the commission exists. (The government, of course, does not volunteer information on the individuals it chooses to keep in jail for crimes of opinion.) Thanks to new information provided by the recently released dissenters, Gerardo Sánchez said, they had only now been able to add to the list of prisoners the name of one man who has been in jail since 1993.

The Sánchezes' personal situation is difficult too. Like every other person who has been a political prisoner, Elisardo will probably never be offered a job as anything other than a menial laborer by the government, which is still the only legal employer in Cuba. Gerardo was a union leader until the day in 1980 when they first arrested his brother and charged him with the all-purpose offense of enemy propaganda. He is also out of work. (Relatives living abroad are the main source of support for the Sánchez brothers, as well as most other dissenters.)

Elisardo has a right to a ration card, but what the card provides these days is not really enough to keep a person alive. (And even that is hard to come by for most former prisoners. Two months after his release, one man still had not had his card "reactivated.") Nevertheless, Gerardo says that over the last few years conditions for those who disagree with the regime have improved somewhat, most likely as a result of Cuba's new need to be more responsive to international pressure. The total number of political prisoners has gone down significantly, Gerardo said, and State Security officers, who in the past have sometimes been regular visitors to the Sánchez household, have lately been leaving the brothers in peace. But Gerardo Sánchez insists that none of these changes are significant because the regime has always blown hot and cold on dissenters, and will have a legal justification for its repressive measures until there are fundamental changes in the Constitution and the legal system.

I asked Gerardo whether he thought that the U.S. trade embargo had been a useful weapon against the regime. He shook his head. "Sometimes I have the impression that the embargo reflects a fear that this economic system might really work, that [the people who support the embargo believe] that if it were lifted today, tomorrow socialism would be viable. It probably couldn't be done overnight, but there should be some thought how to lift the embargo gradually. It would put an end to the regime's great excuse, which is to say that things are so bad here because of imperialism."

Thinking of how moderate the Sánchez brothers' politics are, and how useful the two might be as interlocutors to a regime suffering from severe interior decay and increasing distance from its subjects, I asked Gerardo if the government maintained any sort of regular contact with them: "Of course," he replied. "In the form of interrogations." It is hard to avoid the impression that the Revolution prefers the radical, invasion-prone opposition in Florida to the unarmed social-democratic and Christian-democratic activists within, as if Fidel and his comrades were grateful for the opportunity to present themselves—and see themselves—in a more flattering, heroic mold, facing enemy gunfire rather than snooping on people who want the right to register their organization as a fully legal political party.

If being outside the Revolution is difficult in Havana, it must be doubly so in Santiago, a small, sweltering seaport ringed by the hills of the Sierra Maestra, where generations of rebels, including Fidel Castro, have found shelter. Santiago is a fascinating place, but it is not the cosmopolitan center that Havana has been throughout its history. The visual landscape of Havana has remained pretty much unchanged since 1959, but the visitor to downtown Santiago has the impression of having traveled back in time straight into the nineteenth century: tile-roofed houses fronting on empty narrow streets, an ornate (but empty) galería of shops, and—one result of Cuba's ongoing fuel shortage—spindly

carriages drawn by spindly horses. And if in Havana one is sometimes overwhelmed by the sensation that nothing ever happens—
no news, no movie openings, no political changes—in Santiago
the atmosphere of tedium is ever-present: a weary continuum of
uneventfulness that was once happily interrupted by the bustle
surrounding the pope's visit.

In this small world nonconformists must feel particularly exposed to the glare of official disapproval. I would have liked to ask
Dessi Mendoza Rivero, the physician who revealed the existence of
a dengue epidemic in Santiago and was sentenced to eight years in
prison as a result, how he came to see himself as outside the Revolution and what it was like to be a dissenter in Santiago; but it
turned out that he was on the commission's list of political prisoners who were not released following the papal visit, even though
his name was among those presented to the Cuban government on
behalf of the pope.

It may be that Dr. Mendoza was not released because he is considered a particular enemy of the people. What seems undeniable
is that he did not overstate the extent or the dangers of the dengue
epidemic. I talked to a woman who lives in Santiago and whose
husband was hospitalized during the epidemic. She says that the
resources of the very large general hospital in Santiago were
stretched so thin at the height of it that many dengue victims had
to lie on cots on the lawns of the hospital grounds awaiting treatment. One morning when she arrived to visit her husband, she
found him in a state of great agitation. He begged her to take him
away. "The young man in the bed on the other side of the aisle
died last night. I don't want to die here," he said.

With some trepidation, I looked up Dr. Mendoza's wife, doubt-
ing that my visit to her would go unnoticed, or that she would be
willing to expose herself by talking to me, but Caridad Piñón
turned out to be a fearless woman. A physician herself, she told me
that her husband had been fired from his hospital job in 1995,
after he set up the College of Independent Physicians and joined
the Human Rights Commission, and that from then until the day
of his arrest he had contributed to the family income by selling

fritters at the door of the crumbling nineteenth-century house the couple occupy with their three children.

Dr. Piñón is on maternity leave still (her youngest child was twenty days old when Dr. Mendoza was arrested), but she knows that when she returns to work she too might lose her job, as outspoken relatives of political prisoners tend to. Still, she talked to me, and all of her answers to my questions seemed to come ringed in exclamation marks. "Me, afraid?" she said when I wondered aloud yet again why someone like her would talk to someone like me. "I told them [State Security] that I would say everything that happened. Imagine if I couldn't say what is happening to my husband!"

She went on. A few days earlier, her husband, who suffers from chronic heart problems, had spent five days in intensive care at the local hospital, undergoing treatment for severe hypertension. Even though she was wearing her hospital uniform and carrying her physician's credentials, she said, the guards at the door to his room did not allow her to see him, or even to deliver a basket of food. I could picture her giving the guards several pieces of her mind, loudly, and I decided that what I liked best about her was the sense that she did not feel impotent or inconsequential, the way so many people who disagree with the Revolution seem to. Of course, she had never spent any time in jail, but the fact remained that she was still trying to drive a hard bargain with the people in charge of keeping her husband behind bars.

"I tell them, you let him free and I won't say another word," she said in her exclaiming way, after mentioning that the State Security people had recently suggested that she might want to drop by their offices for a "constructive conversation." I asked her why she thought Dr. Mendoza had not been freed after the pope's visit, and she said, for the first time looking worried and pained, that she didn't know. I thought to myself that it might have something to do with the fact that he will have to serve three and a half years of his sentence before he is eligible for the parole that authorities choose to present as "amnesty." If this is the case, he has more than thirty months to go.

I stared at the rain pouring in through the roof of the room where we were sitting while she saw to some urgent request of her youngest child. Everyone in the family looked healthy, and I wondered what miracles of thriftiness and hard barter were involved in making that possible. I had seen some ration cards for Santiago and other provinces, with the blanks showing that people had not received their allotted quotas of cooking oil, soap, or toothpaste for weeks on end; they were allowed, I saw, ten ounces of beans and one pound of meat substitute per person per month. Whatever food Caridad Piñón managed to acquire on the free market, at dollar prices, had to be stretched to provide for her husband as well; prisoners' ration cards are suspended, on the grounds that they are fed in jail. It was all so difficult it was a wonder that she did not throw up her hands in despair, or blame her husband for the mess he had gotten everyone into. I asked her if she thought Dessi Mendoza knew that he would pay for his statements about dengue with an eight-year prison sentence. "Are you crazy?" she said. "He wouldn't immolate himself like that. He's not crazy!" It had simply not occurred to him that talking about a public health epidemic to an unauthorized audience could be so wrong.

Later, I sat on the terrace of the pleasant turn-of-the-century hotel where I was staying, which overlooks a leafy plaza and the Cathedral of Santiago. At the Cathedral the outspoken bishop of Santiago, Pedro Meurice, holds weekly support meetings for the relatives of prisoners. The hotel terrace too is a sanctuary of sorts, because on the streets that surround the hotel unaccompanied men or women like myself (and even, a Spanish couple told me, men held firmly by the hand by their wives) are targets for relentless hustling by women—or, in my case, men—hoping to obtain a few dollars in exchange for a little adventure. But because the money seekers are not allowed on the terrace unless they are in the company of a hotel guest, a kind of tranquillity prevails there.

The just-formed Cuban-foreign couples who occupied so many of the tables around me were at peace: both partners had what they had come to find. And because Cuba is a place where fantasy and idealism and the pursuit of exoticism have always been intertwined, and because the women are so cheap that they are usually rented by the day, and because it is the hope of so many of the women who rent themselves out that one of their customers will want to keep her for good, the nature of the relationship between prostitute and customer was also different, I thought. A certain amount of trust had time to develop, along with the quest for romance and salvation involved on both sides. It seemed absurd that Dessi Mendoza should be in jail for talking to the foreign press while on the terrace hesitant conversations were taking place between the new couples—in sign language, or pidgin Spanish, or in whatever common language the two people had found.

I had spent some time talking with Bishop Meurice, and been struck by his arguments against the United States trade embargo, which he, like so many other Cubans, refers to always as "the blockade"—perhaps because the word more nearly conveys the besieged feeling of the island. "The Cuban Church has spoken out against the blockade in the past," Meurice said. "It is unjust. But the fact is that there are other realities that also affect the anguish lived by our people: unjust inequalities, state paternalism and centralism, limitations on civil society's ability to participate. The blockade depends on the United States, but the rest of it depends on us. In a situation as hard as the one the Cuban people are living, the truth must be said: the blockade doesn't help. On the contrary. It may prevent us from seeing those other realities."

—June 11, 1998

FIDEL IN THE EVENING

If you are in the neighborhood of forty years old and Cuban, Fidel Castro has been at the center of your heart and thoughts, for however small a second, each day of your life. Perhaps you saw him first in the Plaza of the Revolution, when doves landed on his shoulders as he made his first speech in power. Even if you weren't there, you remember this event as if it had happened to you, because the photographic image of that moment has become part of the national memory. Fidel visited the shiny new infant nurseries and kindergartens and dandled you on his knee and patted your teacher on the back and told you in his papery voice that you were the future of the Revolution. Later he would spread his solemn soaring gaze over Cuba like a protective mantle and you saw him on every poster and wall mural in your barrio. "WITH FIDEL, OUR WHOLE LIFE!" "IN EVERY BARRIO, *REVOLUCIÓN*!"

You think of Fidel when you get your Young Pioneer red bandanna, and your Communist Youth credential. You cling to him for dear life when he is the only solid object standing between you and the great hazy wall of death ninety miles away. Invasion. Nuclear disaster. Total annihilation at the hands of blue-eyed destroyers. Fidel protects you from it all. You are a child, but you are moved beyond words at his courage, which becomes your courage, at his grandeur, which is yours, at his historical inevitability, which you, with your own small courage and your insignificant sacrifice, make possible. Later, when you cut cane against the clock for grueling months on end, you do it to meet his goal: 10 million tons! That endless, agonizing harvest of 1969–1970 turns the island upside down and mobilizes nearly every able-bodied youth in Cuba. It produces barely 8 million tons of sugar, and Cuba's productive infrastructure is nearly destroyed as a result of the effort, but when he offers to resign you are in the Plaza, weeping and shouting "No!" You donate blood for Fidel when he demands your international solidarity for disaster victims overseas, and you are awed and moved to tears again at the endless generosity, the *espíritu de sacrificio* with which his words fill you. Your voice thunders through the *actos,* the revolutionary gatherings where faith is rekindled: "Fi-del! Fi-del! Fi-del!" Such a small island, such a great role in history.

Fidel never visits Angola, but he is there with you in spirit. You are not among the several thousand *internacionalista* martyrs who died in Africa, and for this, although you would not confess it, you are grateful. This is a new feeling, and you may or may not want to dwell on it: martyrdom used to be a blessed gift, a grail Che finally found within his grasp, but after the *aventura africana* you are not sure that this is the destiny you seek. What was it again that your compatriots gave their lives for? Better not to question; better not to ask. Once again, it is time to gather in the Plaza and renew your fervor. "Fi-del! Fi-del!" After all, he needs you more than ever. It's time to throw stones at the 80,000 Marielitos who have decided to flee the Revolution. It's time to remind yourself that the true revolutionary does not question decisions whose intricacies and true causes cannot be revealed: information is the coin only Seguridad del Estado can trade on.

That is why you watch the television screen, transfixed, when the trial of the regime's most popular military commander along with three other officers plays itself out. Drugs, treason, obscene accumulation of privileges are among the charges. When Fidel demands the death penalty for the daring, dashing General Arnaldo Ochoa, humble son of *campesinos,* Hero of the Republic, commander at the legendary battle that crippled the South African invading army in Angola, you swallow hard. Fidel's hand does not tremble, his voice does not shake, his gaze is as firm and soaring as ever. He knows something you don't.

And really it is not a moment to stint on loyalty, because the frail canoe that is the Revolution is about to go under in the tidal wave that history has seen fit to unleash on the world. The Soviet Union is no more; socialism has collapsed everywhere. But not on your besieged island, because, once again, Fidel has determined that he, and through him you, will be greater than any man, will defy history, defy the odds, live for a dream so that others may dream too, dream of a world of perfect equality and perfect justice such as Cuba will one day produce. Socialism will not be defeated! This is a new adventure: Cuba, this beloved and fragile vessel, will ride out the ominous storm. With Fidel at the helm, there is no cause for fear, and yet you are, for the first time, unconsolably afraid.

Suddenly, the Comandante is looking very old.

It is January 16, 1998—nearly ten years after the demise of the Soviet Union, only twelve months shy of the fortieth anniversary of Fidel Castro's Revolution. At nine o'clock, Cubans throughout the island prop chairs in front of the television set or nestle into bed, cushions against their backs, to watch the screen. The Comandante en Jefe de la Revolución is about to give a televised press conference—one of the very few formal press conferences in memory to take place live in Cuba, and exclusively with members of the Cuban press. Because the press conference is taking place only days before the arrival of Pope John Paul II in Havana, and because Fidel is said to be ailing, attention is focused on the political significance of the event (is it a sign of glasnost on the eve of the pope's arrival?). And on his appearance (he has not been looking the picture of health).

It's not as though the viewing audience has been out of touch with their leader in recent times. He is, as always, everywhere—inaugurating seminars, commemorating fateful events, attending receptions, and meeting with world leaders at home and abroad. But a press conference, with its spontaneous give and take, promises to be a novelty. Never mind that the representatives of the press on this particular evening are hardly likely to ask irreverent or troublesome questions. In addition to the moderator, Héctor Rodríguez, a news presenter for the government TV channel, they are four high-level journalists: one each from the National Television Newscast, *Trabajadores*—the official workers' paper—and *Granma,* which is the Communist Party paper; and someone who represents both Radio Havana Cuba and Cuban Television. Probably very few people among those now settling in with a cup of coffee in front of the screen would ever imagine that a troublesome or probing question could be asked on such an occasion.

The first question, from Loly Estévez of the National Television Newscast, sets the tone. She requests Castro's opinion of the results of the national elections staged on the previous Sunday, January 11. Castro's answer (as it appears in the official transcription published by *Granma* five days later) is relatively brief: eleven paragraphs in which he extols the people's satisfaction in their own victory. They have, he points out, decisively elected representatives of the Cuban Communist Party to occupy 95 percent of the 494 seats in the Asamblea Nacional del Poder Popular (the Cuban legislative body) despite the hardships Cuba is undergoing. "A miracle," Fidel says of the election in conclusion. "That is my impression. I won't *fundamentarlo,* I hope I will have to [provide my arguments later on], but you asked me for my impression."[1]

No news so far, but Cubans have had the opportunity to study their leader in greater close-up and at greater length than usual. The quaver in the Comandante's silvery voice, the thick white spittle that keeps forming at the corners of his mouth, the odd pout that deforms his lower lip and distorts his pronunciation, have all been noted. Fidel, always upright, always gallant, was also always very handsome. Now, at seventy-one, even his wispy beard denotes infirmity. His viewers pay close attention: Fidel's soaring gaze has been replaced by the hollow, fearful stare of the very ill, as

1. *Granma, Suplemento especial,* January 20, 1998.

if someone within were peering out from behind bars. Is it really true that he's sick?

After the initial discussion of the elections there is a little exchange, in the half-bantering, half-grumpy tone Cubans are so familiar with:

FIDEL CASTRO: The other *compañeros* can ask questions, or you, Héctor, who are part of the panel; you're not just going to be the boss here, giving orders.

MODERATOR: No, I'll ask too.

FIDEL CASTRO: So I'm waiting for your questions.

MODERATOR: Martínez Pírez has asked for the floor.

FIDEL CASTRO: On the same subject?

MODERATOR: Yes.

FIDEL CASTRO: Please, on the point we were just on: don't change the subject.

Pedro Martínez Pírez dutifully comments that before the Sunday vote there had been all sorts of dire predictions in the foreign press about possible electoral sabotage.

FIDEL CASTRO [interrupting]: Listen, Pírez, if you all aren't pressed for time, before I go on to the subject of abstentions and all that, I'd prefer to explain some aspects of what I was talking about before, and then, maybe, in part we'll make some progress [on your topic].

What Fidel is so eager to explain can be summarized in a couple of sentences for a non-Cuban audience: For the first time in these elections Cuban authorities discounted from the total of valid votes those that were not cast at the polling booth where the voter was registered. A total of 119,000 votes were invalidated this way, which means that the valid votes cast did not amount to 99.8 percent of the possible total, but to a mere 98.35 percent. In the transcript this explanation takes up two entire tabloid pages and then some of the special issue of *Granma* (which, normally, because of the paper shortage, puts out an eight-page newspaper every other day). Fidel reviews the history of the Cuban Revolution, the U.S. economic embargo, the heroic role of the teenage *Pioneros* who patrolled the polling booths ("In our electoral system, in our democracy, why would soldiers have to guard the booths?"), in order to mull irritably over the lost 1.45 percent which, he insists, by right should have been included in the total, to the greater glory of Cuban democracy. Too bad the electoral officers decided to be so punctilious.

"Do I make myself clear?" Fidel interrupts himself at one point.

"Perfectly," the moderator assures him, but Fidel returns obsessively to his percentages and fractions for an additional two full pages of the transcript before interrupting himself again.

"Do you think people have gone to sleep on me?"

"No, people haven't gone to sleep, Comandante," the moderator asserts, before adding helpfully, "Besides, you received more than ninety-nine percent, and the minister of the Revolutionary Armed Forces [Raúl Castro, Fidel's brother] did too."

Fidel notes with satisfaction that another Castro brother, Ramón, who also ran for the Asamblea Nacional, came up with exactly the same percentage, right up to the fraction, as he did, and after congratulating him on this happy coincidence, the moderator says, with what one can only assume is a certain desperate briskness, that it is time to change the subject. What, he would like to know, is Fidel's personal impression of the pope [whom Fidel met last year in Rome]?

The audience perks up here: there is great curiosity about John Paul II, but Fidel's answer takes up one succinct paragraph: the pope has "a noble face," he inspires respect, he speaks Spanish fluently, he is "a precise man, he knows how to listen, and listens very attentively." Perhaps having glanced at his watch at this point, Fidel then says that he is obliged to be briefer in his replies, "although if I have to extend myself [in answer to a given question] I will do so, of course."

The opportunity to extend himself presents itself forthwith. The same journalist who asked the evening's second question now wants to know what might be new or unusual about this particular papal tour. A six-page, or approximately three-hour-long, response is what he gets in reply. The history of revolutionary Cuba's relations with the Church; the pope and the Cold War; the tremendous historical error that the Molotov-Ribbentrop Treaty represented for international socialism; the losses suffered by the Soviet army during World War II (80 percent of its officer corps, among other things); the desertion of German soldiers in Japan; why Karol Wojtyla was elected pope; and John Paul II's deep anticapitalist conviction, documented with an entire page worth of quotes from two papal speeches, are all glossed by Fidel, in order to explain how it is that the anti-Communist Wojtyla is actually a friend of the people. A single murmur from the moderator ("[you are quoting from] two different speeches") is the only interruption.

It is now nearly three in the morning, and Fidel's audience, which has to rise at dawn to negotiate the torturous bike-and-bus marathon that getting to work involves these days for most Cubans, is by and large no longer with him. This is a pity, because the Comandante is about to touch on the one issue that lifelong Fidelistas find most troublesome about the pope's impending visit: How are they to greet a man who is the very incarnation of what vanguard revolutionaries know as "religious superstition"? Are they, in fact, supposed to greet him at all? "I remember," Fidel starts,

> when Lucius Walker [the U.S. Protestant pastor] has come here on several occasions to Cuba: more than once I've gone to the church at La Lisa, where they have their temples, I've listened to them and I've even spoken to them. When [Jesse] Jackson came here once, since he's religious . . . I, without any prejudice, went inside the church, and I even spoke to them. . . .

Therefore, after nearly forty years of official state atheism and vilification of religious believers, Fidel instructs his followers:

What should be the most sacred duty of each one of us? This is truly a key point: we invite all the people [to attend the papal masses] . . . but no one must take a single poster, no one must shout a single slogan . . . no one must cheer a single leader of the Revolution; no one must express the slightest displeasure with any word or pronouncement that might displease or seem unjust to us. . . . Let the television networks transmit to the world that image so that Cuba may be known; this Cuba where 98.35 percent of the electorate voted, 95 percent of whose votes were valid, of which 94.39 percent were cast [for the Cuban Communist Party].

Fidel! The Comandante has issued the marching orders at last. It is almost 3:30 A.M. The Cuban national television network, which normally broadcasts only six hours a day, has given him an extra three and a half hours of its time. The exhausted moderator and two panelists have managed to ask a total of four questions. Fidel—ailing or no—is chipper and about to meet with a few foreign correspondents who have been dozing outside the studio, whom he will keep scribbling in their notebooks nearly until dawn. The moderator thanks him.

FIDEL CASTRO: There are many who have been sleeping for a while now . . .
MODERATOR: But it was worth it.
FIDEL CASTRO: Do you [the other panelists who have yet to be heard from] have anything to say?
RENATO RECIO [who never got to ask a question]: You have really answered the doubts that even we had considered, and in my opinion, it was very complete. In that sense, there is nothing to add.

And so the nationally televised press conference by Fidel Castro ends.

Weeks later, in Mexico, I commented to a Cuban friend my surprise at the Comandante's woolliness. Was he, in fact, seriously ill? Did he not understand the purpose of a press conference?

My friend laughed. "No one is better than Fidel at talking forever about nothing when there is something he doesn't want to say."

*

Forty years of political intercourse do not necessarily lead to intimacy, but on a small, lively, gossip-loving tropical island, where everybody who is anybody knows Fidel, and where almost everyone knows somebody who knows someone who does, intimacy of the sort Cubans experience with their leader is inevitable. They are on to his tricks. They gossip about his love life, laugh at his foibles—bitterly, often enough—refer to him familiarly as Fidel even if they happen to be among those who loathe him, and remain in steadfast awe of him. In August of 1994, when the Habanazo—or first full-fledged riot against the regime—broke out on the streets of downtown Havana, he stopped the rock throwers in their tracks by appearing, on foot, in the very thick of the fray. As the observant and thoughtful correspondents of the Mexican weekly *Proceso*[2] noted at the time, the protesters' tune changed the moment Fidel appeared on the scene. "This is over, El Caballo [The Horse, a favorite name for Fidel] has arrived," someone said, and another man was heard to murmur, "He really has balls, coming here." Yet another: "The Old Man doesn't change. There's no overthrowing him." The ability to inspire feelings of intimacy and awe in equal measure is what has kept Fidel Castro in power even through the years of awful hardship that followed the collapse of the Soviet Union, and it will, foreseeably, keep him in power as long as his remarkable energies remain.

How well anyone in Cuba knows Fidel is another matter entirely. The gossip about his love life does not mean that anyone outside his immediate circle of Party faithful and bodyguards knows whom he sleeps with. He is reported to be shy, and to mask

2. Homero Campa and Orlando Pérez. Their book *Cuba: Los Años Duros* (Barcelona: Plaza y Janés, 1997) is the source for much of the background information in this article.

this he fills his private conversations with the same torrent of statistics, historical ruminations, and revolutionary exhortations that overwhelm his public discourse. He has not been forthcoming with his biographers, and he is elusive even in the two book-length interviews with him that have been published. One is with the Brazilian activist Frei Betto (*Fidel Castro y la religión: Conversaciones con Frei Betto*),[3] the other with the Nicaraguan sometime revolutionary leader Tomás Borge (*Un Grano de Maíz: Conversación con Fidel Castro*).[4] In the conversation with Borge the two comandantes feed each other spoonfuls of revolutionary treacle. Fidel plies Frei Betto with sugar and percentages too, but at least Betto, the cheerful friar, is genuinely curious and persistent. Reluctantly, Fidel gives a portrait of his childhood that is unexpectedly emotional.

He is the son of Ángel Castro, a prosperous and nearly illiterate immigrant from Galicia, in northern Spain, who in Cuba acquired large amounts of land in the district of Birán (near the city of Santiago) through less-than-transparent business deals. The *finca* of Birán, where some three hundred families worked for or rented land from his father, is where Fidel was born. Fidel tells Betto that, although the family was prosperous, he suffered hardship in his youth: along with an older sister and a brother, he was sent to Santiago to board with the family of a schoolteacher. Fidel remembers bitterly that the teacher stinted on the children's food, and that he was always hungry. He was five at the time, and, although his relations with his family were apparently always affectionate, he would never again live at home. He also remembers that at the age of seven he was sent away to boarding school, but his recollection sounds like a particularly Fidelian reinterpretation of history. In his telling, he decided that life at boarding school would be preferable to life with the schoolteacher, and so, one day, having perceived that he was "the object of injustice . . . I deliberately

3. Mexico City: Siglo XXI Editores, 1986.
4. Mexico City: Fondo de Cultura Económica, 1992.

refuse to follow all orders, disobey all the rules, all the discipline. I shout, I say all the words it seemed to me were forbidden, *in a conscious act of rebellion so that I shall be sent as an intern to school"* [my italics]. In other words, he is in charge of his destiny.

He is in charge of it because he is alone. In general, Fidel speaks fondly of his days in three different Catholic schools and of his idyllic vacations back at the *finca,* but there is no mention of childhood friends or teenage pals, nor is there much about his parents or any stories about him and his brothers—just Fidel setting himself challenges: climbing the highest mountain in the region ("I didn't imagine that I was preparing myself as a revolutionary"), physically attacking a priest—a school officer—who had slapped him twice on the face ("It was something unworthy and abusive"). When he was allowed to go to boarding school, he was always happier than when he was sent to stay with a family: there he could not help observing that there was "a certain different relationship. [We] weren't their children, they couldn't treat [us] as their children."

It is a father's absence he feels most, although he never says so in so many words. Rather, he expresses sorrow at the fact that "really, I never had a mentor." Later, talking about his religious education and how little influence it had on his politics, he says it again: "I have really had to be, unfortunately, my own mentor throughout my life." And later still, when he reflects on his first incursion into politics: "I say that I never had a mentor. It must have been a great effort of reasoning in such a little time to elaborate my ideas and put them into practice."

But although he is unusually candid with Frei Betto, he is by no means candid enough to be truly illuminating. Indeed, he leaves out one of the most critical facts of his biography, which is that, like so many other revolutionary leaders—César Augusto Sandino in Nicaragua and both Eva and Juan Perón in Argentina, among others—Fidel Castro was born out of wedlock to a poor woman and her wealthy and lighter-skinned lover or attacker.

The monstrous Latin American class division split these children in two even when, as in Fidel's case, the father loved the washerwoman Lina Ruz—the future revolutionary's mother—eventually married her, and favored Lina's children over his legitimate ones. What this meant was that, although Fidel Castro grew up in comfortable circumstances, he was socially unacceptable. Fidel does not mention this directly to Frei Betto, but we know from other sources that the "good families" of Cuba always saw the brilliant, athletic, tall, and handsome Castro boy as "the bastard," "the upstart," the *gallego's* son. He was *un cualquiera*—an "anybody." What Fidel does mention several times is that because he was not baptized until he was six—probably because his parents did not get married until then—he was also known as a "Jew," a term that was fully intended to be offensive.

Small wonder that Fidel soon developed the underdog's obsession with honor and dignity. And also an obsession with the strategic first strike. As a child, his brother Raúl says, he picked fights constantly. And he did so again once he found politics. As a young university student, he carried a gun, joined in street brawls, signed up for a failed expedition against the dictator Trujillo in the Dominican Republic, and, during a visit to Bogotá in 1949, raced to change into a borrowed police uniform in order to join the fighting when the popular leader Jorge Gaitán's assassination set off a national revolt.

He also learned the first rule of the pugnacious: never acknowledge when you're beaten. Although he has been defeated, knocked down, and forced to backtrack in tests of will against a broad array of enemies (particularly against his principal one, the United States), he has said so in public only rarely. More importantly, he has in fact refused to back down or acknowledge defeat in circumstances that threatened not only his survival but—as in the Cuban missile crisis—the very survival of civilized life. (It was the Soviets who backed down then, not he.) *Era cuestión de dignidad,* he has said over and over to explain these moments of breathtaking defiance. It is a particularly Latin American, Spanish-inspired vision of what dignity consists of, and it comes out of the twinned obsessions with virility and with being condemned by the gods to the loser's fate. Romantic this posture may be, and unreasonable, but it would be a mistake to consider it foolish. From the reasonable perspective of those with less deeply riven histories, the smart premise is that it is virtually impossible for the poor worker to win the millionaire's daughter (a favorite Latin romantic conceit), or for Fidel Castro to overthrow the United States. Therefore, it is better not to try. But if one must reach for such a goal, the logic goes, then a gradualist and conciliatory policy is the safest option. As Fidel has shown, however, in a confrontation where the underdog's chances are virtually nil, reasonableness may not be the best option at all. Better to tip the scales in your favor by knocking them over. Sometime the policy will have to work, and when it doesn't, the element of *dignidad* provides a better aesthetic than the middle-of-the-road alternative. Who is more beautiful: the poor man who elopes with the rich man's daughter, or the poor sucker who slaves away as an accountant under the rich man's scorn, saving up his pennies toward a small purchase of respect? Fidel knew the answer: *Socialismo o muerte!*

The heroic compulsion alone does not account for the dreamlike trance that Fidel's exhortations in the Plaza have produced in so many Cubans for so many years. Nor is the revolt against itself that colonial capitalism seems to breed in its entrails enough to explain how socialism should have come to establish its most enduring outpost on a tropical island. (And on a tropical island that was by no means the poorest or most backward nation in Latin America when Fidel took power.) Anti-imperialist sentiment, that gelatinous explosive, had an enormous role, of course, all the more so because in Latin America, and in Cuba particularly, the most radical haters of the United States were often young men who, like Fidel, chose *el gigante del norte* as their honeymoon site (it was New York he took his young bride to in 1948). There is also the extreme allure of young men—Che, Camilo Cienfuegos, Fidel—who have gone up to the mountains to fight for the nation and then descended again, gaunt, branded with fire and sacrifice and the glory of combat, and cloaked in victory.

But in the end, it is Fidel alone who accounts for Fidel, Fidel who, with his supernatural will, historic sense of moment and of mission, quick trigger finger and massive ego, has single-handedly led Cuba into its encounter with history and kept it there. Never, during the forty years of alleged plots and power plays and desperate efforts to finally be rid of him, has anyone claimed that he could substitute for Fidel or be his equal, and that is why, of course, he endures. All the more riveting, then, to read the accounts of those who have fallen out of a trance with him.

*

Notable among them is the memoir written by Alina Fernández, *Alina: Memorias de la hija rebelde de Fidel Castro.*[5] Fidel and his women, his biographer Tad Szulc has noted,[6] is in itself a worthy subject. There was his clueless first wife, who went to work for Batista's Interior Ministry while her husband was in prison (following the failed assault on the Moncada barracks), apparently without realizing that this decision would enrage him. There was the gorgeous Naty Revuelta, the society beauty who helped him set up the Moncada assault and with whom he had a curiously chaste affair,[7] and there was Celia Sánchez, who handled many practical tasks for him, ensured that he had the protection of the Afro-Cuban deities of *santería*, and was his true helpmeet from the day they met in the Sierra Maestra to the moment she died in 1980. Then there is Alina, the product of the relations between Fidel and Naty Revuelta.

Her name is Alina Fernández, and not Alina Castro, because until she was ten years old she thought that her father was Orlando Fernández—Naty Revuelta's eminently respectable physician husband, who went into exile shortly after the Revolution's triumph.

5. Barcelona: Plaza y Janés, 1997. Published in English as *Not in My Father's House* (New York: St. Martin's, 2000).
6. *Fidel: A Critical Portrait* (New York: Morrow, 1986).
7. A wonderful account of this affair is the central subject of *Havana Dreams* by Wendy Gimbel (New York: Knopf, 1998).

By the time Alina's real father offered to help her change her name to Castro, she wasn't interested. In her own telling, she had by then already developed a highly eccentric personality. How much one can believe a woman who is fuzzy on dates and chronology, joyfully venomous, and, by her own account, emotionally erratic and professionally inconsistent—and who has a less than clear sense of the truth or of the importance of fairness, according to several people who know her[8]—is a problem. And yet *Alina* is a fascinating book, and a real one.

The story of what it was like to grow up as the neglected daughter of a man who is also one of the century's mythical figures is well worth telling. Fernández writes surprisingly well, even if her tone is often irritatingly coy or edgy. And although there seems to be a sad difference between the way others perceive her and the way she sees herself, she has a wicked eye for those around her, notably Fidel Castro. One doesn't have to read the following account as truth to recognize the accuracy of the portrait. Alina describes how one night, after a two-year absence, her father suddenly appears again in the Revuelta home:

> The following night Mommy was radiant. She was an archangel at the side of the Comandante, who was lying on my bed, arms behind his head.
> "I've been too busy these past couple of years. Time turns to nothing on me. It's very hard to keep up a Revolution. Lately I've been negotiating with Japan for the purchase of some machines to make sno-cones with, and I'm very satisfied. In two more months they'll be installed. At least one in each barrio. That way people are going to be able to have their little ice cream, with the weather as hot as it is. But the best part is that I've negotiated the purchase of an ice-cream cone factory, and we'll be able to produce them in this country."
> At least the cones wouldn't have to be imported. . . . I didn't applaud because we were alone.

8. See, for example, Wendy Gimbel's history of Alina's family in *Havana Dreams*.

"The Japanese are also going to sell me a plastic shoe factory with an incredibly large daily output of plastic shoes. It's incredible: you put in a little petroleum-derivate ball of plastic and out comes a pair of shoes—heels and all. For men, women or children. You can manufacture several different models. I've bought the machinery very cheaply. I think that in the long run it will solve the footwear problem of the population."

An image comes to mind, and it is of Yul Brynner as the king of Siam, fascinated with the bells and whistles of European modernity, stubbornly committed to making his country new and prosperous. Forceful, macho, immune to self-doubt and all the other self-conscious weaknesses that plague European males, he keeps the wonderfully progressive Englishwoman he has hired to tutor his myriad children in thrall to him. But he loses the will to live— and dies—when she thrusts upon him the realization that Siam will not be modern until he stops being king.

Fidel, of course, has yet to abdicate from being Fidel. In Alina Fernández's portrait of her father, she captures the abrupt, oddly innocent, maddening logic of the true monarch. "People don't change," he tells his daughter.

"I'll give you an example. A man tried to assassinate me. That was ten years ago. I saved him from being executed and I gave him the minimum sentence. I talked with him several times. Later we even gave personal attention to the family. They let him out of jail and it wasn't three months before he was taken prisoner again."

"Did he try to assassinate you again?"

"No, he was trying to leave the country illegally with his entire family."

And again—musing on this occasion about some of the perplexing details with which he seems to fill a large part of his day, he ponders the uniforms for nationwide boarding schools:

"The uniforms have been selected according to the criteria of comfort and modernity. Although it is true that synthetic materials are hot, they have the advantage that they don't wrinkle easily. Which avoids the use of irons in the boarding schools, reducing the possibility of accidents and fires."

Et cetera. Et cetera. Et cetera.

Several other memoirs of life in revolutionary Cuba have appeared since 1994, a year that saw the Havana riot, the pathetic, deadly exodus on life rafts and assorted floating contraptions that became known as the *balsero* (rafter) crisis, and the final submission of socialist goals to the pragmatic requirements of getting a full-throttle tourist economy under way. A great many Cubans escaped from the island at that time or have negotiated their departure in the years since, and a number of them are now writing interesting books.

Memorias de un soldado cubano,[9] by "Benigno" (Dariel Alarcón Ramírez), is by far the most valuable historically, as well as the most painful and astonishing of these. A movie or two could be made out of any given chapter of this remarkable man's life. Born in 1939, he was a seventeen-year-old farmer in the Sierra Maestra—illiterate, industrious, and very poor—when a couple of bearded men in olive-green uniforms came to his *bohío* asking for food. Frightened, thinking they were government soldiers, he gave them what they wanted, and more. So began his unwitting collaboration with Fidel's *barbudos.* It turned conscious, and purposeful, when the real government forces murdered his teenage wife as a revenge for the help he'd given the rebels.

"Benigno" is the pseudonym Dariel Alarcón used in Bolivia when he fought alongside Ernesto Guevara. By then, he had already served under him as a machine gunner in the Rebel Army and infiltrated the leadership of the counterrevolutionary bands in the Escambray hills. Benigno's wholehearted love for Che and

9. Barcelona: Tusquets, 1997.

Fidel led him to volunteer for every shoddily put together suicide mission his leaders dreamed up. "We had a tremendous fever for internationalist struggle," he says, recalling how eager he and other Cuban volunteers were to depart for Bolivia, where their chances of survival were so small.

Che's love of harsh punishment does not diminish Benigno's loyalty. Once, Benigno recalls, he removed his boots while trying to move a heavy load of supplies across a river in Bolivia, and when the raft he was using broke, he lost his boots. To set an example Che forced him to go barefoot, carrying his usual ninety-pound load. "The pain was terrible, frightful," Benigno says. But Che also made a point of teaching him to read and giving him the basics of an education, which led to Benigno's eventually getting a degree in history:

> On December 30, by the light of a campfire in the Bolivian jungle, at the end of a lesson, Che said, "You've got sixth-grade level now." I felt like the king of the jungle at that moment, and I dared to say to him, "If I get out of here alive, I'll make it at least to the first step of the university stairs." . . . He hugged me and said, "That's the kind of commitment worth making."

Benigno's adventures continue after he and two other Cuban fighters make a Houdini-like escape from Bolivia into Chile following Che's murder. After a few weeks' rest, he is off to Peru on another special mission Fidel has designed for him. He is equipped with an explosive device wired to his crotch, which he is to detonate if anyone tries to open a briefcase he is carrying. Inside, according to Benigno, is a blueprint Fidel has written up: instructions, supposedly, for the military coup that brought the pro-Cuban General Juan Velasco Alvarado to power in 1968. Having delivered the briefcase, Benigno volunteers again for a second attempt to create a guerrilla movement in Bolivia—where he is not recognized, he says, despite the fact that his picture has been all over the papers, "because they'd given me a very good plastic surgery just a while back."

After this last adventure Benigno more or less settles down, training Latin American guerrillas at the special clandestine schools that the Central Committee's quasi-autonomous Departamento Américas has set up on the island. While his own education is postponed, he suffers whenever he has to write something for his trainees on the blackboard, and the *internacionalista* comrades mockingly correct his spelling.

It is at this point that we begin to learn about Fidel's Cuba. Fidel offered training to guerrillas from Uruguay to Mexico—denying the fact all the while to the Mexican government, Cuba's one real ally in the hemisphere—but leaving the various countries' rebel groups parked on the island for months.[10] (All the rebels' papers were confiscated on their arrival on the island, where they lived on a miserly stipend and under strict supervision.) Particularly instructive is the case of the Dominican Republic's Francisco Caamaño Deñó—an army colonel from a military family who was one of the few would-be liberators with any real following. Fidel kept Caamaño on hold for almost four years without granting him so much as an interview. Caamaño was killed in 1972, soon after his poorly equipped and poorly informed expedition (set up by Cuban intelligence) finally landed on Dominican soil. "That is when I realized that my Revolution was not what I had dreamt," Benigno writes.

Benigno dwells on this and other instances of Cuban inter-

10. In their book about Subcomandante Marcos of Mexico (*Marcos: La genial impostura,* Madrid: Alfaguara, 1997), Bertrand de la Grange of *Le Monde* and Maite Rico of *El País* offer a different interpretation of Cuba's role in training Mexican guerrillas. Having looked at some Mexican intelligence documents from the 1970s, the authors speculate that Cuba trained these guerrillas with the full knowledge of Castro's old friends in the Mexican intelligence apparatus. In this way the Cubans helped the Mexican government to dismantle would-be rebel armies with a minimum of losses for its side and a maximum of public relations profit. (Castro, who owed the Mexicans for the easy treatment he and his fellow revolutionaries got while they were conspiring from Mexico against the Batista dictatorship, has a reputation for undying loyalty to his friends.)

national revolutionary solidarity that end in disaster because he is tormented by one question: did Fidel deliberately leave Che to die in Bolivia? He never understands why Fidel withdrew the key liaison agent between himself and Che from Bolivia and never replaced him, or why communications were allowed to die, or why no rescue mission was launched when it became evident that Che was encircled. Was it, in truth, because Cuba's financial backers in the Soviet Union had made it clear that they would not stand for it? Once Benigno works up his courage and asks his commander-in-chief point-blank what, specifically, Cuba did to try to save Che. In answer, Fidel "throws his arm over my shoulder, walks me away, strokes his beard with his left hand and says, 'This is a case requiring study . . .'" then offers Benigno yet another delicate mission.

It takes the aging fighter years to formulate the question that follows from his doubt, and years more to act on it: if the Revolution's purpose is to improve everyone's life, and to make life in general more meaningful, why did it not care about *my* life, why did I mean nothing to Fidel? Coming after such experiences, the question is anything but disingenuous.

While his disillusionment grows, Benigno moves up the ranks of the Special Troops. He becomes one of the three rotating chiefs of Fidel's personal security. He tells us about the East German–type security measures that guard Cuba's political elite, and about the curious precautions taken before Fidel is to visit a given work center:

> The first thing Counterintelligence had to do was look in the files and see what personnel in that specific place were not supporters of the revolutionary process: those people were given the day off. . . . Their workplaces and lockers were checked to see if they weren't hiding anything that could be used for sabotage or assassination attempts. . . . This was so routine that many workers, if they happened to find out about an upcoming visit by Fidel, would go ask their supervisors:
> Well, do I show up tomorrow or not?

From his fly-on-the-wall position Benigno is privy to all sorts of performances by Fidel. Typically, he remembers, a meeting with him would be called at the last minute, the participants would come rushing in to hear Fidel lay out the subject at hand, and then, one by one, give their opinion "while Fidel stroked his beard and looked at them very attentively."

At the end, a vote was taken, and when everyone thought that the point had been approved by the majority, Fidel stood and summarized the meeting, whether it was of the Politburo, the Council of State, or the Central Committee, since he presides over all three. And then one realized that the meeting had been called practically for the hell of it, because there was nothing in the summary about what had actually been discussed. . . . Then [Fidel] would start to give everybody their tasks according to how he saw things, and each one left the meeting with some relief because these tasks were now not his responsibility but Fidel's.

In meetings where the flaws or failures of a high-ranking official had to be discussed, Fidel would lash out at him in front of everyone until the humiliated official hung his head and swore to mend his ways. "Then Fidel would get up, throw his arm over the man's shoulder and walk him to the door. . . ."

"The 'blockade,' or U.S. economic embargo, is Fidel's last resort for holding on to power," Benigno writes, echoing the conviction of so many dissidents still living in Cuba.

The incident with the planes [in which two light aircraft flown by members of an anti-Castro organization based in Florida were shot down over Cuban airspace on February 24, 1996] happened precisely when the United States was disposed to turn over a new leaf in its relations with Cuba. After the planes were shot down, the United States evidently had no other option but to harden its position again. Fidel needs to continue egging on the North Americans, and the day the North Americans don't react he'll go and pinch them so that they do. The day the blockade stops existing, so will Fidel.

How much can we believe Benigno? For the moment, his stories remain impossible to verify. He is not an academic—or a writer. Often we suspect that he knows more than he is willing to say (about Cuba and the drug trade, for example). At other times he makes assertions or engages in speculations about important events without offering anything but anecdotal evidence. Did Castro, in fact, simultaneously encourage guerrilla movements in order to keep up his standing in Latin America, and sabotage their operations in order to keep peace with the Soviets? This is a serious charge, but the confusion, delays, and tragic errors Benigno cites in support of his thesis could just as easily be the result of Cuban bureaucratic incompetence.

We do know that Benigno's account of his days with Che coincides with those of the only two other survivors (both Cuban), and we know that he held the positions he claims to have held. He was for a time in charge of the Cuban prison system, and his description of jail conditions coincides with those of former prisoners.[11] Cubans who know him well say that he has been telling the same stories for a long time. His ghostwriter-editor, Elisabeth Burgos, was formerly the wife of Régis Debray, having married him when he was in a Bolivian prison, and she also ghostwrote and edited Rigoberta Menchú's first book. She knows Latin America—and Cuba particularly—extremely well, and one assumes that she took the trouble to check whatever could be checked.

Whatever his accuracy, Benigno's amazing autobiography is a precise mirror of Cuba's revolutionary upheavals, and the change

11. Benigno estimates the current prison population in Cuba at over 100,000, or 1 percent of the island's total population. His estimate of the number of political prisoners is larger than that of most of the human rights organizations. Sensibly, he points out that a great many "common prisoners" are in jail for attempting to leave the island, and that this is a political crime.

in the author's feelings about "his" Revolution is also a mirror in which many once-fervent Fidelistas can find themselves. Guerrilla heroes become corrupt bureaucrats or commit suicide. A regime that prided itself on its ability to feed, clothe, and educate its youth turns out to have been the late twentieth century's last true colony, unable to survive even modestly once its ties to Great Mother Russia have been severed. Glorious battles are fought for unwinnable causes, or to support cowardly sluggards, like Laurent Kabila in Africa. Why were we in Angola? Benigno asks himself, having, he writes, nearly died there too.

The watershed event for people of his generation as well as those much younger was the summary trial and execution of Colonel Arnaldo Ochoa in 1989.[12] Of course, Benigno knew him: they fought together as teenage *guajiros*—hillbillies—in Fidel's Rebel Army, but Ochoa rose higher than Benigno. From his post as head of Fidel's security, Benigno observed the late commander of all Angola's Cuban troops, and virtual proconsul there, who could enter El Caballo's office time and again without an appointment and without going through the official X-ray machine. Once, Benigno says, he heard Ochoa joke in his usual carefree way after a meeting, "So, I'm going to be the Al Capone of Cuba!" and Fidel told him to watch his mouth.

Benigno is convinced that Ochoa, arrested on corruption charges, was offered as a sop to the United States at a time when the CIA and the Drug Enforcement Administration were threatening to reveal what they had on Cuba's involvement with the drug trade. Again, he gives no proof, but then, this is not an unlikely or even a particularly new theory. What is important is that, in Cuba, where there is so little information about the setting of international intrigue in which the trial took place (and where cocaine is more and more available), there is a widespread

12. Ochoa and thirteen other members of the military and security forces were arrested on June 12, 1989, accused of corruption and drug trafficking. Ochoa and three others were executed on Fidel's direct request, on July 13, 1989.

conviction that Ochoa did whatever he did on higher orders, that nothing happens in Cuba without Fidel's knowledge, and that, facing the firing squad, Ochoa died bravely.

Incredibly, Fidel seems not to have been aware of the consequences of killing a hero. Or perhaps he did understand that Ochoa was not only an official Hero of the Republic but also a wildly popular field commander. In the absence of any other credible explanation, one can conjecture that Ochoa was engaged in some sort of plot against Fidel and his brother and designated successor, Raúl.[13] Perhaps what Fidel did not understand was that his own rule was about to become an anachronism, and that the wound caused by Ochoa's execution would never have time to heal, to diminish and fade, in the rebound of joy and prosperity in an ever more perfect, more socialist Cuba, because the Soviet Union was about to expire in a matter of weeks.

In retrospect, it is hard to imagine a more absurd marriage of conflicting interests. In 1961, when serious talks between the two countries began, the triumphant Cubans wanted to race headlong to utopia and were convinced that the Soviet Union's only possible desire would be to help them get there—whatever it took. The Russian leadership was rather less interested in the fate of 6 million dark-colored, Spanish-speaking people living under palm trees on the opposite side of the world. Their goal was to gain the upper hand in the looming Sino-Soviet split, and to get a nuclear foothold in the Western Hemisphere. In his biography of Che Guevara, Jon Lee Anderson tells us how Che pressed Nikita Khrushchev in 1960 for a million-ton steel factory, against the older man's wise counsel that in Cuba there was no coal, no iron, no skilled labor, and no consumers for such a venture. On a subsequent trip to the Soviet Union, according to Che's other indispensable biographer, Jorge Castañeda, Che and a Cuban revolutionary

---

13. Certainly, Ochoa's execution and the subsequent purge of the Interior Ministry's upper ranks would indicate that a singular political crisis occurred. See Julia Preston in the *New York Review of Books,* December 7, 1989, pp. 24–31.

buddy negotiated the nuclear weapons deal with Khrushchev while shivering on a pier in the Crimea. Through an interpreter (how good was his Spanish?) they listened with misgivings to the chubby old bureaucrat's proposal that the missiles be kept secret.[14]

Castro shared their worries, but he accepted the missiles. Years later, he explained:

> Had we known then what we know now about the balance of power, we would have realized that the emplacement changed intermediate-range missiles into strategic weapons. In the light of what we know today, this must have been the real Soviet motive—not the defense of Cuba. We did not know how few missiles the Soviets had. We imagined thousands. If I had known the real ratio I would have advised Nikita to be prudent. . . . But we had unlimited trust.[15]

In the event, Fidel advised Nikita to be anything but prudent. In a letter that Fidel referred to many times, but that was made public in Cuba only eight years ago, the Cuban leader exhorted his Soviet counterpart, in effect, to nuke the territory of the United States "if . . . the imperialists invade Cuba with the goal of occupying it." At that moment, Khrushchev and Kennedy were working against the clock on the agreement that avoided a nuclear war, offered assurances that the United States would not invade Cuba, and saved face for all parties concerned—or so Kennedy and Khrushchev thought. When Fidel found out that the two had gone over his head to negotiate, however, he felt humiliated. He returned to the National University, where he had made so many

14. See Jon Lee Anderson, *Che Guevara: A Revolutionary Life* (New York: Grove, 1997), and Jorge Castañeda, *Compañero: The Life and Death of Che Guevara* (New York: Knopf, 1997). Both biographies give extraordinary portraits of Che and his times.

15. Quoted by Arthur Schlesinger, Jr., in the *New York Review of Books,* March 26, 1992, p. 25.

crucial and fiery speeches before, to declare that the Russian had no *cojones*.[16]

Conceivably if one is going to invite one of the two contenders for nuclear supremacy to bring in weapons that can destroy the whole world, one takes into consideration at least two factors: (a) Is the possible outcome of nuclear annihilation good for the world? and (b) Who's got the most weapons? But Fidel's enthusiasms don't work this way. Khrushchev had told him that the stationing of Soviet nuclear missiles ninety miles away from the United States was good for the Cubans, and that was good enough for him.

"Nikita, you little faggot, what you give can't be taken away," Cubans chanted after Kennedy and Khrushchev came to an agreement on the missile withdrawal. That extraordinary slogan and its circumstances, the missiles under the palm trees, the improvised agreement hammered out on Crimean shores between four people who spoke not a word of each other's language and had barely spent a few hours in each other's company, the utter improbability of the alliance that was forged on the ashes of this agreement between a leaden bureaucratic empire and a fiery young revolutionary . . . Nearly forty years later, it is hard to believe that any of this could ever have happened. But it did, because of Fidel. What will happen when he is no longer around to cast his shadow on the world is anyone's guess. What will be the future of the exemplary education and health systems, now in shambles, that the Revolution set up? Where will jobs come from if the state apparatus is dismantled? And what about Miami, what about the predators who are assumed to be sharpening their fangs and talons there in expectation of Fidel's demise: will they, perhaps, be kind? Raúl

16. At a conference about the missile crisis held in 1992 in Havana, and described by Arthur Schlesinger, Jr., in the *New York Review of Books,* Fidel told Schlesinger and Robert McNamara, among others, that he wrote the letter in an effort "to strengthen [Khrushchev's] position from a moral viewpoint." This conference was also the first time that the Americans learned that some of the nuclear warheads Khrushchev had sent to the island were actually armed.

Castro, Fidel's younger brother and designated successor, is not the man to answer these questions or calm the bewilderment, anger, cynicism, and fear that now pervade the conversation of so many of his countrymen. Nor does anyone else on the Cuban political horizon currently appear capable of doing so. Fidel is growing old, and it's getting late.

—October 22, 1998

MARIO VARGAS LLOSA

THE BITTER EDUCATION

OF VARGAS LLOSA

Mario Vargas Llosa belongs to a long tradition of the politically engaged Latin American intellectual. In the absence of a professional and competent political class, and in the face of an abundance of vile regimes, people with an education and no stake in the system—the kind of people who used to become journalists in the United States—have stepped in to fill a moral and ideological void. Often they too, like Vargas Llosa, have started out as journalists and ended up as fiction writers or poets. Often they have achieved professional acclaim and moral recognition. A great many have courted, and met, death courageously. But few would have been willing to risk extreme ridicule, as Vargas Llosa gamely did in his most recent political adventure. Apart from Václav Havel, no other writer in recent memory has taken his ambition as high as the presidency. And in a part of the world where a leftist revolutionary position is synonymous with intellectual honor, certainly none but the Peruvian Vargas Llosa would have tried to save his country by running for—and almost winning—the presidency of his country as the candidate of the right.

Now he has written an account of his life, *A Fish in the Water: A Memoir,*[1] that concentrates largely on his run for office in 1990, when, after a very strong start that took everyone, including Mario Vargas Llosa, by surprise, he lost by more than 20 percentage points to Alberto Fujimori. One is relieved to learn in the part of this book describing his life before politics that his disastrous

1. New York: Farrar, Straus, 1994.

campaign was but one episode in a life generously filled with drama, and that a sense of proportion and irony provided by experience has allowed his ego a swift recovery. Three years ago he published a first version of the part of this memoir dealing with the campaign in *Granta*. He called it "A Fish Out of Water" then, and was holding a lot of grudges. Plunging into his subject now, he has changed the title for this edition, expanded his economic disquisitions, and reworked his campaign memories in ways that give the narrative detachment, amusement even, and some forgiveness.

Despite these revisions, Vargas Llosa's account of his run for the presidency is not the most fascinating part of *A Fish in the Water,* and perhaps that is why he has constructed the narrative oddly, inserting chapters about the campaign between others that seize our attention from the first; chapters that trace his life from childhood through his early development as an intellectual, a political activist, and a novelist. The youthful narrative breaks off too soon (as the twenty-two-year-old author prepares to leave Peru for a sixteen-year-long stay in Europe), and we are left with characters hanging mid-plot and a great hunger for more of the stay-tuned sequences of his early life; the end of his marriage to his aunt, his experience of Europe, his readings, the writing of his first book. Vargas Llosa, author of some of the finest novels of this century, has written this book to explain himself as a politician, but he is first of all a writer and it is as a writer that we must first try to understand him.

I interviewed Mario Vargas Llosa in Lima in the fall of 1987, just after he had made a reasonably successful debut as a political speechmaker (at a rally to protest President Alan García's nationalization of Peru's banks), but before he had decided to turn this semitriumph into a full-fledged run for the presidency—or, at least, before he had made his decision public. It was, during the first part of our interview, a perfectly useless conversation: he was evasive about his intentions, plodding about his objections to President García, and not at all quotable about the awful situation of his native country. Then I asked him about his writing, and he relaxed. He told me about his first trip to the Amazon, at the age of twenty-two, an adventure that continues, he said, to provide him with the richest flow of imaginative material for his life as a novelist, and which was the inspiration for *The Green House, Captain Pantoja and the Special Service,* and *The Storyteller.* I asked what had moved him to write *The War of the End of the World,* a novel about a fundamentalist sect that fought a millenarian war in the parched northeast of Brazil in the late nineteenth century, and he answered that it was his lifelong fascination with fanaticism, with the complexity and danger of the fanatic's *impulso totalizador.*

He told an amusing story about a campaign against him in the Amazonian *departamento* of Loreto, provoked by his book *Captain Pantoja and the Special Service* (which describes a touring group of prostitutes at the service of the military in Loreto). The local radio announcer's selective readings from the book were followed by impassioned claims that the novelist's intention had been to defame Loreto womanhood, and calls for that womanhood to impede Vargas Llosa's imminent arrival in their region by blocking the airport landing strip with their bodies. But although the story was funny, Vargas Llosa himself, in some curious way, was not. I had the impression of a profoundly inhibited man, someone who had spent a lifetime learning that he had a right to be himself, and who, despite his effort, was still trying very hard to behave as was expected of him, to please, to avoid giving offense. It seemed to me then that beneath his attentive charm, and his calm and modest awareness of the importance of his work, was an anxious, even timorous, core of personality.

The very first chapter of *A Fish in the Water* tells of Vargas Llosa's encounter with terror at the age of ten, in the form of his long-lost father, a man the child Mario has never met and presumes dead. Mario's mother, who is living with him and her large and loving family in the desert town of Piura in the north of Peru, announces the reappearance of the man she still loves passionately despite the fact that he left her ten years earlier, in Lima, newly wed and pregnant with Mario. She takes the child to meet his father at the local hotel, warning him on the way that if they run into any of Mario's many cousins, aunts, or uncles, he is to say nothing about where they are going. Mario is shocked when he greets his father, because he does not recognize this menacing gray-haired man from the photograph of him on his night table. Then father, mother, and son all pile into a car "for a drive," and don't stop until they reach a hotel in the town of Chiclayo, where from an adjoining room Mario listens anxiously in the night for indications that his parents are doing "those filthy things . . . that men and women did together to have children," and retches at the thought.

"We're going to Lima, Mario," his father tells him in the morning. " 'And what are my grandparents going to say?' I stammered. 'What are they going to say?' he answered, 'Shouldn't a son be with his father?' . . . He said this in a quiet voice that I heard him use for the first time, with a cutting tone, emphasizing every syllable, which was soon to instill more fear in me than the sermons on hell given by Brother Agustín when he was preparing us for first communion." In Lima, Mario was to live years of fear and rage under his father's roof, belittled and bullied by him, censured and confined. The terror is so great that the bookish (or, as his father might put it, "queerish") Mario agrees to enroll in a military academy merely to escape home.

But long before we've got to that point in the narrative—right on page 5 in fact—Vargas Llosa explains the reasons for his father's raging turbulence, and with it, he recognizes his father—and himself—as Peruvian, a citizenship he can claim on the basis of a carefully nurtured, devastating, and specifically Peruvian tradition of rancor:

> But the real reason for the failure of their marriage was not my father's jealousy or his bad disposition, but the national disease that gets called by other names, the one that infests every stratum and every family in the country and leaves them all with a bad after-taste of hatred, poisoning the lives of Peruvians in the form of resentment and social complexes. Because Ernesto J.

Vargas, despite his white skin, his light blue eyes, and handsome appearance, belonged—or always felt that he belonged, which amounts to the same thing—to a family socially inferior to his wife's. The adventures, misadventures, and deviltry of my paternal grandfather, Marcelino, had gradually impoverished and brought the Vargas family down in the world till they reached that ambiguous margin where those who are middleclass begin to be taken for what those of a higher status call "the people," and in a position where Peruvians who believe that they are *blancos* (whites) begin to feel that they are *cholos,* that is to say *mestizos,* half-breeds of mixed Spanish and Indian blood, that is to say poor and despised.

In particolored Peruvian society, and perhaps in all societies that have many races and extreme inequalities, *blanco* and *cholo* are terms that refer to other things besides race or ethnic group: they situate a person socially and economically, and many times these factors are the ones that determine his or her classification. This latter is flexible and can change, depending on circumstances and the vicissitudes of individual destinies. One is always *blanco* or *cholo* in relation to someone else, because one is always better or worse situated than others, or one is more or less important, or possessed of more or less Occidental or *mestizo* or Indian or African or Asiatic features than others, and all this crude nomenclature that decides a good part of any one person's fate is maintained by virtue of an effervescent structure of prejudices and sentiments—disdain, scorn, envy, bitterness, admiration, emulation—which, many times, beneath ideologies, values, and contempt for values, is the deep-seated explanation for the conflicts and frustrations of Peruvian life.

Disdain, scorn, envy, bitterness, admiration, emulation . . . this hopeless litany that defined Ernesto J. Vargas as Peruvian shaped the work of his son, who has dedicated a lifetime to exploring the nuances and interstices of rancor, beginning with *The Time of the Hero,*[2] his explosively tense first novel, which was written when he was twenty-four and based on his miserable years at the military

2. New York: Farrar, Straus, 1986.

academy. Rancor, which also informs the poetry of César Vallejo and the novels of José María Arguedas and Manuel Scorza, dominates Mario Vargas Llosa's best novels, but it is a literary territory first claimed explicitly by Miguel Gutiérrez Correa.

Gutiérrez Correa's novel *La violencia del tiempo*[3] is set in the same desert city of Piura and in the same period used in several of Vargas Llosa's works, and is even based—I am guessing—on some of the same real-life characters, and its reiterated obsession throughout one thousand pages of fury is to explore *las posibilidades del rencor* to their ultimate consequences. Vargas Llosa's work compares to Gutiérrez's as a sacramental wine does to a potion made of fingernails and toad's blood. Vargas Llosa—a *blanco* in relation to Gutiérrez—wants to order the world and, as his candidacy would indicate, to save it. His Piura is a nostalgic place, idyllically remembered in *A Fish in the Water.* There is the crowded, welcoming family house, and the whorehouse (La Casa Verde), where, "as I remember it, the atmosphere of the place was happy and poetic, and those who went there really had a good time," and also the Indian and Zambo (mixed Indian and black) enclave of La Mangachería, "the joyful, violent, and marginal neighborhood on the outskirts of Piura . . . always identified in my memory with the Court of Miracles of Alexandre Dumas's novels." Gutiérrez Correa's novel, by contrast, is set in and seen from a neighborhood like La Mangachería, narrated by the grandson of its ferocious Indian inhabitants. There are no good times and no lively music here, only despotism, murder, rape, as the child narrator traces his family's disgraceful history and discovers it to be one long act of impotent defiance against the hated white landowners of Piura (with whom Vargas Llosa would presumably be lumped in the narrator's mind).

Gutiérrez Correa's son died in a 1986 uprising by jailed militants of the deliriously Maoist guerrilla group Shining Path. The prisoners' revolt culminated in a government massacre in which

3. Lima: Milla Batres Editorial, 1991.

more than 250 prisoners died, most of them killed in cold blood. His wife died in another Shining Path prison uprising in 1993, in which 38 prisoners were killed. One might imagine from such a brief glimpse into his biography that Gutiérrez Correa's literary work is the result of a larger accumulation of resentments than Vargas Llosa can boast of, but this is not necessarily so. *A Fish in the Water* shows that the more *blanco* writer's claim on disdain, scorn, envy, bitterness, admiration, and emulation is justified, as much as by anything else, by his fictional and autobiographical character's relation to the other essential component of rancor. This is machismo, which really is indispensable to, and in many cases virtually indistinguishable from, the class and race ferment that is the raw material of both novelists.

As is the case with his recollection of the city of Piura, Vargas Llosa's understanding of how relations with the opposite sex worked during his oppressed adolescence is put to hideous good use in his novels, and remembered more rosily in the memoir. Here is how he deals with the topic at various points in *A Fish in the Water:*

> To make a girl fall for you and formally declare that she is your sweetheart is a custom that was to decline, little by little, until today it is something that to the younger generations, speedy and pragmatic when it comes to love, seems like prehistoric idiocy. I still have a tender memory of those rituals that love consisted of when I was an adolescent and it is to them that I owe the fact that that stage of my life has remained in my memory not only as violent and repressive but also as made up of the delicate and intense moments that compensated me for all the rest.

And here, in praise of the brothel:

> Seeing a naked woman in bed has always been the most disquieting and most disturbing of experiences, something that never

would have had for me that transcendental nature, deserving of
so much tremulous respect and so much joyous expectation, if
sex had not been, in my childhood and adolescence, surrounded
by taboos, prohibitions, and prejudices, if in order to make love
to a woman there had not been so many obstacles to overcome
in those days.

This is ideal machismo, made up of sharp lust and delicate sentiments, and in some way redeeming. But the novelist Vargas
Llosa knows better than the autobiographer about the torments
of life under machismo, filled as it is for the men who suffer its
weight with constant anxiety about their innumerable class- and
race-related inadequacies: their lack of style, of height, of wavy
hair, of power, of sleek new cars, tailored suits, a foreign accent,
and all the other accoutrements that can provide access to the
right category of woman. It is an anxiety which, despite the disclaimers quoted above, surfaces even in *A Fish in the Water,* in
the form of endless adolescent debates about whether women (of
one's class or beneath it) are cunts with tits or (of one's class or
above it) sainted apparitions, and, in either case, about how to
"get inside their slits," as Vargas Llosa's teenage friends put it.
This is machismo as it really exists, a castrating condition that
has to do primarily not with sex but with power. Its pain can
often be made bearable only with large amounts of alcohol, or
through explosions of violence, and in his novels Vargas Llosa's
characters suffer from it in meticulously and accurately observed
detail.

Here, in *The Time of the Hero,* a character who will be baptized
the Slave by his classmates in the military academy endures an
inaugural hazing. He is instructed to get on all fours and fight like
a dog with another freshman:

The Slave doesn't remember the face of the boy who was baptized with him. He must have belonged to one of the last sec-
tions, because he was small. His face was disfigured by fear, and,
as soon as the voice stopped, he lunged against him, barking

and foaming at the mouth and suddenly the Slave felt a rabid dog's bite on his shoulder and then his whole body reacted and, as he barked and bit he had the certainty that his skin had become covered with bristling fur, that his mouth was a pointy snout and that, above his torso, his tail was whipping back and forth.

"Enough," the voice said. "You've won. On the other hand, the dwarf deceived us. He's not a dog but a bitch. Do you know what happens when a dog and a bitch meet up on the street?"

"No, my cadet," the Slave said.

"They lick each other. First they sniff each other affectionately and then they lick each other."

And here, the protagonist sees the prostitute Goldifeet, with whom he is about to lose his virginity:

The woman was now sitting up. She was, in effect, quite short: her feet barely touched the ground. There was a black layer under her dyed hair, which was a disordered tangle of bold curls. The face was thickly painted and smiled at him. He lowered his head and saw two mother-of-pearl fish, alive, earthly, fleshy, "that you could swallow whole and without butter," as Vallano had said, and which were absolutely alien to the chubby body that rose from them and that insipid and formless mouth and those dead eyes that were now contemplating him.

The early part of the narrative of *A Fish in the Water* traces the not untypical coming of age of a Peruvian-born survivor who inhabits the ragged edges of the ragged middle class: a childhood shaped by adult incomprehension and violence as much as by the nourishing warmth of a large and loyal family. An adolescence spent in a military school, enduring and learning to avoid humiliation and—once again—violence. An apprenticeship in sex at the whorehouses and an apprenticeship in writing as a very cub (age fifteen) reporter on the sordid crime pages of a Lima daily.

Love as betrayal, sex as frustration, and friendship as the enduring source of loyalty. Resentment and rancor in generous doses.

What is exceptional, of course, is the novelist, whose consuming need is to deny rancor, to transcend the moral squalor around him. At the military academy he reads Dumas from cover to cover and translates his own life into French adventure novels (*La Mangachería* becomes *La Cour des Miracles*). He courts the neighborhood girls breathlessly, not daring to imagine sex with them. He despises his father, but he remains polite, well-behaved, obedient even, when around him. At the age of twenty-one, timid and dreamy still, he marries his mother's sister-in-law, and one can speculate that he does so not only out of infatuation with the sexy Aunt Julia (a thirty-two-year-old divorcée), but out of a need to keep faith with the purest love he knows, that of his mother's family. (Having divorced Aunt Julia, Vargas Llosa is now married to his first cousin Patricia.) It is the tension between the vulnerable boy Mario's need not to be disillusioned and the novelist Vargas Llosa's fascination with the threats to his vulnerability that keeps *A Fish in the Water* moving forward powerfully in the chapters dedicated to his early life. And it is the adult Mario Vargas Llosa's ways of transcending his disillusionment that make him so unfit to be a politician.

*

"Perhaps saying that I love my country is not true. I often loathe it," Vargas Llosa states in his memoir. And, "Although I was born in Peru, my vocation is that of a cosmopolitan and an expatriate who has always detested nationalism." This, in the course of explaining how he happened to decide to run for president. Can such a man triumph in politics? Should he?

Mario Vargas Llosa debated whether to run for president in 1987, arguably the worst year Peruvians had endured in this century. Drought parched the land. Whatever can be described as the industrial sector (a handful of manufacturers of cement, hairpins, and Inca Kola, more or less) was decrepit and near extinction. Unemployment was well over 50 percent. Inflation would soon reach the breathtaking high of 7,600 percent a year. A huge and inept bureaucracy gobbled up whatever small proportion of the government budget was not devoured by graft and interest payments on a foreign debt equivalent to 45 percent of the GNP. Shining Path, the guerrilla movement led by Abimael Guzmán—a stolid former small-town college professor otherwise known as Presidente Gonzalo—rampaged through the countryside, bringing the art of murder to new levels of senselessness and gore.

Presiding over this mess was Alan García, a toothy opportunist of some charm and no scruple, who was about to seal his country's financial disaster by declaring a moratorium on all payments on the foreign debt. By the end of García's term, Peru had been declared ineligible for foreign loans, its per capita gross national product had shrunk by 13.7 percent, and net government reserves were $142 million in the red. "The Peru of my childhood," the author writes, "was a poor and backward country: in the last decades, mainly since the beginning of [General Juan Velasco Alvarado's] dictatorship and in particular during Alan García's presidency, it had become poorer still and in many regions wretchedly poverty-stricken, a country that was going back to inhuman patterns of existence." It was clear to everyone that the 1990 presidential elections would be decided on economic issues, even more than on the urgent question of dealing with the Shining Path. One can gather from this memoir that other things were not so clear to Vargas Llosa. One was that his country's disaster could not be laid exclusively at the door of the populist demagogues he despised, that it belonged also to the conservative politicians he admired. The other was that a successful electoral campaign would have had to provide the famished, humiliated poor of Peru—that is, the great majority of his countrymen—with something that was utterly irrational under the circumstances: a sense of dignity and hope.

Barnstorming the country, addressing Amazonian Indians in Iquitos, Quechua speakers in the Andes, mulattoes and mestizos on the coast, everywhere braving crowds he had no appetite for ("I had to accomplish miracles to conceal my dislike for that sort of semihysterical pushing and pulling, kissing, pinching and pawing"), Vargas Llosa eschewed facile promises in his speeches and campaigned instead holding aloft the banner of reason. He might have known better, but, after all, rationalism and *cordura*—level-headedness—had been the ropes he had used to pull himself out of his own Peruvian chasm: although *A Fish in the Water* skips over the author's middle years, we know that by the time he gets into politics the disorder of his earlier life has been replaced by an orderly contemplative existence in which reading and discussion have their scheduled places. Why now should he not offer the same salvation generously to his compatriots? In the early part of the memoir he describes his extended flirtation with Marxism and the world of clandestine conspiracy so beloved of the Latin American left, but rationally, over the years, he had concluded that Marxist movements were doomed. He had evolved into a neoliberal who admired Mrs. Thatcher, and it was as a Thatcherite neoliberal that he campaigned in Peru.

One hardly knows whether to wince or laugh at his description of some of his rallies. Addressing the country's largest labor confederation toward the end of his campaign, he instructs his listeners on the evils of job security, which make it impossible for Peru "to attract investment and stimulate the creation of new businesses and the growth of ones that already existed." The workers who benefit from job security are a tiny minority, he points out gently to his audience—to those very beneficiaries, that is, of job security, men and women clinging with their nails to the last raft in the economic shipwreck. "It was not a happenstance that the countries with the best job opportunities in the world, such as Switzerland or Hong Kong or Taiwan, had the most flexible labor laws," he tells them. And then he adds, describing this scene, "I don't know if we convinced anyone."

Whether he did or not was actually not important at the beginning of his campaign, because it so happened that Vargas Llosa decided to run for president at a time when there was absolutely no other candidate on the field whom people might be prepared to vote for. Alan García had brought his nationalist populist party, the APRA, to ruin, hopelessly tarnishing any would-be successor. The parties of the right, embodied by former president Fernando Belaúnde Terry, could not hope to offer—and furthermore, programmatically did not want to offer—any remedy for the impoverished majority's urgent desperation. The left in Peru historically had never obtained more than 20 percent of the vote in any national election. More to the point, as Vargas Llosa's campaign consultant at the New York public relations firm Sawyer/Miller understood all too clearly from the first, the traditional politicians who had ransacked Peru and bartered away its future were a lost cause.

"Peruvians wanted a break with the old politics. They despised the old politicians," writes Mark Malloch Brown, the Sawyer/Miller consultant, in a brief memoir also published in *Granta*.[4] To the degree that Vargas Llosa represented a break with politics as usual, his audience was willing to give him a hearing, despite the message he preached. For the first few months of the campaign, Sawyer/Miller's polls looked more than encouraging. The candidate's mass rallies had masses in attendance. His organization, Libertad, grew nationwide. But by early 1990, Vargas Llosa was starting to show up in the polls as a potential loser. It wasn't just the candidate's great distance from the destitute masses of his native country that turned out to be a fatal problem. It was his closeness to the people those masses most loathed: the politicians and business class.

And yet, who but the novelist Vargas Llosa has done a better job of describing the mechanisms of power, despotism, and corruption as practiced in his native country? *Conversation in the Cathedral,* published in 1969, begins with the memorable question *En qué momento se había jodido el Perú?* (At what point did Peru lose it, lose all hope, fuck itself, fuck itself over, fuck itself up?) The novel is an investigation of that problem, focusing on the corrupt intimate life and intimate relations between the rich and the powerful of Peru. The two central characters on whom the plot hinges are

4. "The Consultant," *Granta,* no. 36 (Summer 1991).

Cayo Bermúdez ("Cayo Mierda"), in charge of repression, espionage, and torture for the Odría dictatorship, and Fermín Zavala, the wealthy, suave father of the protagonist, whose sordid connections to the dictatorship are forged in the course of the novel. In *A Fish in the Water* the author points out that Peru is so *jodido* that there are barely any rich people left, but for his campaign he chose to ally himself with these few survivors, and to predicate an economic program on the private sector's selflessness, ingenuity, discipline, initiative, courage, and acumen, although the historical evidence is that the business class of Peru is almost entirely lacking in these virtues, and that its complicity with the most dreadful regimes is central to the country's political history. Why did Vargas Llosa the politician fail to see what his novels know?

Partly it is because, in his own mind, the candidate was allying himself with the middle classes—"office workers, professionals, technicians, tradesmen, state employees, housewives, students"— who seemed to him more capable of reason and civilized political action than the masses whose greedy enthusiasm made him cringe at rallies. But office workers and tradesmen were not the people who put up the money—variously estimated at $4.5 million (by the author) and $10 million (by skeptics equipped with a calculator)—for the most expensive campaign in Peru's history. The novelist decided that as president he would be able to avoid any unethical obligations to his campaign financers by the simple expedient of refusing to be told who was contributing what amount, and he made the crucial, foolish, and innocent mistake of confusing his financial backers with his potential voters. One could suspect the author of *A Fish in the Water* of disingenuousness, were it not for the image that lingers throughout the memoir of the teenage Mario, endlessly shuttled, according to the family fortunes, between the seedier Lima neighborhoods of the lower middle class and the dazzling beachside district of Miraflores. There is, as an explanation for so much political ineptitude, the possibility that, as an adult, he never ceased feeling illegitimate and deferential in the presence of the moneyed class, and willing to suspend disbelief.

The voters held him accountable for this, and for a parallel mistake: a few months into the Libertad movement's existence, Vargas Llosa decided that he would not be able to build a nationwide organization in time for the elections capable of giving him a broad mandate for his drastic program of economic reforms, and he chose to ally himself with two traditional right-wing parties, one of whose leaders, the worldly, literate former president Fernando Belaúnde Terry, Vargas Llosa admired. As his consultant, Mark Malloch Brown, understood immediately, this alliance with politics as usual was the kiss of death for his campaign. "To most Peruvians, it marked a betrayal. . . . He had bartered away his most precious asset, his independence."

Vargas Llosa's campaign thus came to grief because of his failure to take into account the nonrational needs of the electorate, because of his own irrational, respectful faith in his most powerful backers, and because of his intense reliance on his family and its immediate circle of associates. Brown writes:

> Mario's wife, Patricia, shared our fear of what the politicians would do to Mario's public image and fought to keep him out of their clutches, but her alternative was to build a political base among blonde ladies from upper-middle-class suburbs of Lima. They began as a Libertad group that worked in the Lima slums, and it was said against them, by men, that they had persuaded their husbands to contribute the funds to construct the feeding centres, schools and playgrounds they operated. The women, many of whom were impressive and strong-willed, were fighting a battle with their husbands and a male-dominated Peruvian upper class. Their slum work did not help Mario's battle for the barrios. The ladies, often wearing Paris and Milan fashions, were representatives of Vargas Llosa, the rich people's candidate.

His decline was swift. By the spring of 1990 the candidate was exhausted, but despite his nonstop campaigning, the polls showed that he was arousing hostility in certain crucial sectors of the population and that his remaining support was not enough to guarantee him the 50 percent needed to avoid a runoff election. Closing in on him was the unknown, untested, untarnished, ideologically uncommitted candidate the voters had been waiting for. It could have been anyone. It could even have been Mario Vargas Llosa, if he had known how to play his cards. Instead it was a then fifty-one-year-old agricultural engineer who had never tried his hand at politics and who is now the strongman of Peru, Alberto Fujimori.

He was the rector of the Agrarian University of Peru, and he had absolutely no previous political experience. His presence on the presidential ballot was something of a fluke; a quirk in the Constitution allowed anyone registering for the senatorial races to register simultaneously for the presidential candidacy, and, almost as a lark, Fujimori, the founder of a small businessmen's movement called Cambio 90, had decided to take advantage of this option. Methodical and hardworking, he had campaigned on a shoestring, promising Honesty, Technology, and Work. To his astonishment, the voters paid attention, because he had no record at all, and, in the minds of the voters, this meant that he did not have the record of chicanery, mendacity, and sloth that they perceived as indistinguishable from professional politics. His spectacular rise in the polls paralleled Vargas Llosa's decline.

The drama of Mario Vargas Llosa's failed campaign culminates, in *A Fish in the Water,* with a rally outside his beloved Piura:

Armed with sticks and stones and all sorts of weapons to bruise and batter, an infuriated horde of men and women came to meet me, their faces distorted by hatred, who appeared to have emerged from the depths of time, a prehistory in which human beings and animals were indistinguishable, since for both life was a blind struggle for survival. Half naked, with very long hair and fingernails, never touched by a pair of scissors, surrounded by emaciated children with huge swollen bellies, bellowing and shouting to keep their courage up, they hurled themselves on the caravan of vehicles as though fighting to save their lives or seeking to immolate themselves, with a rashness and a savagery that said everything about the almost inconceivable levels of deterioration to which life for millions of Peruvians had sunk.

What were they attacking? What were they defending themselves from? What phantoms were behind those threatening clubs and knives? In the wretched village there was no water, no light, no work, no medical post, and the little school hadn't been open for years because it had no teacher. What harm could I have done them, when they no longer had anything to lose, even if the famous "shock" [the package of neoliberal economic reform measures Vargas Llosa was proposing] proved to be as apocalyptic as propaganda made it out to be? . . . Despite the shower of stones . . . I made several attempts to talk to them over a loudspeaker, from the flatbed of a truck, but the outcries and the contention made such a din that I was forced to give up.

This is the Piura of the novelist Miguel Gutiérrez Correa's savage fictional landscape, and, on coming face to face with it, Mario Vargas Llosa may have had his first inkling that he had been campaigning in the wrong country. An insult offered during a televised debate by the man who was to beat him at the polls still rankles. "It seems that you would like to make Peru a Switzerland, Dr. Vargas," Alberto Fujimori said, with his characteristic tight-lipped smile. But, typically for Fujimori, his gibe was a few degrees off the mark: the point was, Vargas Llosa had campaigned as if Peru already were Switzerland.

On April 8, Mario Vargas Llosa got 27.6 percent of the vote and Fujimori 24.6. In the sixty days that elapsed between that date and the mandatory second round, electoral politics in Peru, such as they were, sank to shameful lows. The previously penniless Fujimori—now backed by President Alan García, according to strong rumors—spent money almost as recklessly as his rival on television ads that showed bits of a video clip of Pink Floyd's *The Wall*, in which a monster devours what the campaign depicted as the Peruvian electorate martyred by Vargas Llosa's conservative economic program. To Vargas Llosa's horror, his supporters' campaign against Fujimori was, if anything, more dirty, but then, it was no longer really a campaign, and it was no longer Vargas Llosa's to control.

It was class warfare, decreed by the upper-middle-class blond people of Lima against the darker-skinned multitudes now swarming at the gates. Peru's conservative Church hierarchy leaped into the fray with religious parades against the evangelical Protestants whom Fujimori had cannily wooed to his side. The press and television made fun of El Chinito—as the Japanese-descended Fujimori was universally known. The ruling classes' xenophobia, racism, and conservative prejudices found expression in Mario Vargas Llosa's campaign, even as the candidate haplessly defended his own agnosticism, decried racism, and took refuge in his daily readings of Karl Popper and the Spanish Golden Age poet Luis de Góngora.

The attacks on Alberto Fujimori were proof to the most desperate voters—who made up the vast majority—that anyone the ruling elite hated as much as it also appeared to despise them must be worth supporting. On June 10, 1990, Alberto Fujimori was elected president in the second voting round with a 23-point advantage over his rival, and he took power in July. It was the end of politics for Vargas Llosa, who boarded a plane with Patricia two days after the elections and headed back to the peace of his study and the libraries of Europe, where he became a Spanish citizen. But it was not, unhappily, the end of politics for Peru.

*

At this writing, Alberto Fujimori has been in power for nearly four years. He has brought down inflation to what is, by Peruvian standards, a modest 50 percent a year. The scourge of Peru, Abimael Guzmán, leader of the Shining Path, is now in prison, reading statements to his followers in which he orders them to put down their arms and praises the sagacity of his captors. Fujimori has built up Peru's reserves, and even attracted a little foreign investment to the country.

He has also closed down Congress and replaced it with a puppet National Assembly, jailed a number of his enemies within the military, arrested dozens of journalists, set up an intelligence service that some people think rivals that of *Conversation in the Cathedral's* Cayo Mierda, and turned the hatred of politicians into something of a cult. He is popular. In fact, he may enjoy the most sustained popularity of any Peruvian president in history, and the easy betting is that, if he runs for reelection in 1995, as he appears eager to do, he will win. What did he offer Peruvians that Mario Vargas Llosa could not?

Perhaps it is easier to ask what Vargas Llosa offered the electorate that they did not want—at least, not at the price he was selling it. He offered Liberty and Democracy, and voters sizing up the offer decided that this meant the liberty of businessmen to fire workers in the name of the bottom line; the liberty of the state to fire tens of thousands of bureaucrats in pursuit of administrative efficiency; the liberty of the poor to fend for themselves without even token recognition from the state—their state—that it might owe them some protection from hunger and chaos. Fujimori wisely offered little beyond his campaign slogans, the second of which, for the runoff elections, was "A President Like You."

This presumably meant a president who was like the poor, who understood the poor's need for a little respite; but what Fujimori did on taking power was impose a package of economic reforms as harsh as anything Vargas Llosa might have proposed. Thanks to the sudden unfreezing of prices, Limeños lost 25 percent of their income virtually overnight, a blow struck against a population that had already lost half of its purchasing power during the preceding five years. Cholera and tuberculosis—diseases directly linked to poverty—reached epidemic proportions in the first year of the new regime. "The present reforms have put the economy on a sounder footing, but they have failed to further social justice, because they have not broadened in the slightest the opportunities of those who have less, so as to enable them to compete on equal terms with those who have more," Vargas Llosa writes in the postscript to *A Fish in the Water.*

But what of his other campaign offer, Democracy? It was a word that in the midst of the Peruvian maelstrom sounded infinitely less appealing than Order, and that even today, despite Fujimori's quasi-dictatorial status, does not seem to have a strong market among most of Vargas Llosa's countrymen. Democracy in Latin America has been the keystone of United States policy for the hemisphere for a decade now. Previously, it had been Anticommunism, with a concomitant high degree of tolerance for dictatorial and murderous regimes. Under the new priorities, elections are taken as virtually sacred proof that a country is on the right track and deserves Washington's encomiums and loans. What is one to make, then, of Alberto Fujimori, whose freely elected Constituent Congress provided the necessary rubber stamp for his April 5, 1992, *autogolpe,* the coup against his own elected government? Or of Fernando Collor de Mello, freely elected to plunder and despoil Brazil? Or of Guillermo Endara of Panama or Carlos Menem of Argentina, both of whose elections served to mask high degrees of corruption? Or of the reelection, in El Salvador, of the party whose name is inextricably linked to the country's death squads? What is one to hope for Mexico, where carefully supervised elections in August could conceivably lead to the first loss in sixty-five years for the party in power, and thus, quite possibly, to national breakdown?

Throughout Latin America, elections and despair have proved to be a scary combination, and a decade of economic contraction and antipopular economic reform measures—however urgently needed many may have been—have led inevitably to extreme levels of popular despair. Everywhere half-mad but extremely wily candidates—television game-show hosts, drug money launderers, astrologers, experts in the art of promising all—have run for office and come close. One wonders if the television emcee who ran briefly against Collor de Mello in Brazil—Silvio Santos—could have done a worse job than the people's choice.

In this particular case, and in a few others, the electorate has been able to rectify its mistakes. Collor de Mello became the first president in Brazil's history to be impeached. In Venezuela a corrupt old populist, Carlos Andrés Pérez, was stripped of his powers as president and ordered to stand trial on charges of misappropriating $17 million in public funds. In Panama, on the other hand, following Guillermo Endara's embarrassing term in office, the likely victor in next month's elections is the leader of the party founded by the dictator Manuel Antonio Noriega, back with some more of the demagogic, wasteful policies that kept Noriega popular for so many years. (It is worth recalling that the United States spent some effort and inflicted considerable ruin on Panama by invading it in order to depose Noriega and install the popularly elected Endara.) And in Peru, Fujimori looks as if he will last. "The support for the regime is based on a tissue of contradictions," a wiser Vargas Llosa writes bitterly, and accurately, in his memoir's postscript:

> The entrepreneurial sector and the right hail in President Fujimori the Pinochet that they were secretly yearning for, the military officers nostalgic for barracks coups have him as their transitory straw man, while the most depressed and frustrated sectors, which racist and anti-establishment demagoguery have penetrated, feel that their phobias and complexes have somehow been explained, through Fujimori's deliberate insults of the "corrupt" politicians and "homosexual" diplomats, and through a crudeness and vulgarity that gives these sectors the illusion that it is, at last, "the people" who govern.

And yet. . . . For all its horrors, Vargas Llosa is wrong to say that the Peru he tried to save is now worse off than the Peru of his childhood. Fujimori is not the same as the bloody dictator Manuel Odría, and he could not be because some things have changed in Latin America. Internationally, respect for human rights is becoming an established criterion for loans. Domestically, the hordes that terrify the novelist are, to my eye at least, rather different from his vision of them. They have not sunk to the level of animals; they have been rushed into the late twentieth century, a change that is confusing and threatening for traditional communities, and that has dismantled their sense of identity and purpose and threatens to dismember all the familiar social links and hierarchies. But at the same time, however chaotically, it has pushed them into membership in a civil society that is only now being born.

The new political realities of Latin America are being created between the longing for the false certainties and real order of the past, and the attraction of the false promises and real freedoms of the future. This is the world in which the Indian *campesinos* of Mexico can hold aloft the banner of Emiliano Zapata and call for both democracy and Indian autonomy, and in which an improvised politician like Fujimori can prosper. It is not a world without hope, but rather one with too many unfulfilled expectations, and the sad, final truth of Vargas Llosa's campaign is that he too failed to understand and address them. He concentrated instead on reforms that look orderly on paper but are not designed to deal with chaos, and on the formalities of a democracy that does not yet exist. (Elections, while an important step in the direction of democracy, are far from being the thing itself.) While Latin America awaits the emergence of a new, democratic political class that can address the economy's limitations and the citizenry's needs with truly participatory programs, the door remains open for demagogues.

—May 26, 1994

POSTSCRIPT

On May 28, 2000, Alberto Fujimori was elected to a third 5-year term in office, at around the same time that Mario Vargas Llosa published a brilliant novel about Rafael Leónidas Trujillo, the dictator of the Dominican Republic.

As this book goes to press, barely four months after these elections, Fujimori is struggling to retain control of the country, even as his regime disintegrates under accusations of corruption, espionage, and fraud.

LOSING THE FUTURE

It needed a brutal murder—a man lying bleeding on the ground, his brain shattered, the country's ability to predict its future gone with him—to strip the layers of ceremony and rhetoric from Mexico's public life. Until early 1994, even many Mexicans who knew better had been lulled into believing the dream. The Institutional Revolutionary Party, or PRI—the party that had won every presidential election over the last sixty-five years, with only a little fudging of the figures—was going to win again, overwhelmingly, next August. President Carlos Salinas de Gortari, perhaps the most daring of Mexico's recent omnipotent rulers, was going to step down from office in a blaze of glory. His announced choice of successor, Luis Donaldo Colosio Murrieta, had been received, it is true, with some discomfort by those who had assumed that the canny, brilliant former mayor of Mexico City, Manuel Camacho Solís, would be *el bueno*—the Chosen One. But Colosio was a charming man and a tireless and faithful campaigner, and his expected victory would be Salinas's more than his own. The economy was humming, it was said, even if the very poor got poorer while the ranks of the new billionaires multiplied. The peso was stable, and a free-trade treaty with the United States gave the economy room to grow. Even those who never liked Salinas de Gortari are sorry at the way his dreams have shattered, because, as of last night, they have realized, frighteningly, that the stability of their future is tied to the president.

The old Mexico ended suddenly. On January 1, 1994, a guerrilla movement in Chiapas, Mexico's poorest state, marched through the misty provincial city of San Cristóbal de las Casas. It claimed the mantle of the revolutionary peasant Emiliano Zapata and captured the nation's imagination. At the unthinkable prospect of a Central American–style war, Mexico's thriving but highly neurotic stock market, the Bolsa de Valores, suffered an attack of the jitters. Salinas reviewed his unhappy options and chose to negotiate rather than fight, and for a few weeks it looked like a peace agreement with the Zapatistas would be signed soon. A relieved PRI once again turned its full energies to refueling what is called here *la aplanadora*—the multicolored, flag-spinning, money-spouting campaign machine that steamrollers through the country every six years at election time and squashes all trace of opposition. A return to stability seemed guaranteed.

And then, last night, with two bullets, Mexico lost its illusion of a peaceful, unchanging future. In a shantytown in Tijuana where Colosio had just finished a campaign speech, a young man stepped out of a crowd and shot him point-blank, once in the abdomen and once through the head. Three hours later, Colosio died in the operating room of Tijuana's general hospital.

In Mexico City, cinemas and restaurants emptied, and the streets grew silent as people gathered before their television screens to watch the stone-faced Televisa anchorman, Jacobo Zabludovsky— as seemingly eternal as the PRI itself—monitor phone calls from reporters at the Tijuana hospital, from opposition candidates announcing that they would suspend their campaigns until further notice, from notables expressing their obligatory horror. Eventually, President Salinas was heard reading a statement, even as television crews scrambled to set up their live-broadcast equipment. It was an odd speech, coming from the man who took office, in 1988, looking like the PRI's wimp-designate and almost immediately proceeded to unsettle the nation with his acute sense of command. In a series of canny moves against the corrupt *oficialista* union leadership, against the entrenched bureaucracy, against established precedent of every sort, this flute-voiced man of unprepossessing height and blank features established himself as an unflappable ruler with an extremely firm hand. He was so powerful that he was expected to continue to govern through his successor, although this was against the unwritten rule that grants a president absolute power only during his single, six-year term. Now, as Colosio lay dying in the operating room, Salinas's message was brief and almost alarmingly out of focus: "The law will be applied with all due rigor," he said. "And I am certain that if we all add our feelings of warmth and serenity in the positive direction [of Colosio] it will do him good and it will do us good."

An hour later, after Zabludovsky impassively informed the nation that its presumed next president was dead, the newsroom of *Reforma*—Mexico City's newest and wealthiest paper, financed by conservative capital from the country's industrial north—was buzzing with reporters who were still trying to figure out what questions to ask. Was the assassination the work of the same unidentified people who were responsible for the kidnapping ten days ago of one of Mexico's most influential multimillionaires and were now reported to be asking $50 million for his ransom? And were these two events related to the guerrilla uprising in Chiapas, in the south? Already, wild rumors were circulating: the same people who once theorized that Salinas had engineered the guerrilla uprising to strengthen his own hand now wondered if he had ordered Colosio's assassination to get rid of a candidate who was looking unexpectedly weak. Others speculated, somewhat more plausibly, that the right wing of the PRI might have been involved in the murder—or that perhaps it had been the work of the military, out of frustration at Salinas's decision to negotiate with the guerrillas rather than exterminate them. There was speculation that the millionaire's kidnapping could be a war-chest investment by the guerrillas, although few people seemed to think that they would have interrupted the peace talks with an assassination.

Or could it be that all the dreadful, unexpected events of the last three months were the result of one vast conspiracy? Raymundo Riva Palacio, a veteran reporter, thought that this was impossible, for the simple reason that no genius could coordinate so many disparate ground-shaking events. He conferred with the paper's business editor, Francisco Vidal. Would the stock market crash? Would it even open the next day? "If it does, it'll get wiped out on Wall Street," Vidal opined. (The market closed.) Another reporter came up to Riva Palacio with the latest on the murderer: he had been identified as Mario Aburto Martínez, a twenty-three-year-old factory worker who had come to Tijuana from the state of Michoacán.

Who would be the replacement candidate? Riva Palacio had checked the Constitution; by law, anyone who has held a Cabinet post within six months of the elections is disqualified. This left only two contenders in the line of succession: Manuel Camacho, the former mayor who, the first of a series of mad rumors in the street already had it, might have had Colosio killed in a fit of spite because he was passed by as Salinas's candidate-successor, and Ernesto Zedillo Ponce de León, who had resigned from his post as education secretary to coordinate Colosio's campaign. The most looming questions at *Reforma* and throughout the city were: What would happen to the peace talks with the guerrillas? Would the assassination inevitably lead to a new hard line on all questions of national security? Already, new troop deployments were taking place in Chiapas.

In the course of a very long night, it became evident that the murder had revealed a terrifying schism within the PRI, and that Camacho could not succeed Colosio. At midnight, at the PRI's national headquarters—a compound of massive buildings that had been decorated for the campaign with enormous banners bearing the single word COLOSIO—an impromptu meeting of the dead man's supporters was taking place. *"Justicia!"* the crowd of Party apparatchiks and local community organizers shouted, and then, astonishingly, "Colosio *sí!* Camacho *no!*" *"Compañeros!"* a stocky, swarthy man shouted. "We are all Party militants of great conviction—this is not the moment for factionalisms."

"Shut up!" someone in the crowd yelled, and the peacemaker was hissed and booed into silence before the cry "Colosio *sí!* Camacho *no!*" went up again.

Although Camacho—a Princeton-educated intellectual famed

for his ability to converse with the left and with the restless poor who had staged demonstrations in front of the National Palace during much of Salinas's rule—had seemed to many the obvious choice to succeed the president, there were reasons that Salinas had selected Colosio instead. "The PRI has had to swallow a lot of bitter pills under Salinas," a friend of mine who is close to the ruling circle of technocrats had explained to me after Colosio's candidacy was announced. "Salinas has allowed the opposition to have governors in three states. He's cut back on the bureaucracy. He's privatized the sacred cows. The president chose Colosio because he felt that he couldn't impose another of his *perfumados*"—fancy intellectuals in European suits—"on the Party." I pointed out that Colosio also seemed to fit that mold; he was, after all, the holder of a postgraduate degree from the University of Pennsylvania and, as head of Salinas's key social-works project, Solidaridad, was part of the inner circle of reform-minded technocrats.

My friend replied that Colosio was, nevertheless, a hail-fellow-well-met sort of technocrat, who projected an easy, middle-class, very Mexican friendliness. "He was Party chairman during Salinas's most difficult years, and he soothed the Party traditionalists and talked them into accepting the changes." I gathered that my friend, a wealthy businessman and a PRI member who had always spoken glowingly of the president, was not a Camacho supporter, but, in true PRI fashion, he was circumspect in his criticisms. "Camacho is arrogant," he said. "Colosio makes a lot of friends."

Now, in a late-night phone conversation following the murder of Colosio, my friend surprised me with his bitterness. "This country does not obey the law, it obeys authority," he declared. "And authority disappeared in Mexico as of the first of January"—when the guerrillas of the Zapatista National Liberation Army burst on the scene in Chiapas. "It's time for the president to act like a man and grab the bull by the horns, so that all the people, and the opposition, and all the sons of bitches who are wandering loose out there, know that there's a rule of law here. If the government sits down to bargain with a handful of bastards wearing ski masks, there's no law—there's only an atmosphere in which anyone can feel free to do whatever he fucking pleases, and you get disasters like this."

At last, my friend was speaking frankly, his reserve—like the national myths—undone by Colosio's murder, by the brutal new realities laid bare. The PRI's vaunted *unidad monolítica*—the discipline that has kept it in power for such an astonishing number of decades—exists no longer. On Wednesday night, the all-powerful president was revealed as simply a mediator between opposing and potentially explosive forces. Among the factions are the military and the right wing of the PRI, which want to crush the guerrilla movement by force and put an end to a cautious *apertura democrática;* the booming business sector, which has been Salinas's most influential source of support for both economic and political reforms but now wants him to rule with an old-fashioned iron fist; the technocrat prophets of modernization, led by Salinas himself, who have no real political base of their own, and no source of support, other than what appeared until last year to be their unlimited success in pushing through a program of drastic economic reform; a previously feeble opposition, which owes its relative freedom to operate to Salinas but certainly owes him no fealty (particularly since Salinas came to power in elections that are widely believed to have been fixed); and, last, a citizenry that constantly veers from rage at its own poverty and political helplessness to apathy and then to fear of a different future.

Shortly before midnight, I stopped by the Plaza Garibaldi, where foreign tourists and local merrymakers congregate to be serenaded by mariachis, and found that although the city's fancier restaurants were empty and the streets were silent, the plaza itself was humming with song and activity. I asked a group of mariachis waiting for customers why this was so.

"Who knows?" answered a chubby man with a crew cut and the obligatory mariachi costume of tight black pants and short black jacket. "Perhaps it is because those who come here are mostly from the pueblo, like us. We have no big stake in politics." I asked my taxi driver to turn on his radio for the news, but when I got out of the car he turned it off. Again, I asked why. "As a person, I feel sorry that Colosio was killed," he said. "But, speaking politically, I couldn't care less. We are poor and we keep getting poorer, and we are tired of promises."

We drove by the Zócalo, the central plaza, which was the seat of Aztec power and remains the symbol of the blind, centralized authority that has ruled Mexico for centuries, but it was empty and dark. For several years now, Salinas has ruled from a distance, from the official residence of Los Pinos, and I headed there. It was nearly 1 A.M., and Colosio had been dead for nearly three hours, but Salinas had not yet addressed the nation. At the huge wooden gates to the residential compound, a procession of the country's most powerful men was arriving for a meeting that was taking place inside: former President Miguel de la Madrid, military commanders, the PRI hierarchy.

By Thursday morning, and in the absence of real information, the country was watching for portents of the future. As Colosio lay in state at the PRI compound, Salinas, shaken and exhausted, arrived to form the first honor guard. On his right he placed Ernesto Zedillo, the former education secretary and Colosio's campaign coordinator. An immediate consensus formed that Zedillo was the next Chosen One. And then the unthinkable happened again. At this moment of high solemnity, the president of Mexico, in his role as leader of the national mourning, was met not with reverential silence but with enraged cries for justice from the PRI militants, and as he made his way to the exit, he faced a squabbling crowd. Indisputably, it signaled the end of an era.

—April 4, 1994

ZAPATA'S HEIRS

What all of Mexico understood when it awoke last New Year's Day to discover a ragged congregation of peasants calling themselves the Zapatista National Liberation Army, or EZLN, marching through the streets and proclaiming the overthrow of the regime was that the Mexican Revolution had finally arrived in the state of Chiapas. Things take a long time to get here. The Revolution did not arrive in 1911, when Emiliano Zapata and his *campesino* battalions, in the state of Morelos, northwest of here, rose up to the cry of *"Tierra y Libertad!"* It was defeated by the Chiapas gentry when the troops of Venustiano Carranza, a liberal landholder, arrived in 1914 and tried to impose decrees abolishing indentured labor and *latifundios*—extralarge haciendas.

The Revolution did not even really get here in 1940, when President Lázaro Cárdenas made a legendary trip to San Cristóbal, the first ever by any Mexican ruler—involving several days' travel by car, steamboat, train, and, finally, horseback—all to enforce his land-reform program in this renegade region. A highway to San Cristóbal was inaugurated in 1946, some *latifundios* were reduced in size, and the state's political chieftains perfected a system that every six years, at election time, allowed them to deliver 100 percent of the votes to Cárdenas's party, the Institutional Revolutionary Party, or PRI. Nevertheless, Chiapas and the center of its counterrevolutionary power, San Cristóbal, remained largely beyond the reach of modern comforts and of the hegemonizing ambitions of the regime that declared itself the guardian of the ideals of Carranza, Cárdenas, and Zapata.

To make up for lost time, the new revolution has proceeded to turn not only Chiapas but the whole country upside down. At this stage, Mexico feels as if it were precariously balanced on the head of a pin. Luis Donaldo Colosio, whom President Carlos Salinas de Gortari appointed to succeed him in August, has been assassinated. The stock market is teetering. One of the wealthiest men in Mexico, kidnapped two months ago, is still pleading for someone to pay his ransom so he won't be killed. Another multimillionaire was kidnapped late last month. The private sector has been taking its money out of the stock market and putting it into dollars at a rate that threatens the stability of the peso. The PRI is badly split. It is unlikely but conceivable that another party could win the elections, for the first time in sixty-five years—an idea that would have seemed ridiculous right up to December 31, given Salinas's ratings in the polls then. All these crises are linked in indefinable ways to the arrival of the new Zapatistas on the national scene, but each has taken on a momentum of its own.

In the meantime, the Chiapas crisis itself continues, even though Salinas—a man of remarkable political flexibility—took some of the wind out of the Zapatistas' sails by appointing a peace commissioner and calling for a cease-fire just twelve days after the New Year's Day takeover of San Cristóbal. Today the president looks a great deal less powerful than he did six months ago, and this change of aspect, in turn, affects his ability to assure the Zapatistas that his successor, to be elected next August 21, will be able to enforce any peace treaty that might be negotiated.

Colosio's murder, on March 23, looked to many people like the work of the right wing of the Institutional Revolutionary Party—which is furious about, among other things, the president's soft treatment of the Zapatistas. After the assassination, the Zapatista National Liberation Army reportedly feared that a major military offensive—or even a coup d'état—was on the way. It then called a halt to internal consultations it had carried on regarding a tentative agreement that had been reached during talks in February between its representatives and the government's peace commissioner. In effect, this means that the dialogue for peace, as the ongoing talks are called, is suspended indefinitely. A brief meeting between the two sides this week led only to a promise of further meetings. The cease-fire that was declared when the peace talks were announced is holding, but it is constantly threatened by the ferment that was generated in the Chiapas countryside on January 1. Land-hungry peasants have invaded nearly 100,000 acres of agricultural land in the state, while the cattle ranchers whose land is threatened mutter about their willingness to take up arms themselves. These ranchers are the political descendants of the original *mapaches*—the counterrevolutionary guerrillas of the time of Carranza—and, given their very recent use of murder and intimidation against the peasantry, their anger is not to be taken lightly. So far, the military, which mobilized some 1,200 troops in the state after the uprising, has shown a remarkable degree of discipline, but everyone is wondering how quickly the conflict could escalate if there were a cease-fire violation.

Meanwhile, the revolution that was once broadcast live is disappearing from the media. Gone are the images of ski-masked combatants, which reminded the nation of a past whose legacy has been turned into rhetoric and honored in the breach. Gone are the equally mesmerizing images of the interior of the San Cristóbal Cathedral, where these same Indian combatants sat down to talk as equals with a government that, a month into this unlikely war, was hemorrhaging politically, although it had suffered few military blows. (The Zapatistas' only military near-success was an assault on a garrison outside San Cristóbal. Elsewhere, they did very poorly—a disappointment that might explain *their* willingness to sit down at the negotiating table.) The Zapatistas have pulled back to their stronghold, the Lacandón jungle region of Chiapas, near the border of Guatemala, and the deforested, mountainous area there known as Las Cañadas—the canyons. That is where one must go to look for answers to the many questions no one had time to ask in the dizzy excitement of the first few weeks. Why did several thousand *campesinos* decide to go to war? What did they set out to achieve on January 1, and how willing are they to deviate from that original plan? What is the relation between the Zapatistas' Indian leadership—something called the Clandestine Indigenous Revolutionary Committee—and a light-skinned man known as Marcos, who gives all the press interviews? What does the Indian leadership want, and how does that differ from what Marcos will settle for? Or should the question be asked the other way around?

Fittingly for Chiapas, it takes a long time to travel from San Cristóbal to the villages under Zapatista control—an area that begins about seventy miles southeast of here. From this town, which now makes its living largely off tourists who are attracted to its tile-roof-and-cobblestone charm, one descends through misty pine forests to the lowland town of Ocosingo, a pitiful splotch of one-story houses on treeless, sunbaked streets, and then to a village that marks the border of the Zapatistas' territory. Access past this point is strictly controlled, but on a recent weekend the Zapatista Liberation Army invited journalists to drive in, having announced that after this visit there would be no further press expeditions in the foreseeable future. After a couple of days' wait at the border village, and stops at a succession of Zapatista checkpoints, we entered a land of hamlets without electricity or health clinics, without passable dirt roads, or even a place to buy anything to eat or drink.

Fifty years ago, this area was mostly highland jungle, but after President Cárdenas came to Chiapas to promote land reform, many *latifundistas* were forced to free their indentured Mayan peasants. Many other *latifundistas* voluntarily expelled their peons, because raising cattle for export to the United States was becoming a big business, and ranching required far less labor than running the traditional, self-sufficient haciendas with diversified crops. The government encouraged the freed peons—Maya belonging mostly to the Tzeltal language group, but also migrant speakers of Tojolabal, Tzotzil, and Chol—to colonize what was then seen as a promising agricultural frontier. That was the former jungle we were now entering, and the first thing we learned here was that the new Zapatistas were not the most backward, or even the poorest, *campesinos* of Chiapas—Maya tied to their exhausted small farms in the highlands by tradition and passivity—but, rather, the innovators: adventurous frontiersmen and women who were convinced that they could make a new world. The original Zapatistas had asked for "land and liberty," but the new rebels' demands are more complicated and more ambitious, because they already have land, and, in that they are the victims of almost total government neglect, they also have liberty.

A man who called himself Vicente told us at a Zapatista village we visited that what he really wanted was a good education. He pointed toward the schoolhouse nearby; it was closed now because of the war, but even before that it had offered studies only up to the second grade, and the teachers, underpaid and underqualified, rarely stayed around for a full school year.

The village was perched at the gateway to the Las Cañadas area, on a promontory surrounded by high peaks. A parched river diminished into a trickle, where women stooped to wash clothes. The steep hills all around were covered with a patchwork of *milpas*—corn plantings—and the remaining forest. The village itself was much like the others in this corner of the state: a stuccoed adobe church, the schoolhouse, a dusty playground, a scattering of mud-and-wattle shacks. A dozen visitors had lined up against the church wall like prisoners, in an attempt to hide from the scorching sun, and eventually we moved into a shed set up as an open-air communal kitchen, where a few noncombatants were getting ready to cook a vat of beans for the Zapatista troops stationed in the village. One of the men there was Vicente, who was reading from San Cristóbal's only newspaper—a three-sheet linotyped daily called *Tiempo,* which someone had just brought in. He was reading aloud and very slowly, working out the words one by one, for the benefit of his *compañeros.*

Vicente told me he would have liked to finish the sixth grade, or possibly even high school, but the nearest full-grade school was in Ocosingo, and so his children's chances of completing even primary school were also pretty slim. His interest in education was all the more striking because the list of his other wants was so basic and urgent. His actual cash income was virtually nonexistent. What there was went immediately for salt, soap, and the like, and toward medicines that the villagers kept stocked for emergencies. His plot of land on the *ejido,* or communal farm— the village was its center—was a two-hour walk away, and was so steep and dry that it was barely possible to raise on it a subsistence crop of corn and beans. Some fifty years ago, following Cárdenas's trip to Chiapas, Vicente's grandparents had been freed from serf-dom and granted the right to set up an *ejido* here, on what was the edge of the Lacandón jungle. But the fertile land at the bottom of the valley somehow wound up in the hands of *los ricos,* in amounts far beyond what the law allowed. And, now that there were so many new mouths to feed, the original *ejido* was not nearly large enough or productive enough to take care of everyone.

The Zapatista battle cry of *"Tierra y Libertad!"*—formulated at a time when fewer than 850 families held 97 percent of Mexico's arable land—was the basis of Article 27 of the Constitution. Until late 1992, this article not only regulated the maximum size for private ranches and farms but also guaranteed all peasants who were banded together in *ejidos* the inalienable right to their land, and the right to claim *latifundio* and fallow land from the govern-ment. For ten years the men in Vicente's village, under the aus-pices of Church-inspired peasant organizations, had pressed their demand for an expansion of their *ejido* at the offices of the Agrarian Reform Ministry in Tuxtla Gutiérrez, the state capital, and then in Mexico City. "But they always lied to us," Vicente said. "They would tell us to go home and get a certificate of this or that and then come back on such-and-such a date. So we would go back on the appointed date, and they would say, 'Oh, no, *el Señor* isn't here, he had to leave, come back another day.' And we would come home again, thinking, Well, it couldn't be, and now we've spent our *compañeros'* money on the trip. And then the government changed Article 27, and now we can't file a claim on that land any-more, and we'll never be able to take out a loan, because the inter-est rates are very high, and if we don't pay our debts on time the bank can take the land we have away from us. The end of Article 27 was what made us decide we'd had enough."

The radicalization of Vicente's village did not happen over-night, though. In 1970, Samuel Ruiz, the bishop of San Cristóbal, decided to follow the long-neglected example of the sixteenth-century Dominican friar Bartolomé de las Casas by preaching a radical gospel in favor of the Indians. Like the Tzeltal pioneers, the bishop saw the Lacandón jungle as the promised land. He commissioned a translation of the book of Exodus into Tzeltal, and, because there were very few priests who could minister to the region, he set up a network of lay preachers—deacons—to serve the scattered pioneer communities of Las Cañadas. Bishop Ruiz's vision of a radical peasant utopia in the jungle coincided with the arrival of a group of Maoist political activists. They were disillu-sioned with the whole idea of armed struggle, and preferred to spend the next decade—roughly, from 1974 to 1984—organizing the Indian communities to fight the government on its own terms: by winning bureaucratic battles and pressing for credits and subsidies as well as land. It was slow work, with few victories, and gradually, as the number of settlers multiplied and came to occupy virtually all the arable land, the communities of Las Cañadas grew impatient. The Maoist-bred leadership in their own ranks was becoming too close to the government, they felt, and was negotiating behind their backs and selling them out. The *caxlán*—white—advisers were made to feel unwelcome, and pulled out. Then, in 1983, a new group of political activists—six of them, they themselves say—arrived with a project of their own. They wanted a new armed revolution in Mexico, and they thought that the utopian communities of Chiapas were the perfect place to begin.

They didn't start proselytizing right away, they say. They lived in almost intolerable conditions in caves in the rain-forest moun-tains along the border with Guatemala, made contact with a few trusted families in Las Cañadas and beyond, and offered emer-gency medical services to whoever might need them. But they let it be known that they were there to offer their armed expertise whenever the communities should decide that that was what they wanted. In the first few years, they made almost no headway; their numbers expanded from six to forty, and that was considered a triumph. Then, in the early eighties, as the jungle lands ran out, the *campesinos* began invading the cattle ranchers' land, and the ranchers, true to their old tradition, reactivated their *guardias blancas,* or terror patrols. Peasant leaders were killed, and entire villages were burned down or threatened. In 1989, the International Coffee Organization allowed the price of coffee to float on the international market. Prices collapsed, to the detriment not of the coffee exporters but of the 74,000 peasants in Chiapas who produce a third of Mexico's coffee exports. Among those who were ruined were the more prosperous *campesinos* in Las Cañadas. Around this time the Indian leaders in the area consulted among themselves and agreed that it was time to call the people in the caves. According to someone who spent many years working as an organizer with the reformist Maoist movement, and who, along with the rest of the Maoists, left the region in 1989, by that date there was virtually not a youth in Las Cañadas who had not gone up to the mountain caves to receive military training. Now the only question was what would be the right moment to act. When the reform of Article 27 was announced, the Clandestine Indigenous Revolutionary Committee of what was already the Zapatista National Liberation Army held a secret referendum in the region. The vote was by no means universally in favor of taking up arms—a good many *campesinos* had defected back to the Maoist-reformist organization and had recalled their *caxlán* advisers—but at the end of the referendum period the followers of the Zapatistas among the people of Las Cañadas told the military mestizo leadership that they were ready to prepare for war.

The Clandestine Indigenous Revolutionary Committee held a press conference at Vicente's village for the visiting journalists. The committee members strolled up to a breezy lean-to overlooking the valley early in the afternoon—eighteen of them, all male, all wearing ski masks or gaily printed bandannas over nose and mouth. I had the feeling that I had seen some of these men just a short time before, chatting on a bench with the other villagers. The one whose Spanish seemed to be most fluent was called Rubén, and he was rotund, cheerful, and outspoken. One of the committee's members had been murdered two days before, and it would have been easy for Rubén to say that the killing had been the work of the cattle ranchers, but he said instead that it might have been the result of an act of *indisciplina* by the committee member, that an investigation was under way, and that the *consulta* on the peace talks' tentative areas of agreement would have to be suspended at least until the murder was cleared up. In any case, he said, the *consulta* would take many months, because the proposal would have to be translated into all the Mayan languages in the region and discussed to everyone's satisfaction, so that the agreement eventually reached could be a lasting one. "We've been at this for years," he said. "Why rush for the sake of a few months?" What the committee wanted, however it was formulated, he went on, was an answer to its basic list of demands: not just Land and Liberty but Health, Education, Housing, Work, and Regional Autonomy, among others. "This is what all the Indian *campesinos* of Mexico want," he said. "And until we get it, we won't stop fighting."

Rubén and the other committee members we talked with were intelligent, soft-spoken, and knowledgeable about their communities' needs, but an abyss yawned the moment a foreign journalist asked about the Zapatista National Liberation Army's demands vis-à-vis the Mexican state. If a peace treaty should be signed granting autonomy to Las Cañadas, a territory of about 2 million acres, would the committee allow state authorities—troops, judges, police—to come into the region? The answer was no. Would the Zapatistas lay down their arms? Never. Could they see the Mexican government, or any government, accepting what was, in effect, an independent state within a state? Again, the answer was that the Zapatistas would never lay down their arms. What about the elections in August? Would the Zapatistas allow voting booths to be installed? Rubén was frank: "We Zapatistas have no opinion about the elections; we don't care who wins, because we have no experience in this business of politicians and

194 | LOOKING FOR HISTORY

votes." The main point of the Zapatista war proclamation that was made public on January 1, the ouster of President Salinas de Gortari, did not even come up.

I then asked three members of the committee—*campesinos* who used pointed sticks to plant the corn kernels in their *milpas*—to assume that the war had ended and the treaty had been signed. In this new future, what would be the most they could hope for, the most ambitious dream they could entertain? It took a long time to get across the point that they could have anything they wished for. "Some good farm equipment," came the reply at last from one of the men. Another said, "A dignified life with a little rest." The third added, "And a school, so that the children can be whatever they like when they grow up."

Much has been made—by, among others, Subcomandante Marcos, the dashing military leader of the Zapatistas, and Bishop Ruiz, who is now the mediator of the peace dialogue—of the unique cosmogony of the Indians of Chiapas, of their acutely different sense of reality and time. But it seemed to me then that the distance between Rubén and me, say, had less to do with these mystical elements than with the breathtaking differences in our needs. The Zapatistas burst on the scene January 1 and galvanized the country with their first war proclamation, which announced their troops' imminent arrival in Mexico City and called for the overthrow of the "dictator" Salinas de Gortari. They demanded respect for the indigenous people of Mexico, cancellation of the North American Free Trade Agreement signed last December, and the establishment of fair and free elections. The appeal was twofold, and the citizenry responded on both levels. In a mestizo country where people take great pride in their Indian blood—their membership in *la raza de bronce*—and train themselves to ignore the suffering of the 9 million people who identify themselves as Indians in the census, the spectacle of a Mayan insurrection made a tarnished self-image glow brightly again. And at a moment when the government of Salinas de Gortari appeared to have scored an unequivocal triumph with a program that overturned all the old nationalist, populist tenets and opened Mexico to an avalanche of gringo merchandise and culture (Michael Jackson's last concert, it should be recalled, was in Mexico City), nothing could have been more moving than the spectacle of a band of impoverished Indians tearing down the Salinista myths. The Zapatistas said, "This country is not rich, and it is not democratic. It is corrupt, it is poor, it is Indian, it is us, and we are going to save the rest of you." But Rubén's priorities, it was now clear, were not fair and free elections and a freer press. They were more arable land, a tractor, and a sixth-grade education for his children and Vicente's. The divide between the committee members and mestizo, urban Mexico was one of inconceivable want.

After the committee members left, one of our number started to build a cooking fire from scraps of garbage and corn husks lying about. A woman stepped up and invited us to use her hearth instead. She spoke halting Spanish to us (something that most of the women in the region are too shy to do, preferring to stick to Tzeltal), and she wore a faded modern-style dress instead of the multicolored, ribbon-and-lace-trimmed frocks customary among the Tzeltal. Before I walked into her house, I had decided that these were signs of prosperity; and perhaps, by the standards of the village, they were. The hearth was set in the back corner of a one-room shack. The furniture was a rickety wooden table, a chair occupied by a very old woman with tangled gray hair, and, near the door, a tiny hammock in which an eight-day-old baby lay sleeping. Señora Ana, our hostess, told us that this was her tenth child. She looked about forty years old, and exhausted, but she said that she had married when she was fourteen, and had had a baby just about every year since, so she couldn't have been much older than twenty-five. All her children were born on this dirt floor, which was densely inhabited by voracious ticks. The midwife had been her mother—the old woman, who was now helping me extract a swelling tick from my hand, and was amused that I should be so horrified by it. The household children scampered about, the littlest girl carrying her toddler brother on her back. Every woman in the village had ten children, or twelve, or even more, Señora Ana said as she moved her family's meal of boiled beans off the fire to make room for our pot. We prepared our packages of instant noodle soup feeling hot with shame, because the other women in the village had lined up to watch us through the wide gaps in the wall planks and shrieked with laughter when we opened the seasoning packets and sprinkled them on the boiling noodles. *"Vitaminas!"* I heard them say to one another in Spanish. "The *caxlanes* put vitamins in their food; that is why they are so big and strong."

That night, we put up our hammocks and sleeping bags in a large shack that served as the *ejido*'s meeting room, and the children crept in silently and poked at the sleeping bags, wondering at their softness, and sniffed our cameras, our drinking water, and our notebooks. It was late when we put out the candles to go to sleep, but they were still lined up behind the gaping planks, staring.

President Salinas's son is named Emiliano, after Zapata. So is one of the sons of the new PRI presidential candidate, Ernesto Zedillo Ponce de León. Prominent in this administration are former student-movement leaders and radical activists, like Arturo Warman, the agrarian attorney. Salinas appointed the former rector of the National University, an intellectual with a reputation for probity, first to set up a National Commission of Human Rights, then to direct the attorney general's office—a Medusa's head of institutionalized violence and corruption—and, now, the Ministry of the Interior, which is in charge of internal security. Salinas does not get much credit for these moves, or for the fact that he has faced down the military and the right wing of his party and has handled the Chiapas conflict with remarkable restraint. The lack of enthusiasm can be attributed to the fact that he has also restructured the state and the financial system in ways that have finished ruining the likes of the people of Las Cañadas and in addition have allowed about two dozen families to monopolize half the country's private wealth (not including income from the illegal drug trade). The fact remains, however, that the social-welfare and governmental-reform programs of the Salinas administration have drawn on a large pool of committed and skilled administrators, many of them former militants of the radical left or, like Manuel Camacho Solís, Salinas's designated peace commissioner in Chiapas, from the reformist wing of the PRI.

I talked to Camacho recently here in San Cristóbal, where he had returned in the hope of jump-starting the stalled peace dialogue. Camacho, forty-eight, was appointed the mayor of Mexico City in 1988 and served until last year, when he resigned, indignant that President Salinas had not designated him the PRI presidential candidate. The former mayor did not disguise his anger over Salinas's choice of Luis Donaldo Colosio, even though he was offered the Foreign Ministry as a consolation prize. His lack of party discipline enraged the PRI and contributed to the impression, once he had been named peace commissioner, that he was a man acting very much alone. As a foreign-educated, modernizing technocrat who believed that Salinas's economic reforms should be tempered with additional social programs for the poor, Camacho had more in common with Colosio than with the old-time Party hacks, who loathed the reforms and turned every social program into a private till. It must have been particularly painful for him when, following Colosio's murder in Tijuana, he was accused of plotting the crime by the Party rabble at the candidate's wake.

On the evening of the day of Colosio's murder, troops surrounded the hotel here where Camacho had his Peace Commission headquarters, and the city was plunged into what felt like a virtual state of siege. The reporters who were staying at Camacho's hotel, and who had developed some respect and even affection for him over the weeks, watched in silence as the peace commissioner, a lanky figure, paced up and down for hours on the veranda, alone in the gloom. He left for Mexico City the following morning, and he had not returned or made any public statements until the day I saw him. But he had accomplished a great deal during his first stay here.

Together with his team, the team from the Zapatista National Liberation Army, and the visionary mediator Bishop Ruiz, Camacho had worked out specific solutions to all but two of the Zapatistas' thirty-four demands. (The government refused to consider the Zapatistas' demands having to do with the elections and Salinas's overthrow.) The solutions included budget provisions and administrative measures approved by the government ministries involved in each case.

On the morning I talked with Camacho, he seemed optimistic that the peace dialogue would soon begin again. The Zapatistas had just put out a communiqué expressing their continuing commitment to the talks. A difficult agreement had been reached between the federal government and the many activist *campesino* organizations in Chiapas: the peasants had agreed to stop taking over haciendas and the government had agreed to review all their land claims on the previous two months' takeovers. The Mexican army had issued a communiqué in which it expressed its unconditional support for a political solution to the Chiapas crisis, and the country's leading intellectuals, who have in general terms been supportive of the Zapatistas, had put out a statement calling on them to return to the negotiating table. The Mexican Episcopal Conference had expressed its support for Samuel Ruiz's role in the peace talks. Reforms of the electoral law of Chiapas had been proposed at record speed to curtail the power of the local caciques, who deliver votes to the PRI and devour the money from the federal government. It seemed then that the stasis could be broken. I asked Camacho how it had happened that the most significant outbreak of armed revolt in Mexico in the last fifty years had ended in peace talks after just twelve days of war, and he replied that this had been the result of (a) the high cost of the war for both parties, and (b) Salinas's "political imagination" in designing and applying a strategy to deal with the Zapatistas swiftly enough to allow the government to retake the initiative.

I asked him if, given all the changes he had just outlined, it could be said that the war had worked. He appeared startled for a moment, but then he said, "Up to now. But if it starts up again, it won't work. It'll be a civil war."

The effect that the war had had on the government's thinking, he went on, had indeed been great. "Because every idea we had

had up to then had to be reexamined," he explained. "Violence begins where politics ends, and we had to come to terms with the fact that, politically, what worked before no longer works.

"What this led us to in the negotiations was to realize that there could be no ambiguity in our answers. This is not to say that we had to be soft—only that we had to offer basic, simple discourse as a way of recovering a legitimacy that had been lost. So how do we offer a new legitimacy that takes the Zapatistas into account? That is the central question. We can't offer more than we can accomplish, and we have to figure out how to offer concrete things in the short term."

True to his PRI background, Camacho has a knack for producing *conceptuoso* statements that on second look turn out to have little substantial information in them. By these standards, he was unusually frank in our talk. I asked him what could cause the negotiations to fail. "An accident," he replied—meaning, presumably, another sinister event like the murder of Colosio. "Or if the EZLN fails to realize that things changed with the murder—that there is a conservative backlash in the country. If the Zapatistas believe that they can maintain their popularity even if they do not come back to the negotiations, they will lose a great deal of strength. In practical terms, if they consolidate what they have won so far, they can go down in history as one of the most successful armed movements ever, but if they do not work out the political mathematics of this correctly, they can lose a great deal of what they've already achieved."

At this writing, the area that the Zapatistas control is surrounded by troops. The Mexican army took the measure of the Zapatista fighting forces in January, and since then has conducted frequent surveillance of their territory by air. Food and other supplies have been allowed through in strictly regulated and limited quantities. The rainy season is about to start, and if the *campesinos* don't plant now, the corn and beans that they subsist on will not be available for harvest in the fall. The ostensible reason for the journalists' visit to the Zapatista zone was a military ceremony commemorating the seventy-fifth anniversary of Zapata's assassination in an ambush laid for him by his Carrancista fellow revolutionaries.

The ceremony was a moving event, because so much effort had clearly gone into mobilizing the region's meager resources for the benefit of journalists, but militarily it was not impressive. The village where the ceremony took place produced an electric generator and sound equipment. A platform was set up for the Clandestine Indigenous Revolutionary Committee and the military command. The village women turned out in freshly laundered dresses trimmed with bright-colored ribbon and lace, and adorned their tiniest babies' bald heads with caps made of ribbon and crocheted flowers. Speeches were made on the platform, in Tzeltal, but with frequent references in Spanish to the *cabrón gobierno*—the son-of-a-bitch government—and to the *traición,* or betrayal, of Zapata by Carranza, which was the watershed act that stood as a warning to all *campesinos* never to trust a government. And then there was the centerpiece of the ceremony: a parade by the Zapatista troops, 300 of them, sweating through their ski masks, wearing homemade ammunition belts and bike packs over their hand-stitched brown-and-green uniforms. It is not clear what message the Zapatistas wanted to convey to the press about their present situation, but the message we got was that, if the current assortment of aged hunting weapons and machine guns is any indication, the Zapatista National Liberation Army is not a modern army in any sense of the term. (This could change overnight, of course, if it should turn out that the Zapatistas are behind a wave of kidnappings of millionaire Mexicans during the last two years. A great many weapons could be acquired with the ransom money.)

Do the Zapatistas really believe that they can march to Mexico City and overthrow the regime with whatever weapons it is that they do have? This is the question I put to the military head of the EZLN, the light-skinned man who calls himself Subcomandante Marcos.

"The war isn't over yet," he said. "You'll have to wait and see."

He is good at entrances. There had been four days of waiting in

Zapatista territory through a succession of yes-no-maybe replies to my request for an interview. Late on the last night, I was awakened by a flashlight shining in my face. Behind it stood Marcos, smiling. He turned out to be an insomniac in desperate need of conversation, and to be more articulate, cosmopolitan, humorous, and coquettishly manipulative than any guerrilla leader of El Salvador or Nicaragua who ever locked horns with the press. (But no less narcissistic than any other politician.) And—perhaps this is the secret of the great goodwill he has generated in the media—he did not pretend to offer easy replies to difficult questions.

He has become famous for the long letters that he pens apropos of anything at all, which appear regularly in the press, but his talk is better. On paper, his prose is frequently treaclish and self-eulogizing; his speech is clear and imaginative, and comes out in perfectly constructed sentences that sound as if they had been written. Puffing thoughtfully on a pipe through the mouth hole in his ski mask, he elaborated on the answer to my question about whether it was really possible for the Zapatistas to take the capital. "The war isn't over," he repeated. "We will take Mexico City, although not necessarily in physical terms. Weren't we there already by January 2? We were everywhere, on the lips of everyone—in the subway, on the radio. And our flag was in the Zócalo"—the central plaza. "How often does it happen that an armed group's declaration of war is read in public just a few feet from the National Palace, or that the government negotiates with a group that brings its weapons to the table? None of this was planned. We won the lottery: we thought that it would take years to achieve what we accomplished in twelve days! What helped us was Salinas; he was always our best ally, because he constructed such a big *tramoya*"—a jury-rigging of false appearances—"on a base so fragile that it fell apart almost immediately.

"The way Mexico is entering the new economic order is based on a lie," Marcos went on. "Farmers in the United States have tractors and machinery, and we are planting our corn with a stick and using slash-and-burn methods. But the government says, 'Our problems are over—we're now a part of the First World.' It has to take a step back and say, '*This* is the country we are and *this* is what we have, and anyone who wants to deal with us will have to take this reality into account.' "

There was nothing fervent about Marcos, and his objections to the unappetizing triumphalism of the Salinas administration hit home. Of medium height, broad-shouldered, and, at a guess, in his mid-thirties, his chest crisscrossed with bandoliers, he slouched easily in the passenger seat of a car where we were talking, to take advantage of its lights, and produced a flowing historical narrative (it is his version of the Zapatistas' origins that I have given), a critique of guerrilla theory, and a vision of the Zapatistas' role in bringing injustice to an end that were totally captivating. Only slowly did it dawn on me that he too was a utopian, dealing in closed universes, good and evil, and dreaming of egalitarian, redeeming poverty just as the visionary Church does, or the *campesino* communities so eager to pursue a vision of hope. He was a hip Anabaptist with a gun who had replaced the narrow dogmas of the left with a shimmering vision of *communitas*.

Skimming easily over the fact that *campesinos* who chose not to take up arms are now under surveillance and not allowed to leave the Zapatista-controlled zone, he explained how the magical army in the jungle had come about. "We gave military action second place to organization of the population," he said. "As a result, it's very difficult to draw a line between the combat force and the support population. We say that here even the hens are Zapatistas. If your tendency is to become a mass-based army, then you can't put so much emphasis on the old, traditional vertical guerrilla discipline—the you're-with-us-or-you're-dead school of thought. You can't raise the step so high that nobody can climb it; you have to make room for all the people to participate to the best of their abilities, and so you are always in the process of looking for what unites people, and not what separates—what adds, and not what subtracts. That's why we are not a party and we are not a guerrilla force: we are an army with a flag wide enough to embrace everyone—liberty, justice, and democracy. And that's why our goal can't be the creation of a New Man or a New World, in the old guerrilla style. The Zapatista Army wants to open the door to the waiting room of a New World—to create a space in which people can think about what is needed to create a new world, in which armies will no longer be necessary."

According to one rumor, the Zapatistas were fully prepared to be slaughtered on January 1, and convinced that this sacrifice would ignite a political brushfire that would redeem Mexico. According to another rumor, admittedly biased, they were so prepared for victory that the leadership told the troops to pick out the houses in Ocosingo that they wanted to live in after the war was over. What the Zapatistas, and Marcos, do not appear to have been prepared for was what happened: a wave of national joy and solidarity at their appearance, followed by an urgent plea to negotiate before any more blood was shed (total losses in the two-week war were estimated by the Church at around 400), which, in turn, was followed by the current creeping onslaught of indifference. Marcos is far too alert and intellectually curious to have remained willfully oblivious of the truth, and, indeed, it appeared to be gnawing at him.

"We cannot make the leap into the New World ourselves," he said. "We're just an army. If there were a political movement right now with our same banner—democracy, justice, and liberty—the EZLN would subordinate itself to that. We do not want to—we are not able to—take on the political leadership; there has to be a party, and a mass movement. The problem is that this movement is scattered at the moment, and that it expects too much from us. At the beginning of the dialogue, we placed a great deal of hope in civil society. We thought that it would be able to do a lot, but, after the dialogue ended, that society said to us, 'Tell us what to do,' and we said, 'We can't, we're just an army.' It seems that the population doesn't have enough of a consensus, and the regime is betting that this mass movement will never come together, and that it will be able to remain in power through Zedillo."

What if Zedillo should win fairly?

"We will recognize him as a legitimate interlocutor for us."

And why did the negotiations seem to be stalled?

"It's an impasse that doesn't worry us," he said. "We doubt if it will be possible to carry out the changes we want without more deaths. Whether the dialogue continues or not, we are still at war: we are still saying that we want Salinas to leave, and he is still calling us 'transgressors.' "

Marcos focused obsessively on Salinas, the way he focused on the poverty of the *campesinos* of this state, but Mexico is more complicated than that: along with the humiliated Maya of Chiapas and Huichol of Hidalgo, there are farmers in Jalisco who use tractors, and middle-class accountants in Querétaro who send their kids to college; and the government that the Zapatistas would like to depose was until recently quite popular. Even if the attack on San Cristóbal on January 1 unveiled a deep underlying dissatisfaction with Salinas and with the PRI in general, the Zapatistas' bet that people outside Las Cañadas are willing to go to war to overthrow either or both is, at best, chancy. Is the risk worth it? If the war proceeds, will the people of Las Cañadas be better off than they were before? If the revolution triumphs, will a devastated war economy (even the present economy had zero real growth in the last decade) allow for the subsidies and public works that Salinas de Gortari is now willing to pump into the region? If the revolution's organizers had preached birth control and handicrafts for the export market, say, instead of utopia, would the results in the end have been less spiritually rich and more materially advantageous? Would *that* trade-off have been worth it? I told Marcos that I thought the Zapatistas had obtained much in the last few weeks in their struggle to transform Chiapas—and, indeed, the electoral process in Mexico. Wasn't it time for them to cash in their winnings and call off the bet?

"The coin is still in the air," he answered. "There's still a considerable way to go to know if we were right or not."

We had been talking for a couple of hours, and Marcos showed no sign of being ready to retire for the night. Feeling like a participant in a relay marathon, I went to wake up another reporter and a couple of photographers who were sharing a car with me on this trip. It was the new moon, the breeze had turned chilly, and all the stars were out. We sat in a circle while the photographers worked and Marcos waited expectantly for more questions. He needed to talk. He had been convinced, he said, that he would be killed on January 1, and the days he had been living since then felt like a bonus. Soon, he was certain, he really would be dead. Perhaps that was why he was writing so compulsively, he mused, and why he was unable to censor his answers to us or stand on formality. When you stare death in the face, he warned us, pretense seems useless. "Am I moving too much?" he asked the startled photographers.

Assured that he wasn't, he amused himself by inventing an autobiography, inspired by the odd questions that foreign journalists came up with. One journalist, not long ago, had asked him his opinion on gay rights. Now he told us—he wasn't serious—that he had worked in massage parlors and had been fired from a job as a waiter in San Francisco for being gay. Then he returned to the task of fielding the questions we were halfheartedly lobbing.

Why had the Zapatistas chosen January 1 to attack?

"Because we weren't ready before," he said. "In January of '93, the Clandestine Indigenous Revolutionary Committee gave us a year to prepare for war: 'Choose the date and the time and let us know,' they said. We didn't want a date before the PRI announced its new candidate, because we didn't want it to look as if we were trying to influence the succession. We thought of Columbus Day, but we weren't ready. We thought of November 20"—the anniversary of the Mexican Revolution—"but one of our units couldn't get there in time. We thought of December 25, but something or other happened to change that. Then we decided on December 31, but, typically, we were late, so the war started on January 1."

We hinted that we had a long drive ahead, and that it was nearly dawn, our departure time, but Marcos was not to be stopped. He went off to fetch one of his lieutenants, a Major Rolando, whom he had decided I should interview. For thirty minutes, I asked the yawning, shivering Major Rolando as many questions as we could both handle about how he had joined the Zapatistas when he was a construction worker in San Cristóbal. The Subcomandante was still chatting with one of the photographers—a comely young woman, whose charms were evidently not lost on him. I thanked Major Rolando for his time and fell into sleep. An hour later, Marcos shook me awake. "You'll be late," he said. "I already woke the others. Go get some coffee." And then, before I could realize that this was the last I would see of him, he trudged down the path toward the valley and was gone.

It was daylight by the time we were ready to leave, and the children were clustered around again, transfixed by the wondrous contents of our car trunk. People came up the footpaths to say goodbye as our car lurched and bounced along the gully that passed for a road. A few asked for things we might think of bringing back if we ever returned—a basketball for the kids, a pair of reading glasses for an old man who had lost his. Mostly, they just waved. It was hard to think that a series of errors of judgment or pride by the parties in charge of this war could lead to a scorched-earth attack on this village, an aerial bombing, death. The trip back would be long, as the members of the Clandestine Indigenous Revolutionary Committee whom I talked to the previous afternoon had solicitously pointed out. Were there many *campesinos* in this city I wrote for, New York? I informed them that, in truth, there were very few left. That was too bad, one of them said—they had wanted to send their regards. "But in any case," he added, "please convey our very best greetings to the people you know in that place."

—May 16, 1994

THE UNMASKING

On the evening of February 9, 1995, at a press conference in Mexico City that had been announced less than two hours before, an aide to the attorney general played a strange game of peekaboo with photographers and a crowd of sweating, jostling reporters. In his right hand the aide held an oversized black-and-white slide of a ski mask and a pair of large, dark eyes, and in his left a black-and-white photograph of a Milquetoasty-looking young man with a beard and large, dark eyes. After we were allowed to study the two for a few seconds, the aide slipped the slide over the photograph. *Voilà!* Subcomandante Marcos, the dashing leader of an Indian peasant revolt in southeastern Mexico, the hero of a thousand fervent letters addressed to the Mexican nation, the postmodern revolutionary who has contributed mightily to what in this turbulent year, with its hemorrhaging economy and political murder scandals, looks like the steady crumbling of a sixty-six-year-old regime—this masked idol is a Clark Kent. His name, the attorney general announced before the media crowd, is Rafael Sebastián Guillén, and he is a philosophy graduate and former university professor. The aide continued imposing the slide of Marcos on the photograph of Guillén and flipping them apart again—now we saw him, now we didn't—until the storm of camera flashes subsided, and then we left.

The revelation of Marcos's identity was part of a two-pronged strategy by President Ernesto Zedillo Ponce de León to break the stalemate that has existed in the state of Chiapas since the Ejército Zapatista de Liberación Nacional, or EZLN—a ragtag army of

Mayan peasants led by Subcomandante Marcos—rose up in revolt there, on January 1, 1994. Even as we watched the slide show, Army troops were preparing to move into the mountainous and overwhelmingly rural southeastern part of Chiapas—almost on the border with Guatemala—where the Zapatistas had maintained their unofficially recognized *territorio liberado* for thirteen months. Villages were being retaken without a fight, and their inhabitants, the armed Zapatista fighters among them, were fleeing into the jungle-covered mountains and ravines. President Zedillo said that the army was going into the area only to provide backing for the federal agents who would attempt to serve Marcos with an arrest warrant, but this was a transparent excuse, for thousands of troops swarmed in, and have continued to take positions farther and farther inside the territory.

Before the offensive began, the stalemate between the Zapatistas and the government had lasted so long that it seemed permanent. All actual fighting ended barely twelve days after the New Year's Day rebellion got under way last year, in the lovely town of San Cristóbal de las Casas. The peasant army had vowed in its declaration of war that it would march to Mexico City and overthrow the government of President Carlos Salinas de Gortari, but, instead, it suffered significant losses and scored no military victories. It did, however, capture Mexicans' imagination: televised interviews of Mayan peasants in makeshift uniforms, who said that they were fighting not only for a change in their own desperate circumstances but to rid the nation of a corrupt and slothful regime, brought thousands of demonstrators out into the streets all over Mexico during the first days of January, demanding an end to what threatened to turn into an army slaughter of the poorly armed Zapatistas and their families.

Faced with the politically volatile option of turning the army against its own people, Salinas, on January 12, called for a ceasefire. Thereafter, and through the transfer of power in December from Salinas to Ernesto Zedillo, following the presidential elections last August, talks and attempts at talks promoted by both sides led to no fruitful agreement, but they at least kept the cease-fire from breaking down. Even in December, when the Zapatistas pushed beyond their control zone to protest the stalemate and what they saw as massive fraud in the elections for governor of Chiapas, the rebels and the government troops managed to come within a few hundred feet of each other without a shot being fired.

The army's offensive certainly appears to have taken Marcos completely by surprise. Much of the anxious speculation about what will happen next in Chiapas centers on his personality and his aims—on what he believes in and to what lengths he is willing to take the war. Will he negotiate to keep his peasant troops from suffering further? Does he really want nothing less than the overthrow of the government? And is he in fact the man in the photograph?

As far as I could tell on the night of the attorney general's press conference, as I tried to make the ten-year-old ID shot of a bland Rafael Guillén jibe with my recollection of the masked man I had talked with last April, the ski-masked slide we were being shown could have been slipped just as persuasively over a photograph of Richard Nixon. The Marcos whom I and other journalists interviewed in the Zapatista control zone was a mesmerizing personality—self-possessed, courteous, ironic, and theatrical. He liked to make journalists spend hours, or days, waiting for him, and then he would appear in the dead of night and talk endlessly, puffing on a pipe, tugging at the uncomfortable ski mask, and asking as many questions as he answered—uncannily well informed about the intellectual and media world beyond Chiapas.

While the resemblance between Guillén's eyes and Marcos's—the only part of his physiognomy we are all acquainted with—is not conclusive (Marcos's are a hazel-brown, for one, and the photograph is black-and-white), the account of the EZLN's history and Marcos's role in it that the attorney general's office has been leaking to the press does coincide with much that has been said privately about Marcos in Chiapas for some time.

According to what can be pieced together from these convergent accounts, the EZLN has its roots in the Latin American guerrilla movements that sprang up in Mexico beginning in the tumultuous 1960s. In the early seventies, one of those guerrilla groups, the Fuerzas de Liberación Nacional, or FLN, had a training camp in Chiapas, near Ocosingo, a town that sits on the edge of what later became the Zapatista control zone. In 1974, the army raided that camp, arrested several of the guerrillas, and "disappeared" three others, including a woman whose first name was Elisa. People here have speculated that one of the guerrillas who survived—the brother of one of the disappeared men—took refuge in the north of Mexico for a few years and then returned to Chiapas, using the code name Germán. He was either accompanied by or eventually joined by a dozen others, among them a second-year woman medical student, who had been captured in a raid on another FLN camp. After spending a few months in jail, she had been granted a presidential amnesty. In Chiapas, she took the code name Elisa—presumably in honor of the disappeared guerrilla from the Ocosingo camp. Sometime around 1984, a year after the EZLN's official founding, a young, bright philosophy graduate who was known first as Zacarías and then, much more recently, as Marcos, linked up with these comrades in Chiapas. The government claims that Subcomandante Marcos—that is, Rafael Guillén—is the son of a prosperous furniture retailer from Tampico, and was a leftist activist student and a teacher at a Mexico City university before he left for Chiapas. It also claims that, although Comandante Germán is still at large, Comandante Elisa was captured two days before the February 10 offensive.

At the university, a fairly radical enclave called the Universidad Autónoma Metropolitana, which was founded in 1973, people certainly remember Guillén. In the early 1980s, a friend of mine who taught there recalls, the faculty saw social activism as part of its mandate. "We wanted to put the emphasis as much on practice as on theory, and we understood that it was our duty to give back to the community what we received from it," he says. "We were all radicals, particularly those of us in the Design Science and Arts Division. But no one was more radical than a group of young, brilliant, serious, and hardworking teachers in the Department of Theory and Analysis. Guillén and Silvia"—Silvia Hernández, an

EZLN founding member—"were in the middle of that group. I thought *we* were perhaps too sectarian, but they beat us. They kept strictly to themselves, like a little family. But they came up with very original, very creative projects. They were big on Althusser"—Louis Althusser, the French philosopher—"on his theories of ideology and communication, and on something they called *gráfica monumental.* Before they left the school, they did a wonderful mural for the auditorium—it's still there."

My friend could not say for certain, at twelve years' remove, whether the man he remembered as Rafael Guillén would prove to be Marcos. Most reporters who have interviewed Marcos have no opinion on his likeness to Guillén's mug shot, but none of us could fail to notice how much Marcos talks like one of Guillén's brothers—Alfonso Guillén, a university professor in Baja California Sur, who was shown on television on February 9 being hounded by reporters as he tried to explain, with much of Marcos's striking calmness and courtesy, why he had not seen his brother Rafael in several years. There were other clues as well: before the army incursion, the "capital" of the Zapatistas' *territorio liberado* was an impressively large performance space built out of nothing in a clearing in the jungle. It was presided over by an amphitheater whose benches covered the entire face of a steep triangular hill, and whose rostrum was fronted with socialist-realist paintings—surrealist, in their jungle surroundings—that recalled the mural at the university.

Marcos's preoccupation with symbolic language is certainly worthy of a student of Althusser. He has created his own dazzling image as a masked *mito genial*—his term, meaning "an inspired act of mythmaking." He has staged a very real, threatening war on the Mexican state based on almost no firepower and a brilliant use of Mexicans' most resonant images: the Revolution, the peasants' unending struggle for dignity and recognition, the betrayed Emiliano Zapata. And he has used his writing: what we know about Marcos is mostly what he has written about himself. "How do you manage to write so much?" he asked me enviously when he showed up at last on the night we talked, in a hamlet in the Zapatista control zone in April. I pointed out that writing was what I did for a living, whereas he had a revolution to run and nevertheless managed to produce reams of copy. (Rather more than my output, in fact. The collected letters and communiqués he published in the Mexican press in the first eight months of last year alone have just been turned into a good-sized book.) It had not dawned on me then that the most visible and critical part of the Zapatistas' revolution was the letters that the Mexican press publishes regularly—particularly the long, sometimes poetic, sometimes irreverent, personified postscripts that are the Subcomandante's contribution to epistolary art. Now swaggering, now full of righteous fury, now impudent and hip, the Marcos of the postscripts is at all times both elusive and intimate, and this seductive knack has allowed him to become a faceless stand-in for all the oppressed, an anonymous vessel for all fantasies from the sexual to the bellicose—a star.

Marcos's letters exhibit an intense, self-involved romanticism, and so did Rafael Guillén's senior thesis at the university, which was ostensibly about Althusser and really about himself. Guillén wrote, "One thing is certain: the philosopher is 'different'; he belongs to a strange lineage of 'sensibilities that keep themselves at a prudent distance from the trite'; he can reflect with a brilliant phrase that will eventually pass into posterity on the death of an ant squashed as it tries to cross a busy street at 8 P.M. . . . His hair is disorderly and his beard unkempt, his gaze is continually ecstatic, as in an orgasm not yet achieved; cigarettes and coffee are part of his persona." Marcos too likes to come up with little fables about ants and rather personal things about sex. ("The anchor's long chain . . . groans when it is detached from its moist bed like our sex from the feminine belly," he wrote last August.)

When Marcos arrived in Chiapas to join his friends—lugging too many books through the jungle, by his own account—he found fertile ground for a rebellion. The southeastern part of the state, where the revolt first took hold, and where the Zapatistas eventually set up their control zone, is one of the most backward in all Mexico, but it is also an area whose inhabitants were already familiar with and eager for ideological debate. The region is known as Las Cañadas, or the Canyons. It has no paved roads, no phones, little electricity, hardly any working schools, and a soaring population growth rate. It was settled by *campesino* migrants from other parts of the state and from the rest of Mexico, most of them Mayan Indians who speak Tojolabal, Tzeltal, and Tzotzil, and little Spanish, and came to what used to be the nearly uninhabited Lacandón jungle in search of land where they could grow their corn and raise their families in peace. For years, the bishop of San Cristóbal, Samuel Ruiz, had preached Indian rights and egalitarianism in the hamlets of Las Cañadas, and also for years radical activists had done organizing work in the communities— sometimes in agreement with Bishop Ruiz's network of priests and deacons, sometimes at odds with them.

People from Chiapas who know Las Cañadas well say that Marcos, Germán, and Elisa usurped the Church's existing network of priests and deacons to promote "self-defense brigades," and gained credibility among the population by offering health services. According to several accounts, the guerrillas' work added to the divisions in the by now radicalized communities. Some of Bishop Ruiz's most deeply committed followers abandoned him to join the EZLN. So did many of the *campesinos* initially organized by the radicals, whose leaders had by the late 1980s embarked on a series of close alliances with the government. On the other hand, many *campesinos* who had opted for the guerrillas' self-defense courses were offended by their theories of dialectical materialism and by their denial of the existence of God. (In the process of becoming "Indianized," Marcos told me, "there was a certain amount of clashing while we made the adjustment between our orthodox way of seeing the world in terms of bourgeois and proletarians to the community's world view," and I assume that he was referring to the conflict over religion.)

Sometime around 1993, the guerrillas themselves appear to have suffered, if not a split, at least a serious difference of opinion. People say they have heard stories that Marcos, on the basis of his organizing work, was convinced that Las Cañadas was ripe for an insurrection that would set off a revolutionary spark throughout Mexico. Apparently, neither Germán nor Elisa felt this to be the case, and they left the zone.

It seems unlikely that the government found out what we now know about the EZLN from Elisa and the other guerrillas captured the day before the attorney general's press conference. For all the mystery surrounding the Zapatistas, the rebels had plenty of connections to both the Salinas and the Zedillo administrations, and it makes more sense to guess that information gathered from these sources had been known and kept for use at the moment when the government might decide that further attempts to reach a negotiated settlement with the Zapatistas would be fruitless. One former radical who has joined the establishment is Adolfo Orive, a founder of Política Popular, the radical movement that first organized the Indian peasants in Las Cañadas; he is now Zedillo's chief adviser on rural affairs. Another is a ruling-party *diputado,* or member of the House of Representatives, who for years was part of the EZLN's high command, and is now known to the Zapatistas as a traitor. And then there is Raúl Salinas de Gortari, the "troublesome brother" of the former president, as the newsweekly *Proceso* called him in a prescient cover story last year. Raúl Salinas is a very wealthy man, an engineer with a postgraduate degree from a French university, a sometime littérateur. He has also, of course, just been indicted on charges of conspiring to murder his former brother-in-law—José Francisco Ruiz Massieu, the secretary-general of the ruling party, who was assassinated last September. And he is a former Maoist who, together with Orive and, apparently, Comandante Germán, was active in Política Popular, nearly two decades ago.

The warrant for the arrest of Rafael Guillén announced on February 9 has allowed the Zedillo administration to leak much of its hoarded information and rumor, but the government has not succeeded in what appears to have been its primary goal. The plan to disillusion Marcos's admirers with the revelation that the daring guerrilla is a sappy-looking academic full of old-line Marxist dogma worked for about seventy-two hours. A young acquaintance of mine who used to swoon at Marcos's name took one look at Guillén's photograph and said, *"Guácala!"*—"Yuck!" That was on a Thursday. The following Sunday, the Mexico City papers received the first communiqué from Marcos since he, his troops, and his *campesino* followers retreated from their villages into the hills. It had three of his trademark addendums, in which the postscript itself becomes a character in a drama, and a sign-off:

> *P.S. that rabidly applauds this new "success" of the government police:* I heard they've found another "Marcos," and that he's from Tampico. That doesn't sound bad, the port is nice. I remember when I used to work as a bouncer in a brothel in Ciudad Madero [near Tampico], in the days when [a corrupt oil-workers' union leader] used to do the same thing to the regional economy that Salinas did with the stock market; inject money into it to hide poverty. . . .
>
> *P.S. that despite the circumstances does not abandon its narcissism:* So . . . Is this new Subcomandante Marcos good-looking? Because lately they've been assigning me really ugly ones and my feminine correspondence gets ruined.
>
> *P.S. that counts time and ammunition:* I have 300 bullets, so try to bring 299 soldiers and police to get me. (Legend has it that I don't miss a shot; would you like to find out if it's true?) Why 299, if there's 300 bullets? Well, because the last one is for yours truly. It turns out that one gets fond of things like this, and a bullet seems to be the only consolation for this solitary heart.
>
> *Vale* again. *Salud,* and can it be that there will be a little spot for me in her heart?
>
> [signed] The Sup [Subcomandante], rearranging his ski mask with macabre flirtatiousness.

In five short paragraphs, the Sup reestablished his credentials as an outlaw hero, brought sex into the issue, and, yanking back the mask his pursuers had torn off, donned it once more. Two demonstrations were called by solidarity committees in Mexico City to protest the military attack on the Zapatistas and the arrest warrants on the EZLN leadership; according to press reports, tens of thousands of people showed up.

There was a very real sense in which, during the past thirteen months, Marcos fought the Zapatista war single-handed. It was, after all, a public relations war, and the Indian fighters—most of whom spoke little Spanish, and for whom the government had provided, at most, a few years of elementary schooling—were not equipped for the sophisticated exchanges with the government and the Mexican public that such a war required. It was Marcos who wrote the letters, and also the communiqués signed by something called the Clandestine Indigenous Revolutionary Committee—General Command, which is supposedly the highest authority within the EZLN. (It is more likely the body, consisting of village authorities, that makes the real decisions affecting daily life in the Zapatista zone, while Marcos himself seems to have decisive influence, if not absolute power, in questions having to do with war and relations with the central government.) It was Marcos who granted the vast majority of the interviews—or, at least, the ones that got quoted. It was he who drew up the list of accredited "war correspondents" and signed our laminated mint-green credentials. It was he who stage-managed the moving EZLN events at which glamorous visitors from Mexico City and abroad watched Indian peasants parade in homemade uniforms, carrying hunting rifles and other guns and—in the absence of real weapons—carved-wood imitations of guns. And it was his adroit manipulation of this array of symbolic weapons that mobilized public opinion in favor of the EZLN and kept the war the Zapatistas had invited at bay.

Marcos, however, cannot fight a real war by himself, and, on the basis of the army's stunning advance over the last three weeks, it seems that any attempt by the EZLN troops to take on the Mexican army can end only in tragedy. The total number of dead that reporters have reliably been able to come up with for this week's offensive is fewer than ten, and this is because, rather than fight, the Zapatistas and their families fled by the thousands into the jungly, ravine-crossed mountains that stand between their homes, in the former control zone, and what remains of the Lacandón jungle.

Just about a year ago, the government, desperate to appease the rebels of Las Cañadas, offered a settlement involving a cornucopia of social-works projects—health clinics and roads and electrification programs—and the insurgent peasants proudly turned down the offer, declaring that they wanted democracy as well. Less than a month ago they were a defiant force, the improbable vanguard of a leftist movement that had finally managed to pose a real challenge to Zedillo's decrepit ruling party. Now the Zapatistas are terrified, sick with fear and hunger, and in awe of the display of tanks and cannons the army has ostentatiously deployed throughout the former control zone. Marcos continues to produce communiqués, but they are days late in arriving, evidently because an excellent communications network that included faxes and a satellite phone is no longer in place. As he did throughout the thirteen months of cease-fire, he continues to warn that, although the Zapatistas want peace, and have therefore refrained from war, they can be pushed only so far.

But it is hard to see how much further the rebels can be pushed without calling it defeat. Those of us who watched the repeated Zapatista military parades last year, and saw the carved-wood weapons, assumed that the four hundred or so troops who used to march were representative of thousands of others, and that the wooden weapons could, on the day of reckoning, be turned in for something to fight with. Perhaps we were wrong. "The EZLN is not willing to hold a dialogue in humiliating conditions," a recent communiqué stated. In other words, the EZLN has been humiliated. An amnesty law sent to Congress by Zedillo will most likely be approved. It is a surrender treaty disguised as a dialogue offer, and there is a good chance that the Zapatistas will sign it; significant numbers of their supporters are already starting to return to the villages.

Although the Zapatistas' support network in the United States pumped up the Internet with reports of widespread killing by the army, reporters could find no trace of these events, and it appears instead that the military has behaved with remarkable restraint by Latin American standards. By these standards, restraint means that many peasants who did not flee have been arbitrarily detained in their villages, and are being threatened, beaten, asphyxiated, or deprived of food, so that they will denounce the Zapatistas among them. Essentially, the remilitarization of the Chiapas conflict means that the Mexican army has been turned into an occupying force.

Against the expectation that the living conditions of the Mayan Indians will improve soon, no matter what happens on the battlefield—if there is ever a battle—there is the economic disaster that it has been Zedillo's lot to preside over. The best that can be expected is that the Mexican economy will remain in recession for at least a year, and it is not clear how money can be found to buy stability in Chiapas, where the economy has collapsed. Who will pay the taxes to provide for the public works demanded not only by the Zapatistas but now by virtually all of Chiapas's impoverished peasant population? And where is the land that can satisfy the *campesinos'* hunger, now that so much of the Lacandón jungle has been deforested and settled?

There was a phrase one heard everywhere last year, stated sometimes fearfully, sometimes with joy: *"Los indios perdieron el miedo"*— "The Indians are no longer afraid." Made fearless by the armed Zapatistas, *los indios* invaded some two thousand cattle ranches and coffee farms. The owners are threatening to take up arms in defense of their land. *Los indios* also did fierce, bloody battle with each other over issues of religion and politics, which always had their roots in land disputes. Even if the Zapatistas are brought to their knees, these conflicts remain unresolved.

There is a dreamlike quality about the speed with which the world that the Zapatistas created in their stronghold is being dismantled. Their pride, their monument, the capital of their *territorio liberado*—a ceremonial space baptized Aguascalientes, in honor of the site of the constitutional convention that was called by the revolutionaries of 1914, and in which Emiliano Zapata played a preponderant role—is gone. The Zapatistas built Aguascalientes last July in preparation for a National Democratic Convention called by Marcos, which was attended by thousands of Mexican delegates and hundreds of reporters from all over the world. Mexicans are lavish hosts, and the impoverished Indians of Las Cañadas were no exception. They cleared the jungle to build guesthouses, a kitchen, parking lots, even a library with makeshift bookshelves, so that their literate guests could feel at home. And they built the amphitheater, with a primitive rostrum to rival the one in the national Congress in Mexico City, and gave it as a backdrop two enormous Mexican flags, just like the ones in Congress. In front of the rostrum, there was a parade space for the marching troops. For the audience, an entire hillside was covered with benches made out of split logs. It was a gigantic effort, worthy of the importance that the *campesinos* of Chiapas felt they had attained, and it took army troops less than a week to dismantle the entire compound, log by log.

When I arrived at the site last week, government soldiers were planting the last of several hundred saplings in the holes where Y-posts had once held the benches of the amphitheater on the hill. I asked the colonel in charge of the operation why the government had felt that it was necessary to return Aguascalientes to the jungle. "I think that in Mexico the era calls for more wooded spaces," he said, explaining the issue ecologically. "The problem is that anyone can think of cutting down a tree, but no one thinks of planting one back."

I asked him why the troops seemed so relaxed, as if they had no fear of an enemy attack. "You're the one who says there are Zapatistas," he answered. "I've been stationed in the region eight months and I haven't seen one yet."

It took an hour to travel about ten miles down a gutted road from the nearest town to another village in the region. The *campesinos* there had taken to the hills when they heard of the army's approach, abandoning their yard animals and their supplies of corn, but days later, figuring that if they didn't reclaim their homes the army would take them over, they had returned. Since then, they had not dared to leave the village to work their fields. Yet the radical fury of their discourse, their innocence of the world, their stubborn hope that the Zapatistas might yet manage to terrify the government into giving them a place in the world, was startling. "We don't know what the government looks like, where it sits, or what its palace is like," a woman said in broken Spanish. She was choking with rage. "We are ignorant, but what I want to know is this: Do the bourgeois, the rich people's children, sleep on the floor, the way ours do? Do helicopters come and terrify them?"

"Let the government take its helicopters, tanks, and cars out of here," a man said, "because everyone knows that the Zapatistas aren't just a handful, so if it doesn't they will take revenge. Is it a crime to want what they want? We want justice, liberty, and democracy." And he added, with no apparent sense that one wish was infinitely smaller than the other, "We want the government to take us into account."

I told him that Aguascalientes was no more, and other villagers came close to hear the news.

"They didn't have to carry the logs to build it," the man said quietly. "Was it so much in their way that they had to destroy it?"

—March 13, 1995

POSTSCRIPT

In the five years since Rafael Guillén was revealed as Subcomandante Marcos, the state of Chiapas has witnessed great transformations. Nearly all the ranch land once in private hands has been turned over to *campesinos* who, under the aegis of the Zapatista movement, invaded the ranches and eventually negotiated legal title to them with the local government. This great transfer of property has not made the Mayan *campesinos* any less poor or eased their rage against the politicians of Mexico, nor has it brought peace to the state.

President Ernesto Zedillo directed enormous amounts of federal aid toward Chiapas and visited the state more than thirty times during his term in office. The official figures are impressive: in Mexico's poorest state two hundred miles of highway were built, 250,000 more children were enrolled in school than under the Salinas administration, 650,000 Chiapanecos received piped drinking water. Yet the local and federal governments remained incapable of generating opportunities—in terms of jobs or higher education—for the Indian majority of the highlands, or of ridding themselves of corruption or political intolerance. As of the military deployment of February 1995, President Zedillo and his advisers also chose to escalate the conflict between the federal government and the EZLN. When, later in the year, the Zapatistas agreed to sit down to open-ended formal talks with a government delegation, there was great hope that a settlement might at last be reached with the rebels. These talks lasted from July 1995 to February 1996 and concluded, apparently to the satisfaction of both parties, with agreements covering everything from bilingual education to regional autonomy for the various Maya language groups. Unfortunately, the question of autonomy collided with the Constitution, and President Zedillo did not ratify the agreements. But he also refused to make the political gestures that would have made it possible for the peace talks to continue in some fashion. As a result, his government lost the initiative with regard to a political solution in Chiapas.

For his part, Subcomandante Marcos has not felt the need to peel away at least some of the layers of rhetoric in which the EZLN is now cloaked. For one thing, the Zapatistas are not an army and it appears unlikely that they will become one in the foreseeable future. For another, the Mayan people of Chiapas are as divided—or pluralistic—as the rest of Mexico, in this case between Catholics and members of evangelical Protestant sects, between different language groups, between pro- and anti-Zapatistas, between the traditionalist elders and the young people who are traveling in increasing numbers to the United States to look for work and, lastly, between communities that have become heavily infiltrated by the drug trade and those that have refused to collaborate. Conceivably, if the Zapatista leadership recognized these realities in its language, it would open the way for a more useful view of its future, and the future of its support communities. But this would involve making what appears to be an intolerable admission: that Marcos does not speak for all 10 million of Mexico's indigenous people, and not even for all of the Maya in Chiapas.

The ubiquitous presence of the military—which traditionally has kept a very low profile everywhere else in the country—is now hardly even remarked on. Troops move up and down the highways constantly. Government checkpoints are everywhere, as are the black-uniformed and much-feared members of the local and national Policía Judicial. Partly because its use has become more accepted by all parties, there is some likelihood that violence in the state will escalate greatly in the next few years. Members of the local government provided their followers with high-power weapons as soon as the Zapatista presence became known, and the terrible massacre of Acteal, over Christmas of 1997, in which 45 men, women, and children were killed, was one result. And if the EZLN failed to provide its would-be soldiers with many weapons, the drug trade has stepped in with alacrity to fill the need. Blood feuds, land disputes, drug wars, and even religious conflicts, none of which have diminished in the last six years, may now express themselves through machine guns rather than pistols and machetes. The long epidemic of violence has not yet played itself out in Chiapas.

There are, however, reasons to hope that the political stalemate in Chiapas could be broken soon. There is the recent election to the Mexican presidency of Vicente Fox, who is not a member of the PRI and so has everything to gain by breaking with the old established interests and setting up an effective, goal-oriented dialogue, not only with the Zapatistas but with the many conflicting parties in Chiapas. And there is the parallel election to the Chiapas governorship of the coalition candidate for the opposition,

Pablo Salazar. The new governor is of Maya extraction, and he is a former PRIista who is still on friendly terms with many of his former party comrades. In addition, he is a leading member of the Evangelical Protestant community, which has grown so quickly in recent years and may soon overtake the Catholic community in size. He is, in other words, in an ideal position to forge links between many of the forces in conflict.

Marcos himself has remained worrisomely silent since even before the elections, and at this writing he has yet to comment on the end of the PRI regime or on either the new president or the new governor-elect. The most hopeful interpretation of this silence is that the Zapatista communities are consulting among themselves as to what their next step should be, and that the result will be a decision to lay down their few arms and join the rest of Mexican civil society as a political movement.

When President Carlos Salinas de Gortari traveled by heli-
copter on a recent Sunday to a meeting in the agricultural
community of Tecámac, outside Mexico City, it was a sunny afternoon in the middle of the rainy season, and all the fields were
green. Excited *campesino* men and women dressed in their Sunday
best streamed from dirt paths along a maguey-and-poplar-lined
road, headed for a green-and-yellow tent where several thousand
other farmers were already milling noisily.

Some of the government's bigger guns were up on the platform.
Carlos Hank González, former schoolteacher, former mayor of
Mexico City, former governor of the state of México (where Tecámac is situated), former secretary of tourism, current secretary of
agriculture, perpetual powermonger, and multimillionaire, was at
the president's left. The current governor of the state of México,
responsible for insuring that the crowd for the day's event would
be large and sufficiently enthusiastic, was to his right. The head of
the Confederación Nacional Campesina, the ruling party's peasant
organization, was just beyond him. When the president arrived
on the platform, the crowd whirled noisemakers and cheered and
whistled and clapped for several minutes. It was just six weeks
before the presidential election and, in the time-honored tradition
of the Partido Revolucionario Institucional, or PRI, which has
ruled Mexico for the last sixty-five years, Carlos Salinas de Gortari
was about to hand out money.

No one mentioned the election, or even the name of Ernesto
Zedillo Ponce de León, the candidate who replaced Salinas's hand-

picked successor Luis Donaldo Colosio when Colosio was assassinated in March. All the speakers praised President Salinas and thanked him many times for his visit, on their own behalf and on behalf of the roaring audience, and the head of the *campesino* federation stated that the checks the members of the audience were to receive were not handouts. They were, he explained, a direct subsidy to grain and oilseed growers affected by the flood of cheaper imports of those crops made possible by the North American Free Trade Agreement. As such, he said, the checks represented a great step forward in the modernization of the countryside, and a vast improvement over previous "hidden subsidies," which took the form of guaranteed prices.

The governor of the state of México said that these checks would prevent the massive migration to the cities that has made urban life a nightmare here over the last few decades. A local *campesino* representative swore that this was true. "We will not sell our land! We will associate ourselves in the different associative forms you have created, Señor Presidente, and we will remain faithful to them forever," he shouted, and he added that he would not wish to conclude without asking for the president's understanding and support in the matter of a $70,000 debt his community owed to the electric company. The petitioner handed the electricity bill to Salinas, and the president, smiling benevolently, turned it over to a minion. Then, after listening to a few more *"Viva Carlos Salinas de Gortari!"*s and *"Viva México!"*s, he handed out the first ten checks of a total of almost four million that would soon be distributed, and stepped to the very edge of the platform to address his audience.

"I am very happy to greet the *compañeros* of Tecámac and Zumpango and Ojo de Agua," the president said, and the audience rose to its feet, yelling wildly. "I feel right at home," he said, and the audience rose to its feet once more. "We are here to keep our word!" he shouted, and the audience rose again. Somewhere toward the front of the crowd a drumroll announced each applause line, talk-show style, but Salinas appeared to be the host of a different kind of program. "Why don't you raise your hands and show us the checks?" he ordered, and obedient hands went up. "And now what are you going to do with the money?" He cupped a hand to his ear. "Buy a tractor? Very good! Buy fertilizer? Excellent!" It was *Sesame Street.*

The people of Tecámac, Zumpango, and Ojo de Agua seemed to be enjoying themselves thoroughly, and, indeed, so did the president. The orchestrated ecstatic ritual was at the center of a political culture that has made the regime the longest-lived one-party system in the world today, and has kept Mexicans politically dependent, infantilized, and powerless—trained to accept corruption and grateful to have stability and economic succor, even if it comes at the price of their rights as citizens. It has been a system of such subtle and exquisitely managed controls and gratifications that no one can even prove they exist, and all political discussion takes the form of speculation. Is it true, for example, that peasants who do not cast their vote for the PRI are sanctioned by the *campesino* federation with a loss of such benefits as the subsidy checks? Is it true that Carlos Hank González's fortune grew every time he commissioned a huge public-works program for Mexico City or the State of México, because his transport company ferried the materials and his automotive company provided the trucks? Is it true that the hordes of reporters who cover events like the money-disbursing ceremony at Tecámac receive a small emolument themselves for their pains? Did the fact that all newsprint in Mexico was until recently sold by a state-owned corporation influence news coverage? These are questions that are answered unwaveringly in the affirmative by a populace raised on a near-total absence of truthful information about its governors and persuaded that wisdom lies in believing the worst.

Lunatic conspiratorial fantasies also spring from this lack of information: Was it Salinas himself who ordered the assassination, on March 23, of the candidate Colosio, because Colosio had hurt his feelings? These fantasies are believed by the very people who cash in their subsidy checks and cast their votes for the PRI—willingly, often enough—in election after election, and also by the many millions who have never bothered to vote in their lives. To what end, those millions ask, if the PRI's candidate is selected by the president each time through a secret process known as *el Dedazo*—the Big Finger—and if the PRI's candidate invariably wins?

That voters feel a measurable enthusiasm for this year's elections, however—though this sentiment coexists uneasily with the conviction that somewhere some politician is diddling them—is due to a series of recent electoral reforms that have dramatically altered the voting panorama: for example, for the first time, there are nine candidates for president, three of whom have been considered serious contenders at various points in the eight-month-long campaign; and the vote, on August 21, will be monitored by citizen volunteers. There is, by all accounts, an acute sense of these elections' historic importance. The reforms have been either initiated or made possible by President Salinas, who many people believe did not win the elections in 1988, although he claimed victory over his rival, Cuauhtémoc Cárdenas. Cárdenas, who had broken away from the ruling party the previous year to run as an independent, won big in Mexico City and in four states, but it has never been possible to establish if he won anywhere else or by how much. The days before the 1988 elections were marked by violence: two of Cárdenas's closest aides were killed. Then, on election night, the computerized vote-tallying system "fell" as the first votes—overwhelmingly favorable to Cárdenas—were being counted, and the computer meltdown was followed by a news blackout that lasted two days.

The ballots were stored in the basement of the Congress and were destroyed in December of 1991, by which time Salinas had revealed himself as the most forceful president in many years and also as a great pragmatist. Having evidently decided that the push for democracy was too strong to resist, he let the Partido Acción Nacional, or PAN—the party of the conservative opposition—claim governorships in three states. He also reformed the electoral process and established a National Commission of Human Rights.

Salinas's reformist ambitions were given an unexpected push on January 1, when the impoverished Mayan Indians who form the rank and file of the EZLN marched into a town in the southern state of Chiapas and declared war on the regime. The rebels of the

Zapatista National Liberation Army wore masks, as if they were robbers, but they did not frighten a country persuaded that the real *bandidos* are traffic cops who extort a day's wages for a wrong left turn, and government contractors who build public housing that crumbles a year after its completion. The Zapatistas' masks disguised more than their faces, however: though they performed as a military movement, it turned out that they had no military strength and were in reality an armed pressure group. Nevertheless, they pointed up a profound ambivalence in the body politic toward President Salinas—a distrust and fear of his triumphalist rhetoric and capitalist programs despite his 80 percent popularity ratings—and they mobilized tens of thousands throughout the country with their calls for "Liberty, Justice, and Democracy" and for Salinas's overthrow. Partly in response to the Zapatistas, the regime speeded up the process of reforming itself. The Federal Electoral Institution was overhauled, all PRI representatives were removed from it, and the voter-registration system was redesigned to make fraud much more difficult. The opposition parties have also been given equal time on television to present their programs.

In the presidential office and residence at Los Pinos, in Mexico City, where Salinas works surrounded by glowing Diego Riveras and an elegant life-size portrait of Benito Juárez, I asked him how he felt about the notion that his party might lose the presidency for the first time.

"Democracy introduces political uncertainty, and we welcome it!" he said. "The PRI will have to adjust to this new reality. It has already been going through changes in the last few years, and this new situation implies the acknowledgment that any candidate who wants to win will have to work harder. Democracy isn't an event; it's a process."

Salinas, forty-six, is a scion of the PRI intelligentsia: his father is a former Cabinet member who once aspired to the presidency himself, and his cousins are intellectuals of note. The nuances of the PRI's *nacionalismo revolucionario* allowed him not only to sell off all the state monopolies that his predecessors had nationalized but also to give shelter in Los Pinos to Rigoberta Menchú, the

Guatemalan winner of the Nobel Peace Prize and a radical activist for Indian rights, when it seemed that her right-wing enemies might try to have her killed. Salinas is also a prize-winning equestrian (he won a silver medal at the 1971 Pan American Games), and, by all accounts, an immensely ambitious politician, who is now lobbying heavily to become the first director of the Geneva-based World Trade Organization. He is cosmopolitan, highly educated, keenly observant, and intensely curious about his own country. The old-style one-party system is coming to an end, he told me, for two reasons: "Because a society that has grown more diverse and more pluralistic is demanding different options, and also because we are living in new international circumstances; Mexican citizens looked around them and saw that other societies were opening up to a diversity of options. This government decided to place itself at the head of the demand for change."

The Indian uprising in Chiapas was not evidence that the social cost of his economic reforms had been too high, he said. Quite the contrary: "If this administration had not invested so strongly in social programs for the last five years, the rebellion in Chiapas would have spread like wildfire."

I asked him about the most pernicious legacy of the PRI—the ingrained cynicism about politics, the disdain for what is seen as its inevitable mendacity and corruption.

He begged to differ. "I think that the term"—cynicism—"has to be revised in the light of at least two factors," he said. "The first is that all the polls are showing an unusually high degree of willingness to participate in politics, either as observers or as voters in these next elections. The second is that one should consider this cynicism vis-à-vis the same phenomenon in comparable Latin American countries with similar degrees of industrialization. I don't think that that cynicism is the PRI's doing, and, in any case, it is a mistake to suppose that the PRI of twenty or forty years ago was the same party as today's."

"Por un México sin Mentiras"—"For a Mexico Without Lies"—is the slogan of the PAN leader Diego Fernández de Cevallos, the most enigmatic candidate in the race. Until a few weeks ago, he

was known, wherever he was known at all, as the cigar-smoking, irascible candidate of a party that the government has long excoriated as ultra-Catholic and reactionary. And yet he was also the bully in the Chamber of Deputies who acted most often as an ally of President Salinas and helped push through Salinas's constitutional reforms. He has a prosperous private law practice, an equally flourishing ranch, and a flowing Tolstoyan beard, which he appears to have had trimmed for the campaign to a length that makes him more nearly resemble Mexico's tragically confused Emperor Maximilian of Austria, and which polls said worked against him. The country got a closer look at him on May 12, when he appeared on television with the two other leading candidates, Ernesto Zedillo of the PRI, and Cuauhtémoc Cárdenas (son of Lázaro Cárdenas), Salinas's 1988 rival, who is running again, this time as the candidate of the six-year-old Partido de la Revolución Democrática, or PRD.

Although the event was billed as Mexico's first presidential debate in this century, it hardly looked like one: there was no live audience, and no journalists were present; no questions were allowed from the ladylike moderator; and the cameras were not permitted to focus on anything but the upper torso of the candidate who was speaking. Controlled though it was, the debate was such a groundbreaking event that about 40 million people— almost half the population—are estimated to have tuned in. They watched, transfixed, as Diego Fernández de Cevallos proceeded to tear up his rivals. He cocked his head and fixed his round, glittering eyes on the camera, wagged a stern forefinger, and told Zedillo that, although he was a good boy and got very good grades, he flunked democracy. He waved papers in the air and told Cárdenas that he was two-faced—that he had spent most of his political life in the PRI, behaving in PRI fashion, and now he was pretending to be a martyr of the opposition. He jutted his chin out and puffed up his chest and barked his attacks in the manner that has earned him the title Boss Diego in Congress, and the next day no one needed a poll to know that Fernández de Cevallos was the hands-down winner of the debate. The question was: would people want

Boss Diego as their leader, or did they simply like to watch him bash the mighty?

Diego Fernández de Cevallos received me in his law firm's offices, which are large, if a little threadbare, and are in a posh neighborhood. There seemed to be absolutely no one else there except his secretary and his press manager, and no phone call interrupted our interview for the nearly two hours in which the candidate—genial, extroverted, loquacious, and courtly—expounded his views. Despite a surge in his popularity ratings after the debate to 31 percent (against Zedillo's 38 percent), at the time we spoke he had mysteriously canceled all public campaign commitments for the next two weeks and hardly seemed to be in a flurry of private politicking. I asked him if he really wanted to be president, because it certainly didn't look like it. He answered, jovially, that he wanted to do the decent thing and win by a modest margin, rather than by a landslide, and then he added, more seriously, that modern campaigns are won in the media, and not with old-fashioned village-to-village pilgrimages, such as Cárdenas favors. He said that he was concentrating on activities that are of vital importance to a future president—he had, for example, met the previous day with the British ambassador and with the highest-ranking executives of the Coca-Cola Company.

I asked him why he referred to people he disliked or disagreed with as *peladaje* and *descalzonados*—"rabble" and "people with no pants on"—and why he called their masculinity into question.

"I have no doubt that I am a man for whom hypocrisy and sinuosities are impossible," he said. "And politics in Mexico has by and large been hypocritical. For better or worse, that's my style, and it can cost me some sympathizers—or win them. I am a ranchero, and more cannot be asked of me."

Fernández de Cevallos didn't deny that he is personally close to President Salinas—"and to any number of people in the government," he added—but he maintained that he was campaigning hard against Salinas's designated successor, Zedillo, and declared that he would win. "The debate ended the myth that no one dares speak forthrightly to the official candidate, who had always been addressed before as an untouchable, deified figure," he said. "Mexico is beginning to understand that anyone can win."

What Fernández de Cevallos also showed during the debate, to the great delight of the highest officials in the land, is that the man who insists that he won the 1988 elections is a poor candidate in the current ones. Cuauhtémoc Cárdenas and his party, the PRD, were generally considered to be the only serious challenge to the PRI's Zedillo until the debate in May. But Cárdenas proved no challenge at all to Fernández de Cevallos. While the conservative candidate waved papers in the air and accused Cárdenas of ruling despotically when he was governor of the state of Michoacán, Cárdenas, looking wooden and embittered, made feeble jokes and failed to respond to any of the accusations. He repeated what often seems to be the only heartfelt theme of his campaign, which is that the government will never let him win. Following the debate, he dropped to an 11 percent rating in the polls.

"The debate ended a myth about who was the second political force in the land," a high official told me gleefully. "People hadn't seen Cuauhtémoc Cárdenas before, and so they had imagined him. Then they saw him on television, and they found out that they didn't like what they saw." Other members of the government gave me careful versions of what appears to be the official sotto voce account of what really happened the night the computers "fell" in 1988. "It was lamentable," one of these officials said. "Cuauhtémoc really did get a lot of votes in the capital, and logically those were the ones that were counted first. Unfortunately, people did not respond very well when those first votes came in. There was a panic reaction and . . ." He shrugged helplessly. "But what is definitely true is that, over all, Cuauhtémoc didn't win."

Cárdenas staged his most triumphant rally last month, on the sixth anniversary of the elections he lost, at a bullfight ring that sits in the middle of Mexico City's noisy, polluted industrial sector. The *toreo* was packed to the rafters, but this was not surprising, because all public spaces in Mexico are overfilled; the subway, for instance, with its cattle railings to herd male and female workers into separate cars (a measure to protect the women from harassment), was filled to bursting at the *toreo* stop. On the street level, traffic had solidified into a gigantic clot of cars, the access routes were crammed with buses and illegal transport vans, and the sidewalks were overflowing with hundreds of shacks offering rolls, nuts, sandwiches, candy, quesadillas, for all those who can't afford to eat anything more than a snack between their double or triple work shifts. Dodging buses, picking their way between the shacks, indifferent to a pouring rain, a river of people flowed toward the access gates of the *toreo*, carrying the PRD's black-and-yellow flags and organized, as tradition dictates, by electoral district, by city block, by trade. The Cardenistas who were lucky enough to find a space in the bullring's stands—thousands of others could not fit in—were an amalgam of Mexico's poor. There were squatters, kids from the radicalized public high schools, housewives from radical neighborhood groups carrying banners for the Zapatistas, and peasants who listened impassively to a killer rock band called Santa Sabina. The lead singer sang with a razor-edged soprano and looked like Morticia Addams. The bass player wore a mask, like Subcomandante Marcos. The air smelled of sweat. A man came up and asked if I would interview him. "We are two thousand families who took over the land in Chalco," he said, referring to an area on the outskirts of Mexico City. "The government won't give us title to it. There are no electric lights or sewers, it takes me two hours to get to work, and, now that the rains have come, our shacks are flooding." He had a terrible cough.

When Cárdenas appeared onstage, there was a deafening roar and a cataract of black-and-yellow confetti. He said, "Six years and four days ago, two of our *compañeros* were murdered." He asked for a minute of silence for them, and for all the other Party workers who had died violent deaths since, but before forty-five seconds were up a voice near the rafters broke into the national anthem and was immediately joined by some twenty thousand other voices in the *toreo*.

Yet Cárdenas, who in the very form of his campaign events appears to understand keenly how hard it is to be Mexican, is not what he seems either—or at least his party is not. Formed six years ago, immediately after Cárdenas's defeat, the PRD is structured much the way the PRI was in its founding days—as a conglomerate of warring factions united around certain power-sharing arrangements. The PRD's battling components are various segments of the radical left, and a number of former high-ranking members of the PRI. The leftists are dogmatic; the former PRIistas are strong on pragmatism. The leftists once called on the government to commit a *fraude patriótico* in order to prevent the conservative PAN from winning a governorship. The pragmatists see nothing wrong with their candidate for the congressional race in Chiapas. Her name is Irma Serrano, but she is known as La Tigresa, and it is hard to know whether she is more famous for her early career as a ranchera singer in the sixties, her subsequent flowering as an *artista del desnudo* in kinky theatrical revues, her frightening Kabuki eye makeup, her foul temper, or her liaison with President Gustavo Díaz Ordaz, who was in power in 1968, when an infamous massacre of students by the army took place. "Irma was planning to run anyway," the PRD chairman told me. "We'd much rather have her with us than against us, and she draws a lot of people."

On Cárdenas's campaign bus, I asked him what had changed since 1988. All the other politicians I'd talked to in the last few weeks considered the political *apertura,* or opening, and the greater citizen interest in the elections to be of primary importance, even as they pointed out that the *apertura* was due to their own efforts as much as to any benevolence on the part of the government. But Cárdenas began with a ringing indictment of Salinas's economic policy. "Unemployment has increased," he began. "Agriculture, fishing—the rural sector in general—are in much worse shape. The countryside has been neglected. Public works are needed. Much of this is a result of the international situation; even before the free-trade treaty went into effect, the border had been opened to forestry and agro-imports. Loans for agriculture have been cut back, and there has been almost no productive investment in the countryside. At the same time, the flow of manufactures like textiles and shoes has also brought a great deal of damage. It is true that this government has generated a climate of confidence for foreign investment, but as long as that investment continues to go mainly into stock-market speculation, as it has until now, it will have little or no effect on people's economic situation."

I asked him how the electoral situation had changed.

"There is a much more restrictive legal framework now," he said. "The government is exercising much more control over the electoral process."

I pressed the point: wasn't his own situation as a candidate better now than it had been in 1988, thanks to the reforms?

"We're in the same shape. There is a greater effort by the government to impose controls."

Why, then, was he bothering to campaign?

"It might seem like a contradiction to be calling for a vote and proclaiming the existence of fraud at the same time," he answered. "But it's been proved in other situations around the world that when there are enough votes, and enough organization to protect them, electoral maneuvering is defeated in the end."

Cárdenas and his people claim that the polls showing him in third place lie. He told me that in 1988 his incessant whistle-stop tours had paid off in the campaign's closing weeks. He fully expected this to be the case again, Cárdenas said.

One of the many paradoxes in the current situation is that, while a victory by any of the three principal candidates would not bring significant policy changes—they all want to carry on with NAFTA, the peace talks in Chiapas, and tight-money, balanced-budget economics—in a worst-case scenario, Cárdenas's defeat could lead to chaos. There are indeed millions who feel represented by him, and the line that separates them from those who look on the Zapatistas with sympathy is blurry. Cárdenas has decried the Zapatistas' use of violence, and Subcomandante Marcos, for his part, publicly excoriated the PRD in May, but the people carrying Zapatista banners at the PRD's rallies do not seem really interested in these quarrels.

The other side of this paradox is that the PRI would have to lose in order to win back some credibility, but it seems as though

Zedillo, who came to the candidacy looking like a hopeless loser, might really win. He was not initially in the running for the 1994 nomination, and it is not even clear that he was being groomed to run for the presidency in the year 2000; a former secretary of education and of planning and the budget, he seemed too much "the good student," Diego Fernández de Cevallos likes to say—too much the number cruncher, too little the master negotiator—to make a likely candidate. In December of last year, Salinas's Big Finger pointed to Luis Donaldo Colosio, who was a personable and skillful politician with long experience in the PRI, and Zedillo resigned as secretary of education in order to take charge of Colosio's campaign.

After Colosio's assassination, there were really no other contenders in the ruling party except Zedillo, because a clause in the Constitution forbids anyone to run for the presidency who has served in the cabinet during the six months before the election. The decision to nominate him took place, as usual, behind closed doors, and when the PRI announced the choice (it is never presented as the president's), Zedillo was instantly rebaptized Dedillo—the Little Finger.

Zedillo's campaign managers told me that the candidate had no time for an interview, but I had a chance to observe him when he addressed several hundred businessmen in Tijuana recently. Boyish-looking (he is forty-four), with big glasses, a scrawny neck, and an eager expression, he had a hard time warming up the audience, but he really had no need for charisma, because instead, and in sharp contrast to all the other candidates, he could offer up-to-the-minute information on border industries and local exports damaged by NAFTA, and ten-point programs to reactivate them, with technocrats and loyal Party supporters in place who could guarantee results. The inescapable conclusion among those few businessmen who were not already PRI backers was that Zedillo would govern better, because he was the only candidate who knew—in intimate, exhaustive detail—how the country is managed.

In Lomas Taurinas, the working-class *colonia,* or development, in Tijuana where Colosio was murdered, I talked with half a dozen young men who were taking a rest break from a government-financed, community-organized road-building program. They were all planning to vote for Zedillo, because the PRI had financed the *colonia*'s founding, had sponsored the introduction of running water, electricity, sewer systems, and even a few phone lines, and could be relied on to negotiate all the community's dealings with the state. Zedillo may be short-tempered ("Either your information is wrong or you are a liar," he told a foreign reporter at a press conference who had raised a question about vote buying), and he may be a soporific public speaker and look ill at ease pressing the flesh, but the people who want security and predictability more than anything else will vote for him—or rather for the PRI. At this stage, he is comfortably ahead in the polls.

In the weeks that followed my interview with Fernández de Cevallos, his campaign languished. Compared with Cárdenas's thirty-seven campaign stops and Zedillo's nine broadcast interviews in a typical week in July, for example, Diego gave three interviews and attended only seven rallies. There was nationwide expectation of a second debate, which was agreed on after Diego made mincemeat of his opponents in the first one, but when the PRI chairman declared on July 12 that its candidate had no time for a new televised meeting, the normally pugnacious Diego did not protest. The rumors escalated. Had Mexicans been lied to once again? Had Diego, Salinas's point man in Congress and acknowledged good friend, given up fighting for the presidency when it became clear that he could win? Had he simply acted the part of the *rejoneador* in the bullfights he likes so much—one of whose functions is to gore and tire out the bull (who in this case is Cuauhtémoc Cárdenas), leaving him docile enough for the *torero*?

With typical aplomb, Diego has denied the rumors that he is throwing the election. ("Let them say that to my face if they're man enough!") But there is his reputation as a dealmaker, and the unusual intimacy between the president's inner circle and the opposition candidate who makes it a point of honor to be beholden to no one.

In a sense, it hardly matters whether the rumor is true or not: the effect of it is that Mexicans are back to imagining conspiracies. Imperceptibly, the casual conversations one struck up everywhere just weeks ago about the strange, agreeable excitement of participating in a "real campaign" have shifted to cynical discussions of Diego's halfhearted campaign and what it's like to witness an election that seems almost for real—in other words, one that, when all is said and done, might still be a lie. If Diego Fernández de Cevallos remains quiescent and Cárdenas loses narrowly, Zedillo will find it hard to rule with credibility, and also with authority— particularly because in Chiapas the Zapatistas have let it be known that there are virtually no circumstances in which they will recognize his victory. Of course, either Diego or Cárdenas could actually win in a last-minute sprint, and in that case the PRI's only challenge will be to show that it has learned how to leave.

—August 15, 1994

WHODUNNIT?

On May 24, 1993, as Juan Jesús Cardinal Posadas, the archbishop of Guadalajara, was about to get out of his car at the
crowded entrance to the Guadalajara airport, gunmen forced open
the door and shot him point-blank. The reasons for the cardinal's
death remain in doubt in the public mind, but it is accepted that
the men who killed him were in the pay of a swiftly emerging
drug elite. In March of last year, Luis Donaldo Colosio, the presidential candidate of the Partido Revolucionario Institucional, or
PRI, was assassinated in Tijuana. President Carlos Salinas de Gortari appointed Ernesto Zedillo, Colosio's campaign manager, as
his unlikely successor. Zedillo was duly elected in August, and the
system prepared to move on. But a month later there was yet
another assassination. This time it was the secretary-general of the
PRI, José Francisco Ruiz Massieu, and the realization dawned here
that crime might be the new form that politics was taking in this
unpredictable era.

The murders, dreadful in and of themselves, are terrifying
mainly because they remain unsolved and, as such, are clear evidence not only that the country is falling apart but that there is no
one who can put the old order back together again. Not since the
aftermath of the 1910 revolution, commentators and opposition
politicians keep pointing out, has Mexico lived through comparable times. There is a raging economic crisis, the trade of illegal
drugs has put significant power in the hands of outlaws, and the
PRI's one-party rule is disintegrating, but the emotional center of
the unhappiness and unease that seem to have invaded so many

aspects of public and private life in Mexico remains the bloodshed that destroyed a cherished illusion—that Mexican citizens lived in, and tolerated, a regime that was neither transparent nor just but profoundly, reassuringly predictable.

It's not that the old rules don't apply anymore but that there is no longer any way of knowing when they do. The opposition is allowed to win in some states and is denied victory in others. The government talks peace with the rebel Zapatistas in Chiapas, but in the nearby state of Guerrero peasants get mowed down by the Policía Judicial. Facing a crime wave, the Mexico City police announce that "suspicious-looking" people will be detained at checkpoints, then back down the following day in deference to a civic uproar. Drugs are everywhere—even, it seems, in the government. Former President Salinas's brother is in jail, accused of masterminding the murder of Ruiz Massieu, the PRI leader, and indeed Salinas, who was seen for years in the admiring light in which he cast himself, is no longer the hero of a sweeping neo-liberal economic reform but the protagonist of a grotesque drama and the object of an enraged nation's scorn.

When I interviewed Salinas in August a year ago, shortly before the election of his successor, his administration was still reeling from the Zapatista uprising in Chiapas and the assassination of Colosio, but the president himself had managed to hold on to high popularity ratings and, for a ruler who had less than four months to go in office, to an unusual degree of political control. (Mexican presidents serve a single six-year term.) I told him a story that a Cabinet secretary had once told me about a former president, the easygoing Adolfo López Mateos:

"Adolfo," the secretary asked, "now that it's all over, how did it feel to be president, to enjoy such absolute power?"

"The first year," López Mateos replied, "when people came up to me and said, 'Señor Presidente, you are God,' I felt sickened by their servility. The second year, when they said it, I said, 'Thank you very much.' The third year, I felt rather pleased. The fourth year, when they came up and said 'Señor Presidente, you are God!' I thought to myself, That's an exaggeration! The fifth year, I looked at myself in the mirror and thought, Could it really be?"

"And the sixth year?" the secretary asked.

"The sixth year," the former president replied, "I asked myself why I hadn't committed suicide during the fifth."

Salinas, a man with an immense liveliness that can easily over-shadow an unprepossessing appearance, listened attentively to the story and then laughed it off. Six weeks later, Ruiz Massieu, a trusted and ruthless political ally, and, as it happened, the president's ex-brother-in-law, whom Salinas had elevated through the PRI ranks to the post of Party leader, was assassinated. Ignoring issues of conflict of interest, Salinas appointed Ruiz Massieu's younger brother, Mario, who was then deputy attorney general—and who was to become known, disparagingly, as Super Mario—to head an investigation. In November, Mario Ruiz Massieu held a breathtaking press conference, in which he announced his resignation and charged that high PRI officials had blocked the investigation into his brother's murder. (The president, though, had always supported him, Mario said.) In December, Zedillo took power, gave advance warning of a long-overdue devaluation of the peso, and appointed a new special prosecutor to investigate the three *magnicidios*—or big-time murders—of the cardinal, the presidential candidate, and the Party leader. In January, following a run on the peso, the economy collapsed. On the last day of February, the special prosecutor, Pablo Chapa Bezanilla, arrested former President Salinas's brother, Raúl, and accused him of masterminding the murder of José Francisco Ruiz Massieu.

The days that followed this arrest are the ones that people remember. Mario Ruiz Massieu, after being called in for questioning about his investigation of his brother's murder, fled the country on March 2, but he was arrested at Newark International Airport on charges of bringing in undeclared cash (more than $30,000 worth) and was subsequently charged in Mexico with covering up Raúl Salinas's role in the crime. That same day, at one-thirty in the morning, former President Salinas, looking haggard, knocked on the door of a house in a working-class neighborhood in the northern industrial city of Monterrey and asked the startled occupants if they would mind giving him shelter while he went on a hunger strike.

The hunger strike lasted two days, during which Mexicans had time to ponder many things. Most important, as the first images sent from Monterrey by a flock of dazed reporters landed on the TV screens back home, there was the obvious question: had Salinas lost his mind? We saw him perched on the edge of a cot, with a couple of photographs on the night table—not of his family but of himself at press-the-flesh events. Next to the photographs was the fancy bottled water that he had sworn to consume exclusively as long as the fast lasted. Never a large man, he now looked as if he were being devoured by the glove-leather bomber jacket he was wearing. The former president seemed bewildered. And lonely.

In groups, reporters were allowed into the fasting room. Salinas repeated a single message to each: He was certainly not on strike because his brother had been charged in connection with the murder of his former brother-in-law and good friend; he had faith in the justice system. No, he felt that a historic injustice was being committed by those who implied that he had been involved in the murder of Colosio, and by those others (namely, President Zedillo and his team) who laid the blame for the current economic earthquake on his own long refusal to devalue. He would fast until his name was cleared.

Perhaps this was the moment when Mexico, as those of us who were born and brought up here knew it, came to an end. Or perhaps it was a few weeks earlier, in the state of Tabasco. Elections for governor had been held there last November, and an opposition leftist party and the PRI were both claiming victory. In private negotiations, Zedillo and his people agreed that the PRI candidate would resign and that the opposition candidate would be allowed to take power. On January 19, in what amounted to a mutiny against the president, the Tabasco PRI staged a raid on the Government House in the state capital and installed its candidate, and he remains there. Or perhaps the old Mexico came to an end almost a year earlier, when Colosio was assassinated. The fact is that a system of perfect, unquestioned central authority, in which the absolute untouchability of presidents past, present, and future was the ruling tenet, is no longer in place. Twenty hours after Salinas arrived at the house in Monterrey—the home of Señora Rosa

Ofelia Coronado—he flew to Toluca, the capital of the state of México, adjoining Mexico City, and then back to Monterrey, having either met with or failed to meet with Zedillo (we don't really know) to negotiate about his future. And twenty hours after that, back at Señora Coronado's home, he received Zedillo's agrarian reform minister, an old friend of his, and agreed to lift the hunger strike. Salinas was photographed one last time in his native land, preparing to eat a fast-breaking spoonful of soup under the watchful eye of Señora Coronado and her clucking, affectionate neighbors, and then he departed, first to Mexico City, and, a few days later, to the United States. All the old certainties went with him.

Former Congressman Manuel Garza, a well-groomed, silver-haired, courtly, and effervescent man of a certain embonpoint, is one of the committed few for whom the Institutional Revolutionary Party's contradictory name still embodies a mystique, and he has traditionalist notions both of his party's place in the world and of diet. I talked with him a couple of times at a chic little European-style coffee shop where he regularly has breakfast with friends, allies, and supplicants, and on both occasions he feasted on eggs and wonderfully rich croissants. For Garza, the PRI's traditional way of practicing politics is neither sordid nor archaic but deeply patriotic, hugely entertaining, and, above all, efficient. There are people who refer to him as an *alquimista*—a vote fixer, an unprincipled transmuter of opposition triumphs into PRI electoral landslides—but Garza knows that the one thing that counts is power, and that power works best at higher concentrations. "They," he said, encompassing in the pronoun every suspect modernizer from Salinas to the unnamed incompetents on Zedillo's team, "go on so much about the *distancia apropiada* between the Party and the government, but I say that the appropriate distance is *this*"—he dropped a morsel of croissant to make a tight hugging motion with both arms. "That's how my wife and I are—each of us tending to our own affairs, but nice and close. We tell each other what we're up to, and we help each other out. Now, what could be wrong with that?"

Last year was not without troubles for Manuel Garza. For one thing, he was fingered by the attorney general's office in connection with the murder of José Francisco Ruiz Massieu, but he exonerated himself in the interrogations and in an impressive speech before Congress, and his expertise is once again being put to use in the Party in elections small and large. Now that a series of real electoral reforms agreed to by Salinas is in place, candidates of both the left- and the right-wing opposition parties are actually running for and winning mayoralties and governorships. As a result, polls are all the rage. Garza scoffs at them. "I only need to talk to ten people in a given town to know what our strength is," he said. "The point is, I always know exactly which ten people to talk to."

Garza stood by helplessly for six years while Salinas used his power to force on the PRI his vision of a democratic transition. In 1989, when Salinas allowed the conservative, largely Catholic opposition party Acción Nacional—known as the PAN—to win the governorship in Baja California, not even the conciliatory Luis Donaldo Colosio, then the head of the PRI, was able to persuade Party stalwarts to put aside their fury. "They want a democracy like Switzerland's," Garza told me. "But this is Mexico."

What he means by that is that the PRI evolved out of deeply Mexican political traditions, and that the one sure way to lose an election is to ignore this history. Take, for example, the *acarreados,* or trucked-in demonstrators, invariably poor, who at PRI or other official rallies are equipped with a hat, a noisemaker, a sandwich and a beer, and are told to cheer loudly. Left-wing intellectual types find this practice particularly distasteful. "But why do we have these demonstrations?" Garza asked me socratically. "Because they are demonstrations of the Party's strength, support, and organizational ability. They are the opportunity for our leaders to show—to contribute—what they have. Nowadays, we get sneered at for having *acarreados,* but we say, 'Let's see *you* truck them in!' "

Not long after being sworn in as the presidential candidate last spring, Zedillo made a campaign stop in San Cristóbal de las Casas, in the convulsed state of Chiapas. Zedillo, who is not only a modernizer but a modest and uncharismatic man, had evidently instructed his campaign team to skip the *acarreados* and the hoopla. A couple of dozen of us reporters and a larger security contingent stood in the central plaza of San Cristóbal and watched as the candidate climbed on a park bench and addressed his campaign speech exclusively to us. No one else stopped to listen. Several weeks into this type of event, Zedillo and his people apparently began to fear that he might actually lose an election with a level playing field, and they turned to the Party traditionalists, who delivered one rally after another packed with ecstatic thousands. Zedillo immediately started climbing in the polls, looked much more cheerful, and won 49 percent of the vote in the largest turnout and very probably the cleanest vote in Mexico's history.

Zedillo has repeatedly promised to modernize the presidency by redistributing power among the branches of government, and each renewed promise is a dagger in the PRI *histórico*'s heart. Part of the problem is that the PRI respects power and authority above all else, yet President Zedillo continues to behave as if he were not the country's chief executive but a replacement actor, brought onstage to play a scene or two until the star's throat clears. Zedillo is regarded as a decent, upstanding family man, who has never, to anyone's knowledge, made a dishonest peso. He is fair-minded and extremely intelligent. Unlike all recent presidents, he is of the people. (As a boy, he sold newspapers and shined shoes.)

Zedillo was very much part of Salinas's little team of foreign-educated economists, but he was a second-level member and had never held elected office. He was not on the short list of candidates who are unofficially vetted by the PRI's informal council of elders before the president decides who is to be his successor. After the party's designation of the doomed Luis Donaldo Colosio, Zedillo was put in charge of running his campaign. He didn't do particularly well by the personable, mild-mannered candidate, and in retrospect it seems clear that his weakness as Colosio's campaign manager was the same weakness he has as president—he is a terrible salesman. There is an odd proviso in the Mexican Constitution that prohibits anyone from running for president who has served in the Cabinet within six months of the election, and this left Zedillo as virtually the only member of Salinas's inner circle who was available to run. It is probably the last thing he would have wished to do, but on December 1 he took the oath of office. His inaugural promises were austere, and so was his audience's response, but, to his credit, he recognized that the legitimacy of his presidency depended on the government's bringing the murderers of Colosio, Ruiz Massieu, and Cardinal Posadas to trial. "We will not rest until justice is done," he proclaimed, and, for once, brought his audience to its feet.

Keeping track of the course of justice is a far more complicated task in Mexico than it is in the United States, where the jury system guarantees both public access to criminal cases and a drama-laden context in which to understand them. In Mexico, a judge hears private testimony from prosecutor and defendant, questions both sides, examines documents and other evidence, and, having come to his own conclusion, either clears the defendant or declares him guilty and decrees a sentence. The trial record must be made available to the defendant and his lawyer, but there is no right of public access.

Nevertheless, we know that in the case of the murdered cardinal, Chapa Bezanilla—Zedillo's special prosecutor—examined the same evidence available to earlier investigators and came to what is essentially the same conclusion: that the men who opened the cardinal's car door and shot him as he pulled up to the curb at the airport were gunmen in the pay of Ramón and Benjamín Arellano Félix, drug traffickers who mistook Posadas for the Arellanos' mortal rival, Joaquín Guzmán, known as El Chapo, or Shorty. (All these parties were actually at the airport, and the gunmen left Guadalajara on a commercial flight.)

The Mexican Church, which was only recently granted the right to speak out on political matters, disputes this version. Some people close to the Mexican Bishops' Conference point out that Posadas was not only prelate of Guadalajara and, earlier, of Tijuana, both of which are major drug-trafficking centers, but also vice president of the Latin American Episcopal Conference, based in Bogotá, Colombia. A couple of these Church people told me that, in their view, Posadas could have been acting as an intermediary between the Salinas government and the Colombian drug trafficker Pablo Escobar. The Church people speculated that Posadas could have relayed an offer from Escobar to Salinas to give him a list of Mexican officials involved in the drug trade in exchange for asylum. Salinas refused the deal, the theory goes, and Posadas was assassinated as an act of revenge. This explanation is full of holes, but then so is the special prosecutor's notion that a tall elderly gentleman in full church dress, who was well known to his parishioners, and who was wearing a rather large cross on his chest, could have been machine-gunned to death because he was mistaken for Shorty Guzmán.

These are, however, simple matters compared with the mess of conflicting versions and senseless arrests and releases that have plagued Chapa Bezanilla's handling of the assassination of Luis Donaldo Colosio. Colosio was shot twice—once from the right, near the temple, and once from the left, through the lower abdomen—on the evening of March 23 last year, as he walked away from the site of a campaign speech in a working-class shantytown in Tijuana. So much is known without a doubt.

A confessed assassin has been held in a maximum-security prison since two days after the crime. He has been identified as Mario Aburto Martínez, but there is, apparently, along with the larger question of whether he acted alone, the question of whether there is one or two of him, and which of the two he is. Or so says Mario Ruiz Massieu—Super Mario—who is now sitting in a jail in New Jersey awaiting extradition hearings but who was undersecretary of internal affairs at the time of Colosio's murder and had access to the investigations. The questions that Mario's statement raised were only a reflection of the suspicion, fear, and cynicism provoked by the murder and by the government's failure to solve it. Should one believe a man who was in charge of investigating his own brother's murder and is now accused of covering up his findings? Is there really a Mario Aburto who is the fall guy and a look-alike who did the shooting? Or is the Aburto now in jail the same man who was wrestled to the ground at the scene of the crime, and was the other one a decoy? Why did Aburto confess so soon after he was grabbed close to Colosio's body holding a gun?

In his single press interview to date, given last April to *Zeta,* a Tijuana magazine, he recanted his initial confession, claiming that he meant just to shoot Colosio in the foot, because the candidate had ignored an old lady who wanted to hand him a petition. "My arm was extended when I tripped and that's how the gun went off" near the back of Colosio's head, Aburto claimed in the interview. But is that in fact Aburto's hand in a three-minute video we have stared at, dozens or hundreds of times, shooting straight up and aiming for the temple with a marksman's speed and energy? And, anyway, who fired the second shot?

The video of the moments leading up to Colosio's assassination, which has been used by the government to build its case, doesn't answer these questions. We see a jostling mob pushing forward, away from the camera. At its center is Colosio, seen from the back and encircled by men who do not face in the same direction— Colosio's security detail, trying to communicate with each other and keep the candidate moving. Or are they acting as conspirators, encircling and trapping Colosio as he tries to push forward, so that the killer can do his work? The faces appear and vanish, Colosio keeps moving, and then the deadly hand appears, aims, and fires. At that instant, the camera swerves, and we do not see the second shot.

The first special investigation of the crime, which was commissioned by President Salinas, was run by Miguel Montes, who concluded after a three-month inquiry that Aburto fired both shots. Colosio, he maintained, did not drop instantly to the ground, face forward, as most people do who have received massive injuries to the brain stem from a bullet wound; instead, he executed a swooping counterclockwise pirouette, and thus received Aburto's second shot from left front to right back, with an upward trajectory. Montes placed three people under arrest—all of them connected in some way to Colosio's security detail. Montes's investigation ended with the announcement that Aburto was a Lee Oswald–like obsessive who called himself an "Eagle Knight" and was associated with a weird Tijuana ultranationalist. He had acted alone, according to Montes's report, but the other suspects remained in jail nevertheless.

The public has seen Aburto three times since the murder. During the equivalent of what is known in the United States as the perp walk, he was shown in a bulletproof glass cage—a sullen-looking, bull-necked young man with full cheeks, a big nose, and a receding chin. Later he was videotaped reading his second deposition and, on a separate occasion, reenacting the crime, and when the two tapes were leaked to television newscasts, we learned that Aburto is strikingly self-possessed, articulate, and intelligent, and was capable of attempting a filibuster of the proceedings by means of legal technicalities, even without the help of a lawyer. We know that he kept a notebook full of scribblings and drawings of pre-Hispanic warriors in his mother's house in Tijuana, because the attorney general's office made them public. We know about his parents and siblings—peasants from Michoacán who migrated first to the miserable shantytowns that ring Tijuana and then to California—because they have been willing to have some contact with the press ever since May of 1994, when they fled to the United States for good to request political asylum. We did not know until very recently that the accused assassin was kept shackled and in solitary confinement while Salinas remained president, and that Aburto now denies any role at all in the shooting.

The prisoner is allowed one ten-minute telephone conversation every week with his family, and transcribed tapes of these conversations were published recently in the newspaper *La Jornada*. In the tapes, Aburto sometimes sounds hazy, and sometimes mad—particularly when he is repeating his obsessive desire that the FBI and the CIA be allowed to take charge of the investigation, because only they will obtain trustworthy results. When he is sounding particularly flaky, his relatives try to make sure that the Aburto on the other end of the line is *their* Aburto. "What was the name of the son of the señora who lived on the other side of La Rinconada?" they may ask, out of the blue. Aburto's parents and siblings take turns pouring hasty messages of love and solidarity into the mouthpiece before handing the phone over to their legal adviser for a few precious minutes of consultation. Aburto sometimes cries. He always protests his innocence. On one occasion he scolds his father, because in an interview the old man said that

Aburto used to meet with other suspects in the weeks preceding the crime. He is very much aware that his family and their adviser are not his only audience. "OK, look, I pretended I was guilty in order to save all of you, understand?" he says. "But what I'm saying, what I've always told you, is that I don't know what happened."

In the first weeks of his investigation, Zedillo's attorney general announced (a) that a bullet picked up at the scene of the crime several hours after Colosio died was a plant; (b) that Colosio did in fact drop instantly to the ground when he received the first bullet; and (c) that therefore there must have been a second gunman, whom he identified as Othón Cortez Vázquez, a member of the PRI who was put on Colosio's security detail at the last minute. Since then, the presiding judge on the case has reviewed Chapa Bezanilla's evidence and released all the suspects Montes arrested. Still in jail is Chapa Bezanilla's second suspect, Othón Cortez. When Othón appeared on television the day of his arraignment, he collapsed three times. Prison authorities attributed the fainting fits to diabetes; Othón's family has medical reports indicating that they were the result of torture. He swears that he is innocent. Chapa Bezanilla's evidence is the too-familiar video, in which Othón can be seen behind Colosio, a split second before the murder, nodding sharply through the dense crowd in what seems to be the direction of the first gunman—as if, the prosecution claims, to say "Now!"

But how could Othón have maneuvered the famous second shot, which traversed Colosio's abdomen from left front to right back, if he was standing slightly *behind* the candidate less than a second before the first shot was fired? If Chapa Bezanilla, who is the source for most of the leaks about the case that find their way into the papers on an almost daily basis, has an explanation, he has yet to put it forward.

The third murder that President Zedillo vowed to solve—that of José Francisco Ruiz Massieu, the PRI secretary-general—is even more problematic, because it involves a dizzying cast of minor characters and henchmen and, more important, because Chapa

Bezanilla has formally accused Raúl Salinas, who is both the former president's brother and the victim's one-time brother-in-law, of ordering it.

José Francisco Ruiz Massieu was sued for divorce more than ten years ago by Adriana Salinas de Gortari after she accused him of being a homosexual, the *New York Times* reported recently. Following the divorce, Ruiz Massieu remarried and maintained his political career and his friendship with his former brother-in-law Carlos Salinas, who, in his last year in office, promoted him over the traditional Party leadership to the secretary-general's chair. Four months later, as Ruiz Massieu was leaving a breakfast meeting with PRI *diputados* in downtown Mexico City, a young man wearing jeans and sneakers stepped up to his car and fired a machine gun. The gun jammed almost immediately, and only one bullet emerged, but it was fatal. The assassin had been told to run toward the nearest Metro station, but he didn't remember where it was and ran the wrong way. A bank guard blocked his escape, and he threw down his gun and surrendered. The date was September 28—almost exactly six months after the murder of Colosio.

The victim's brother, Mario Ruiz Massieu, became an instant hero by taking over the investigation that day. The assassin had originally identified himself as a small-time hoodlum from Guerrero, but under Super Mario's ministrations he soon revealed himself as Daniel Aguilar Treviño, from Tamaulipas, a state known for its seafood and its drug traffickers, and, less widely, for a small but influential group of once-radical—Maoist—politicians close to Raúl Salinas and his powerful brother. It was also the birthplace of another bit player in the drama—a wheeling-dealing, two-timing PRI official and freshman *diputado* named Manuel Muñoz Rocha. It was the obscure Muñoz Rocha, Super Mario revealed, who had hired the team that put together his brother's murder. Unfortunately, Muñoz Rocha vanished the day after the murder. Mario not only failed to find him but failed to answer an all-important question: who hired Muñoz Rocha?

Five months later, in February, Chapa Bezanilla, Mario's replacement as special prosecutor, said that Mario knew the answer and had failed to act on it. Muñoz Rocha, Chapa Bezanilla said, had been acting on orders from the president's brother, Raúl Salinas. Chapa Bezanilla's principal—and perhaps only—source for this version of events is Muñoz Rocha's henchman Fernando Rodríguez González, an undistinguished PRI apparatchik with a shady past who, by his own admission, is the man who hired the flustered murderer and some equally incompetent accomplices. He has changed his story nine times since he was arrested, most recently in an interview with the daily *Reforma*. (Unlike Aburto, he has three comfortable cells in a medium-security prison, and was allowed to talk freely to a reporter.) In the interview, Rodríguez González implicated not only Raúl Salinas but the former president himself, charging that Carlos Salinas used his private secretary to pay the killers. Carlos Salinas's motive for killing the father of his own nieces, as presented by Rodríguez González, makes no sense: "José Francisco begins to pressure Carlos Salinas and the latter gradually gives ground. . . . José Francisco Ruiz Massieu knew a lot about Carlos Salinas de Gortari and his personal accumulation of wealth." Yet a majority of Mexicans who have been polled are more than willing to believe Rodríguez González, because they are willing to believe the worst of a man they also blame for the many ills they have suffered since the economy collapsed eight months ago.

Chapa Bezanilla has not called the former president in for questioning, nor has he come up with strong evidence, or even a satisfactory motive, to justify keeping Raúl Salinas in jail. But there is the singular personality of the former president's brother to consider. Raúl Salinas has been in the shadow of his brother, and has been his accomplice, since earliest childhood, when Carlos, aged four, Raúl, five, and an eight-year-old friend were involved in the death of their twelve-year-old maid, whom they shot while staging a make-believe execution. Though Raúl Salinas has repeatedly sworn to the contrary, there is some slight evidence that at one time he was Muñoz Rocha's friend and political sponsor. The day after Ruiz Massieu's murder, the attorney general's office claims, Muñoz Rocha phoned Raúl Salinas's house and, according to Raúl's bodyguard, spoke directly to Raúl. The two agreed to meet in a Mexico City restaurant, according to a friend of Muñoz Rocha's, who drove him to the appointment. Muñoz Rocha (but not Raúl Salinas) was seen leaving the restaurant that day, September 29, and has not been seen in Mexico again. He is presumed dead.

Mario Ruiz Massieu is accused of covering up Raúl Salinas's putative role in his brother's murder, and is awaiting a decision on the second round of the extradition petition filed by the Mexican government. The first extradition petition filed against him in New Jersey was denied by Judge Ronald Hedges of the Third Circuit, in part because the testimony damning Mario—namely, Rodríguez González's second deposition—was probably extracted by torture. For that matter, Mario himself is being charged here with the torture of several of the people he arrested in relation to his brother's murder, and he is also being asked to explain some deposits he made in a Texas bank between March and November last year, the period he served as deputy attorney general. The deposits total nearly $10 million.

Almost a year has passed since the murder of José Francisco Ruiz Massieu. It has been eighteen months since Luis Donaldo Colosio was assassinated. More than two years after Cardinal Posadas was killed, Chapa Bezanilla has concluded that his death could only have been accidental, because no one would possibly have wanted to do in such a nice man. The attorney general stated in passing, in a sidewalk interview a couple of weeks ago, that the investigation of Ruiz Massieu's murder has also ended. There is no real sense that justice has been done, and at this stage Super Mario is only one of the many characters in a topsy-turvy cast who have turned into villains overnight. He remains unimpressive and undistinguished, as does the Party gofer who stands accused of firing the second shot at Colosio, or the former *diputado* Muñoz Rocha. Yet we continue to be obsessed with these minor players, because they are almost all we know of a murderous tragedy that is playing itself out in a darkened theater while we are kept, craning and anxious, on the other side of the curtain.

In the frightening nightscape, anyone can be a murderer, and one's political allegiance is established according to whom one chooses to accuse. Even master players like Manuel Garza can get lost in this shadow world. The last time I talked to him, I had just come back from the state of Michoacán, where gubernatorial elections are to be held in November. I asked him if he was worried about a certain town in which the conservative PAN, which used to get eight or nine votes at election time, had pulled in ten times as many last August. Garza looked at me benignly for a second and crowed, "But we got two *thousand*! Never forget to do your sums!"

Numbers aren't really the issue anymore, though. What counts is not that Garza can still round up the votes but that someone within his party once tried to involve him in a murder, and that he, in turn, is willing to speculate with a stranger about which of his comrades the real murderer could be. Leaks and rumors have become the accepted form of political infighting, and the ghoulish pleasures of speculation continue to replace informed political discussion—in large part, perhaps, because the attorney general's office continues to equivocate about whether Carlos Salinas will be questioned in relation to the murders of Colosio and Ruiz Massieu. But the leaks and rumors are also evidence that although the PRI still rules, it is coming apart. Even more than the blood already shed, they prove beyond a doubt that the old loyalties that were a system's binding force are dead.

—September 25, 1995

THE RIDDLE OF RAÚL

There used to be no point to following the news in Mexico. Hardly anything ever happened, and whatever did happen was kept out of view by the media, thanks to a healthy sense of respect for the power of the long-ruling Institutional Revolutionary Party, or PRI. This has changed: assassinations, kidnappings, and guerrilla uprisings are featured with frightening regularity, along with bizarre spectacles like that of former President Carlos Salinas de Gortari on a hunger strike, or the extradition of a noted drug trafficker—Juan García Abrego—who had to be stuffed into an airplane like a cat into a bag. The tide of events is such that Mexicans have come to approach their radios and television sets with a mixture of dread and anticipatory relish, and so it was on the evening of October 9 last year, when those of us who turned on the news realized from the flushed, wide-eyed look of the anchorman that events of great moment were about to be announced.

Indeed, the anchorman said, there appeared to be a breakthrough in one of the most shocking of the terrible crimes that have recently undone the stability of the country's seventy-year-old regime. For more than a year, Raúl Salinas, who is a brother of Carlos, the former president, had stood accused of planning the assassination of the PRI secretary-general, José Francisco Ruiz Massieu, a rising star in Mexican politics who had once been married to Raúl and Carlos's sister. President Ernesto Zedillo, Carlos Salinas's successor, had staked his credibility on bringing Ruiz Massieu's murderers to justice, but the evidence presented by the prosecution had so far been scanty, at least partly because of a missing link between the imprisoned Raúl Salinas and Ruiz Massieu's actual murderers. The *diputado* Manuel Muñoz Rocha, a minor politician who was identified from the beginning as the man who orchestrated the killing, could have provided that link, but he had vanished on September 29, 1994, the day after Ruiz Massieu was slain, on a busy downtown street in Mexico City. Now, the anchorman said, there were indications that the remains of the fugitive Muñoz Rocha had been found.

Rain had been pouring relentlessly on the city, and on the police, whom the camera showed to be standing ankle-deep in wet red earth. In an awed voice-over, a reporter identified the spot as a luxurious horse ranch belonging to none other than Raúl Salinas. The government's special prosecutor, Pablo Chapa Bezanilla, unperturbed by the rain and, in his triumph, seemingly oblivious of the mob of reporters, squatted by the excavation site and watched as a white-robed technician carefully set a muddy skull on a plastic tray. The camera zoomed in for a closer look, and the skull stared moodily back. This moment of national contemplation was broken when the anchorman, struggling to hide his perplexity, passed on to his audience what was then only a rumor but would turn out to be a fact—that the remains of the person who might be the long-sought Muñoz Rocha had been found with the assistance of a soothsayer.

So it was that the seer Francisca Zetina, better known by her nickname, La Paca, appeared on the scene. To the degree that she has proved to be deeply corrupt, she can be said to be in some sense remarkable, but she would never have become a nationally recognized figure if she had not become a public joke, and she would not have become even that but for one fact: she is a player in the murder trial of Raúl Salinas, who, as the brother of a former president, may well be the most powerful man ever to have been brought to trial in this country.

Officials did not make La Paca available for interviews after the discovery of the skeleton, but eventually reporters tracked her down at her home, and she gave the first of a series of memorable press conferences. Short, stocky, and pugnacious, the special prosecutor's spiritual assistant was carefully made up, had dressed for the occasion in what looked like an oversized Hawaiian shirt, and had a heavy load of amulets hanging on her chest. She said the attorney general's office had provided her with one of the vanished Manuel Muñoz Rocha's old T-shirts, so she could feel his aura. She said that the bones had talked to her. She said that the association between her and Raúl Salinas actually went back a long way: before she helped to find the body buried on Raúl's land, La Paca declared, she used to give Raúl spiritual counsel. When? On this, and on other matters, La Paca was more reticent. Despite her communion with the bones, she couldn't affirm whether they belonged to Muñoz Rocha. But La Paca could with confidence state that certain vibrations at the burial site led her to the conviction that Manuel Muñoz Rocha "rose up from his tomb to point to his assassin." Reporters made an unconvincing attempt to match her straight face: would La Paca please use her psychic vibrations to inform them whether Raúl Salinas would finally be sentenced for the crime?

As it happened, the discovery of the skeleton took place during the season in which Mexico gears up to celebrate not only the traditional Day of the Dead, when ornate skulls fashioned out of sugar are given as presents and laid on altars, but also a new holiday, Halloween, when children knock on neighbors' doors and ask for a sweet contribution with which to feed *mi calaverita,* meaning "my little skull"—a skull-shaped basket with no lid. As it also happened—and for reasons that were quite beyond the attorney general's special prosecutor to explain—the skull found on Raúl Salinas's property was topless too: by means of an electric saw normally used only by forensic examiners, the top of the cranium had been cut off and turned into a neat lid. Cartoonists had a field day; radio talk shows spoke of nothing but La Paca and the trepanned skull; and the mood of the special prosecutor, Chapa Bezanilla, went from triumph to unease. Why were certain parts of the skeleton that were critical to its easy identification, like the teeth and the fingers, missing? Why had the top of the cranium been sawed off? A mystery.

A mystery, La Paca answered, when pressed. The interviews got more aggressive and openly mocking, and La Paca's fluted vowels turned a little raspy as she grew agitated, but she always invoked higher powers. "It's true that I know more than I should," she would say. "In soothsaying and clairvoyance, I have the advantage over everyone else."

La Paca had friends, prominent among them María Bernal, a stunning woman who had once been on intimate terms with Raúl Salinas. It was probably María who provided La Paca with her careful makeup for the first press conference, and it had certainly been María who had turned over to prosecutors a picture seen around the world, in which María is shown straddling a beaming Raúl Salinas in the bow of a yacht. Long before the discovery of the skeleton, María had testified against Salinas to Special Prosecutor Chapa, who then leaked the famous photograph to the press, along with tidbits of María's testimony. (The trial itself had been declared off-limits to the media.)

María seemed to have access to the darkest secrets of Raúl's heart. She was from Spain and she had loved Raúl Salinas ever since the morning they first met, in Seville, in 1992. Drunk, he had wandered into the store where she worked as a salesgirl and asked for her help in getting cleaned up and dressed in new clothes. She had come to Mexico to be with him, but he had betrayed her by marrying another woman—a lissome member of Mexican high society—the following year. Fortunately, she said in interviews, her contact with Salinas had allowed her to meet La Paca, and the seer had given her the only comfort she had known in Mexico. Then after much doubt—after a year of doubt, to be precise—María Bernal had decided to come forward and testify as to what she knew: that a month before José Francisco Ruiz Massieu was murdered Raúl Salinas had come to her house, drunk white wine ("That's what he liked best"), had sex with her, and told her that he was very happy, because "that son of a bitch"— José Francisco Ruiz Massieu, who since his divorce from Raúl's sister had apparently been on less-than-friendly terms with his former brother-in-law, would soon be dead. María, when discussing delicate subjects like her feelings for Raúl Salinas, kept her eyes cast down becomingly.

Then there was the letter writer. Raúl Salinas was arrested on February 28, 1995, five months after Ruiz Massieu's assassination. María came forward with her incriminating testimony on the following September 11. The skeleton was found on Raúl's ranch on October 9 of last year. A few days later Special Prosecutor Chapa apparently became upset by the persistent questions about the trepanned skull. He apparently also felt that it was time to correct the notion of the part played by the soothsayer in his investigation. Chapa had been in charge of investigating not only the murder of Ruiz Massieu but also that of Luis Donaldo Colosio, the PRI presidential candidate, and that of Cardinal Posadas, the archbishop of Guadalajara, who was killed, Chapa concluded, because someone had confused him with a drug trafficker known as Shorty Guzmán. By the time the skull surfaced, Chapa was in trouble, and the future of his job was in question. Except for the spectacular arrest of Raúl Salinas, Chapa had produced slim results in all three investigations, and his reputation for planting evidence was catching up with him: he had unwittingly videotaped himself—unmistakably skinny, red-haired, and foulmouthed—as he coached Raúl Salinas's key accuser on how to testify, and the incriminating tape had recently surfaced. Although Chapa almost never gave on-the-record interviews, reporters had come to expect leaked documents from him, and now he produced one more. It was a letter, allegedly delivered anonymously to La Paca together with a little map, which she had turned over to the justice system. That, and not some paranormal funny business with a T-shirt, had been her contribution to the discovery of the bones.

The author of the letter that was now reproduced in the media did not sign it, and so for the moment we will call him Anonymous. Anonymous began his letter by describing himself as a patriot. He was writing to La Paca, he added, because he knew—he did not explain how—that she had good connections in the attorney general's office.

Seeking to improve his prospects, Anonymous wrote, he had

looked up an old friend who in the fall of 1994 was working as a bodyguard for Raúl Salinas. That well-connected friend obligingly agreed to introduce Anonymous to his powerful boss, and drove him one day to Salinas's house.

"But, oh, what a surprise!" Anonymous wrote of the moment when he and his friend entered the house. A gory spectacle awaited them. Raúl Salinas was clutching a baseball bat and contemplating a bloody corpse lying at his feet, its head bashed in. Salinas "stared stupidly at me," Anonymous related, and soon the bodyguard told his friend that if he wished to stay out of trouble he would have to prove his loyalty. Accordingly, he and the bodyguard watched a mysterious doctor with a "foreign accent" dismember the body with an unspecified instrument and stuff it into a large burlap sack, which was then buried a few miles away, in a bosky corner of Salinas's horse ranch. This information Anonymous the patriot now felt compelled to share with La Paca—two years after the murder—so that justice might be done.

The revelation that Raúl Salinas might be a bat-wielding assassin all but subsumed the original mystery of whether he was the crafty plotter behind the murder of José Francisco Ruiz Massieu. La Paca buffs—that is to say, the nation—were obsessed instead with a series of subsidiary riddles. Did the bones at the Salinas ranch really belong to the fugitive Muñoz Rocha, the man who was said to have organized the killing of Ruiz Massieu? If not, whose bones were they? Who was Anonymous? Where were the foreign doctor and his terrifying instruments? (And why had it been necessary to saw off the top of the skull in order to fit it into a sack?) But the most perplexing question was not any of these. It was, rather, why such large numbers of Mexicans were willing to go to any lengths, including believing La Paca, in order to convince themselves that Raúl Salinas was guilty of a crime for which Special Prosecutor Chapa had yet to assign a motive. At least part of the answer had to do with the fact that Raúl's brother the former president, Carlos Salinas de Gortari, had become the person most deeply hated by most Mexicans. Indeed, today the entire Salinas family is commonly held to be the most corrupt of all the many groups who ever used the imperial power of the Mexican presidency to accumulate untoward wealth.

The former president's brother Raúl had been in trouble for some time before he was put in jail, and by now the essential outlines of his story have been reviewed often: Raúl and his younger siblings—Carlos, Adriana (the murdered Ruiz Massieu's ex-wife), and Enrique and Sergio, who are less well known—are the children of a former Cabinet minister, who wanted very badly to be president himself. Having failed in this ambition (a new president is handpicked every six years by the standing president, and the elder Salinas never got the nod), he groomed both Carlos and Raúl for the post. Carlos was brilliant, funny-looking, and studious. He married young and plugged away at a series of technocratic government jobs having to do with finance. Raúl graduated as an engineer, but he didn't do much work in his profession. He got a couple of degrees in France, worked on and off for the government, taught at the National University, and dallied with revolutionary Maoist organizations. Like his younger, less exciting brother, he was an expert horseman but, unlike him, he loved to have himself photographed in *charro* costume. He was an acknowledged ladies' man (he has been married three times), and he wrote—and published—some erotic ruminations, such as "My Frequency will be your rhythm / and my tongue / a serpent of wisdom."

All of this is part of the public record. What also appears to be true is that in 1992, four years into Carlos Salinas's presidency, his comptroller general, María Elena Vázquez Nava, warned him that there were strong indications that Raúl was involved in particularly nasty forms of corruption. Raúl was at the time a senior official in Conasupo, a government agency that distributes basic products—grains, milk, and the like—at subsidized prices to the poor. It was alleged that he was skimming large amounts of money off Conasupo sales. In addition, it was said, he was known as Mr. Ten Percent, because it was his practice to charge a commission on government contracts that he helped negotiate. Nor was that all: it was rumored that he had friends and business associates among persons wanted by the law for drug trafficking, including the notorious Juan García Abrego, who was extradited so unwillingly to the United States last year.

An official investigation into Raúl Salinas's finances revealed that in 1991 and 1992 he earned about $90,000 working for the government and during that same period he deposited around $7 million in various Mexican bank accounts. This is not such an unusual sum by the standards of Mexican politics, which, as a close relative of Raúl Salinas recently explained to me, lends itself to business. "It's not that they"—politicians—"are dirty, but that they do business," she said. "They buy land when they know that a highway is going to pass through there. They get privileges. If you're in the government, even if you're only the doorman, you get things. It's normal." But it turns out that during the final years of his brother's presidency Raúl also deposited at least $80 million in various bank accounts in Switzerland. There is no way of knowing whether this scale of profit also falls within the norm, because no other public official of equal standing has ever been arrested for the crime of "undue enrichment" or come forward to declare his wealth, but at this stage the sum strikes most people as excessive.

On December 1, 1994, Carlos Salinas handed over power to his elected successor, Ernesto Zedillo. Although the new president's inauguration speech was for the most part indifferently received, it earned an ovation when he vowed to get to the bottom of the three political murders that had alarmed the country—those of Cardinal Posadas, the PRI candidate Colosio, and the PRI secretary-general Ruiz Massieu.

But Zedillo's priorities changed dramatically in the first few weeks of his government. His first major policy move, an abrupt de facto devaluation of the peso, unleashed the country's most extreme economic crisis of the last seventy years. Five billion dollars in foreign portfolio investment left the country in a matter of days. Interest rates soared, hundreds of thousands of people were forced to default on their loans, and the banking system was threatened with collapse. In the first weeks of 1995, the economy came to a near-standstill.

As the president and his Cabinet were seen to flounder, the possibility that Zedillo might have to resign was seriously discussed at dinner parties and in editorials. A joke made the rounds in February: "What do Easter and President Zedillo have in common? Answer: That one never knows whether they will fall in March or April." But in March the likelihood of Zedillo's resignation suddenly ceased to be a topic of conversation, and one of the principal reasons was a televised press conference given on February 28 of that year by the special prosecutor for the Ruiz Massieu, Colosio, and Posadas murders, Pablo Chapa Bezanilla. Chapa announced that Raúl Salinas de Gortari had been charged with the murder of José Francisco Ruiz Massieu and placed under arrest. No evidence was offered and the motive was not explained. Former President Salinas—who had already been condemned in the media and by overwhelming majority opinion for the economic crisis—immediately went on a brief hunger strike to protest his treatment, and then he left the country, perhaps forever.

Compared with the disoriented-looking former president, who let cameras record his fast and the moment when he broke it with some soup, Zedillo at least looked to be in command. And the revelation that another Salinas was responsible for an evil murder—and of his own brother-in-law—was greeted almost gleefully. It must have been tempting for the new president to believe that the Salinas clan was to blame for so many of the country's ills. Certainly, the country as a whole was eager to believe that this was so.

The murder victim, Ruiz Massieu, was a complicated man, a voracious reader, and a scholarly writer on legal and constitutional topics. He was also, it seems, brutal when he felt brutality was called for. During his term as governor of Guerrero, between 1987 and 1993, dozens of members of the left-wing opposition were murdered, and none of the cases were ever prosecuted. If allegations currently being made in the United States prove true, he had connections to the drug trade. He had an unusual love life: his first wife, Adriana Salinas, the mother of two of his children, divorced him some twenty years ago, apparently because he was gay. But his relationship with President Salinas never suffered as a result of the divorce: Carlos Salinas promoted his governorship and, in 1994—around the time his murder was already being plotted—his command position in the ruling party. As a perceived Salinista, Ruiz Massieu must have borne the brunt of the anger that many of the more traditional members of the PRI felt for the president. In other words, José Francisco Ruiz Massieu did not lack for enemies.

Popular speculation abounds concerning Raúl's possible motives for ordering his murder: Raúl wanted to avenge his sister's honor, which had been sullied by Ruiz Massieu's sexual adventures. Raúl resented Ruiz Massieu's closeness to the president. Raúl and his former brother-in-law feuded over money. Ruiz Massieu had the goods on Raúl's shady business dealings. Perhaps. At this stage, the speculation is only that, because the central question of motive has still to be addressed by the prosecution.

Raúl Salinas was arrested on the basis of the testimony of one witness—Fernando Rodríguez González, a former congressional employee who had reported to the missing *diputado* Manuel Muñoz Rocha. Rodríguez was sentenced to fifty years in jail after he confessed to hiring a gunman and several accomplices, on orders from Muñoz Rocha. Since his arrest, two weeks after the murder, and in the course of nine depositions, Rodríguez has given substantially different versions of his original declaration, but the first ones did not implicate Raúl Salinas.

We now know that the attorney general's office paid half a million dollars to Rodríguez's daughter on February 20, 1995, one week after Rodríguez González modified his testimony again. This time, he implicated Salinas. (It was during this period that Special Prosecutor Chapa accidentally videotaped himself coaching Rodríguez González on his testimony.)

Salinas, who remains in Mexico's only maximum-security prison even though he has not been convicted, was moved only two months ago from a tiny "punishment cell," according to his lawyer. He was kept under constant surveillance, with a light always burning overhead. Rodríguez González was transferred from that prison to the more relaxed Mexico City penitentiary after he changed his testimony, and there he was allowed to give a couple of interviews, in his own suite of cells. He held forth on the subjects of power, corruption, and the evil nature of the Salinas brothers, and mentioned a startling assortment of politicians as coparticipants in the murder plot. (None of them have been prosecuted by the attorney general's office.)

Official records show that La Paca, though she worked harder, received far scantier benefits the following year for her collaboration with Chapa and his employers. It is not yet known whether she was acting on Chapa's orders or on her own initiative, but what is known is that the skeleton that was unearthed last October on Raúl Salinas's ranch had been put there by La Paca's relatives in order to give the special prosecutor something to dig up, and that after Chapa's crew failed to find the bones during a first search La Paca and María Bernal came along to help. La Paca also recruited Anonymous—who, it turns out, was one of her longtime associates and also appears to have been the lover of her sister Patricia—to write the letter about Raúl Salinas, and the horrid doctor and the baseball bat.

We know all this because in December, after long-delayed results of DNA tests on the skeleton failed to establish that it belonged to the missing Muñoz Rocha, President Zedillo fired his attorney general and, with him, Special Prosecutor Chapa. Chapa went into hiding in January, and surfaced only in mid-May, in Madrid, where he was arrested pending extradition to Mexico. He has not responded to a statement issued in January by the office of the new attorney general, Jorge Madrazo, regarding the handling of Raúl Salinas's trial. This statement revealed the first details of some liberties taken by Chapa's people in their pursuit of Raúl Salinas, any one of which—a disbursement of half a million dollars to the key witness against the former president's brother, say—might have sparked a small scandal in a different context. But seen in the proper light, these stratagems seem tame, and even cowardly, because what sent cartoonists and vaudeville comedians into a new frenzy of exultation, what inspired a hit salsa song—"I'll Trade You the Shovel for the Bat"—on a nightly satirical puppet show ("Is that a new Metro line they're digging?"

"No, it's Chapa Bezanilla excavating!"), was the account in the attorney general's investigators' report of La Paca's real dealings with the skeleton.

Long before La Paca became a soothsayer, she had played her own small part in Mexican politics. There are newscast images of her from some fifteen years ago, looking stocky, pugnacious, and disheveled, in the aftermath of a squatters' action she helped coordinate. One of La Paca's sisters, Leticia, told me about it. La Paca and her sisters were among many local leaders spawned by Mexico City's population explosion—men and women who mobilized landless people like themselves to take over empty lots on the spreading outskirts of the city. There was a prescribed form for these confrontations, which was followed in 1982 by Francisca Zetina—as La Paca was still known—and some 5,000 squatters she had helped to muster: they squatted, the government sent in the riot police, and La Paca negotiated. In normal circumstances, the government would have paid off the land's original owners, La Paca would have received some portion of the occupied land to parcel out among her followers, a new shantytown would have been born and baptized in honor of a local PRI politician, and La Paca might then have continued in power, providing votes at election time and crowds for the huge rallies that the PRI stages on patriotic occasions. Leticia Zetina is not explicit about what went wrong in this particular case, except to say that the local municipal authority was asking for too much—a house on the occupied land and a car—in exchange for his protection.

"My sister did a good job," Leticia says. "That settlement still exists, and it is what it is thanks to her. The layout of the streets, the sewage system, were all hers." Despite this, the Zetina family had to migrate once again, right across the city to the *delegación,* or borough, of Iztapalapa. They kept a lower profile after this move, partly because of some run-ins with the son of a man who was for years the most powerful member of the PRI in the neighborhood—a man known as El Líder, who ruled over the garbage pickers of the nearby municipal dump.

The whole Zetina family is eager to avoid the press these days, and that is understandable. La Paca and two of her daughters, her sister Patricia, a son-in-law, and a brother-in-law are in jail on charges related to the skeleton. (La Paca's anonymous letter-writing collaborator is on the lam.) But the laws of Mexican hospitality prevented Leticia, who has not been charged, from turning me away when I called on her on a recent hot, dry day.

The Zetina family lives in a particularly cheerless redoubt of what was once the picturesque village of Santa Cruz Meyehualco and is now part of the dusty, barren sprawl of urban poverty that surrounds much of the capital. La Paca's house, which is two-storied and has chrome-colored window frames, can be considered fancy only by the standards of the neighborhood, but it is indisputably large. When I arrived, Leticia had just returned from her daily visit to her imprisoned relatives and their lawyers, and I walked in with her through the main entrance, which leads directly into the kitchen, and on into a dining room, in which an oversized table barely fitted. Leticia, who looks very much like La Paca, was dressed in her courtroom best: a flower-print blouse, a black skirt, and little black heels, none of which were new. In its own way, though, the family is prosperous: at one point in our conversation we were interrupted by an electronic chirp, and Leticia fished a cellular phone out of a fake-leather handbag.

La Paca didn't renounce politics altogether when she moved here. According to published interviews with some of her neighbors, she sold raffle tickets for a fattened pig and kept the pig. She got into fistfights with other neighborhood women for control of the scarce water supply. And she organized. "When we arrived here in Santa Cruz, this was a disaster too," Leticia recalls. "My sister was the one who started to organize the people, to bring in light and water and everything else. And she did it all with the Party. Now the PRI wants to disown her, but she never belonged to any other party. She's been a PRIista to the marrow all her life. Maybe not everybody likes her in the neighborhood, but I've got people gathering signatures for a proclamation of support for her. And people say to me all the time, 'Just say the word, and we'll go to the jail and hold a rally for her.' But it's not time for that yet."

Leticia insists that La Paca "did the thing"—buried the

skeleton—on Raúl Salinas's orders. According to this version (which is believed by the taxi driver who took me to visit Leticia, and by quite a few reporters covering the trial, among others), the whole episode of the bones, so farcical in hindsight, was devised by Salinas as a way of discrediting the proceedings against him. Be that as it may, neither Leticia nor her sister disputes the facts of the story, which centers on the cemetery of Tláhuac, some distance south of Iztapalapa.

Like the village that Tláhuac once was, the cemetery itself, thanks to eucalyptus trees and whitewashed walls, is modest and pleasant. By the grace of what La Paca would probably describe as karma, it is just a block and a half away from a *consultorio espiritual* that she had set up in the neighborhood, and is also very close to a primary school named in honor of La Paca's very often invoked spiritual protector, John F. Kennedy. Tláhuac proudly remains a traditional community, with a Day of the Dead celebration that seeks to outshine all the others in this still semirural part of Mexico City. Accordingly, local authorities tore down much of the cemetery wall for repairs last September in preparation for the big November festivities. Local law also reflects community traditions: only native Tlahuacans and local residents can be buried there, and among them is the father of the man who last year married one of La Paca's daughters.

The father's name was Joaquín Rodríguez Ruiz, and of all the modest graves in Tláhuac his is among the poorest. Instead of a tombstone, the spot is marked by a rusty iron cross, and his name, along with that of his wife, who died in 1995, is painted in whitewash on a small tin rectangle. Rodríguez Ruiz died in late 1993. An autopsy report—which always includes a skull trepanning—names the cause of death as head trauma. His family never managed to pay for a gravestone, and this eventually turned out to be a great advantage for his son, Joaquín *hijo*.

The younger Joaquín had become involved in mystical sessions led by La Paca and presided over by the spirit of John F. Kennedy—so involved that he eventually married one of La Paca's daughters. He turned out to be an unusually pliant son-in-law, according to the attorney general's report, because on the night of October 3 he equipped himself with a shovel, jumped over what remained of the cemetery wall, and, following his mother-in-law's instructions, removed the few spadefuls of earth that covered his mother's coffin. He removed that coffin, uncovered the coffin that lay underneath, which was his father's, and looted its contents. Prosecutors later found that in his haste he left behind some fingers and teeth. From the cemetery he went to Raúl Salinas's ranch (which is called El Encanto, or the Charm) and there, with the help of the night watchman (who is married to but estranged from La Paca's sister Patricia), he buried his father once more. Six days later, Special Prosecutor Chapa presided over the disinterment of the skeleton, accompanied by La Paca and her friend María Bernal.

Asked about the charges La Paca faces as a result of these events, Leticia, who has a highly personal definition of certain words, explained, "She's accused of conspiracy to commit a crime, but where's the conspiracy? It was all in the family. You can't conspire with your family! And then they say that she's guilty of illegal exhumation. But there wasn't a real exhumation." Joaquín's father, she said, was "completely rotted already, and all they took out was the bones."

I recently had a chance to see, if not to meet, Raúl Salinas, in the course of a trial procedure that was open to the press. There are no jury trials in the Mexican legal system—only a series of presentations by lawyers for the prosecution and the defense, dictated depositions by witnesses, and a procedure called a *careo,* a confrontation between accuser and accused in front of a presiding judge. Public access to the Salinas trial has been severely restricted in the past (and trial records are secret), but last month reporters—without their cameras and tape recorders—were allowed into the maximum-security prison where Raúl Salinas is kept, some forty miles west of Mexico City. The occasion was a *careo* between Raúl and María Bernal, the woman who accused him of telling her after a night of passion that he, Raúl, had decided to arrange for the murder of José Francisco Ruiz Massieu. She had been arrested with La Paca after Chapa's downfall on charges related to the skeleton. The confrontation between María and Raúl promised fireworks, so there was a large contingent of local correspondents from the nearby city of Toluca—reporters who are covering the country's most important trial for the various national media and who are, by and large, undertrained, underpaid, and overworked stringers. Also present in the small, windowless courtroom were Raúl's children from his previous marriages; Raúl's wife, Paulina; and her children by a previous marriage. (Another frequent visitor is Raúl's sister, Adriana, the former wife of the murdered José Francisco Ruiz Massieu. She has defended her brother's innocence all along.)

Although María Bernal is still remarkable-looking—doe-eyed, dark-haired, and Gypsyish—she appeared skinny and unhappy after her weeks in prison. Raúl—mustachioed, partly bald, dark-eyed, and physically fit—looked bored and disgusted after his two years in prison, but he still has about him the self-assurance and the polite cordiality of the Mexican upper class. He cheered up immensely when the judge told him that he could, for once, speak without interference—unless one counts as interference the fact that he had to deliver himself of his declaration slowly enough for a fumbling stenographer to take it all down. Despite this, and in the course of some five hours, he gave a riveting performance. Or, at least, I thought he did. My reading of the event was that Raúl used the hundreds of pages of María Bernal's earlier declarations against him—he had them read into the trial record once again— to establish that their relationship had lasted barely two weeks, in September of 1993 (part of the court record is a letter that María wrote two years later to Raúl complaining bitterly about his long indifference); that he had then hired her to do small jobs for him, for his father, and for his new wife, Paulina (María, in her depositions, freely admits this, and refers to Raúl's wife as *la señora* Paulina); that it was Paulina—who may have known nothing about the earlier liaison—who gave María permission to live in her old house; that Raúl and Paulina fired her at last, in 1994; that shortly before she was dismissed from a new job, a clerical position Raúl had recommended her for, and at a time when Raúl was already in prison, María started making the rounds of the Salinas family, asking for money and threatening revenge in meetings that the family took the precaution of taping.

Raúl also quoted from a letter that María had sent him in prison, which has been part of the court record for months. In it she wrote, "There is a person whose name I can't say, who is pressuring me to testify against you, saying falsehoods." This person was threatening to deport her if she did not comply, María wrote, and in the courtroom Raúl concluded that he could be none other than Special Prosecutor Chapa Bezanilla, who had it within his power to issue a deportation warrant. (In September of 1995, days before she testified against Salinas, Bernal began receiving a monthly allowance for rent and gasoline, and a car, from Chapa.)

Almost all this information was new to me, since it had been reported only glancingly in the local press, and I could imagine what the following day's headlines might be: SALINAS, SPEAKING IN HIS OWN DEFENSE, MAKES A STRONG CASE FOR HIS INNOCENCE. But what Raúl could not prove—since there had been no witnesses—was that he did not tell María after having sex with her (some time after the period in which she complained that he was ignoring her) that his former brother-in-law, "that son of a bitch" José Francisco Ruiz Massieu, would soon be dead. The courtroom dispute between María Bernal and Raúl Salinas over the truth or falsehood of the statement soon degenerated into a shouting match (it was late in the evening by then), and this spat—"a lovers' quarrel"—was the focus of the next day's stories.

It is, of course, entirely possible that Raúl Salinas ordered the death of Ruiz Massieu. The fact that at this stage all the evidence to that effect is tainted, that Special Prosecutor Chapa is now in a jail cell in Madrid, that his boss, former Attorney General Lozano Gracia, has acknowledged authorizing payments to witnesses who testified against Salinas ("The president knew," the former attorney general said in his defense, though the president denies it), and that the new prosecution team has still to come forward with conclusive evidence and a motive does not prove the contrary. But the new attorney general, Jorge Madrazo, and his deputy, José Luis Ramos Rivera, are adamant that the case against Raúl Salinas remains strong. "I am convinced that the payments"—made to La Paca, María Bernal, and Rodríguez González—"did not induce them to lie," he told me in a recent interview.

It is far more likely, however, that Raúl Salinas is guilty of some very questionable financial operations, which could include money laundering on a vast scale, and this is why his murder trial, for all its farcical proceedings, is ultimately not funny at all. There are, after all, at least $80 million sitting in various banks in Switzerland that are still to be accounted for. Raúl insists that he can explain the legitimate origins of his immense fortune, and that only the fear that this information might be used against him "for tax purposes" prevents him from clearing his name immediately. But the office of the prosecutor general of Switzerland, Carla del Ponte, is looking for alternative explanations. After sixteen months of examining the paper trail of the Swiss bank deposits, the prosecutors say they believe that Raúl Salinas de Gortari acquired his fortune by laundering money for Mexico's flourishing drug exporters. The evidence gathered by the Swiss will probably be presented at a trial for undue enrichment that should get under way in Mexico sometime this year.

This new trial of Raúl Salinas should have momentous consequences not only for him but for venerable institutions like Citibank, which handled the transfer of more than $50 million from Mexico to Europe for the former president's brother without, it appears, asking any uncomfortable questions. If Raúl Salinas is indeed guilty of money laundering, a successful trial would go far toward bringing to light the complex international web of legitimate and criminal business interests that makes it possible to reap profits from cocaine. It would allow Mexicans to understand how politics and business became infiltrated and corrupted by the drug trade in a relatively short time. It would bring an unprecedented degree of accountability to the business of politics, by bringing to justice a ranking member of the country's previously untouchable ruling elite.

But the likelihood that this will happen—or, for that matter, that the crime against José Francisco Ruiz Massieu will be satisfactorily explained—looks small, to judge from the goings-on in the trial of Raúl Salinas for the 1994 murder of a man who was not only his former brother-in-law but also the secretary-general of the PRI.

—June 2, 1997

POSTSCRIPT

In Mexico, it would seem, stories never have a final chapter. Raúl Salinas de Gortari, brother of Carlos, remains in prison, having at last been convicted of the murder of his brother-in-law, José Francisco Ruiz Massieu, on the basis of the bizarre assortment of false, coerced, and questionable evidence accumulated by Special Investigator Pablo Chapa Bezanilla. He was sentenced to fifty years in prison in January 1999. The investigation carried out by the Swiss attorney general's office on the source of the $80 million-plus that Raúl Salinas had salted away in Switzerland under various assumed names has been suspended indefinitely. That is to say, the brother of the former president has not yet faced international charges of money laundering, as once appeared imminent. In Mexico, the attorney general's office has accused Raúl of "illegal enrichment," but in four years it has not yet gathered enough evidence to bring him to trial on this charge.

Chapa Bezanilla, who was responsible for the arrest of Salinas, has faded into one or another of the obscure corridors of power where he first achieved his small prominence. Dismissed from his post after the scandal of La Paca and the trepanned skull, he surfaced in Madrid in May of 1997, from where he was extradited back to Mexico with record speed and efficiency. The extradition petition filed by the Mexican government charged, among other things, that Chapa Bezanilla may have induced La Paca and her family to exhume the trepanned cadaver and bury it again on Salinas's property. But it did not accuse him of having bribed the key witness against Salinas with half a million dollars, as substantial evidence indicated. (Of the two charges the latter was by far more serious.) A few weeks after his return to Mexico Chapa Bezanilla was released on his own recognizance and ordered to check in every week with the attorney general's office. The public has never heard from him again.

Francisca Zetina, better known as La Paca, remains in jail for her role in the exhumation of the skeleton of her son-in-law's father. Her friend María Bernal, former lover of Raúl Salinas, also served time in prison but, presumably because she was not held to be directly involved with the exhumation of the corpse, her term was short. She has just published a book on her brief fling with Salinas in which she alleges, among other things, that she and her lover once had dinner with the king of Spain.

Only Mario Ruiz Massieu, the weird and literary-minded brother of José Francisco—the victim of the crime Raúl Salinas was accused and convicted of—appears to have had a sense of dramatic closure. After almost three years under house arrest in New Jersey, and as he was preparing to face trial in the United States in relation to the $9 million he had deposited in a Texas bank, Mario swallowed an overdose of antidepressants, in April 1999. Unfortunately, the suicide letter that was found after his death contained only vague and incongruous accusations against, of all people, President Ernesto Zedillo, and, yet again, not the slightest trace of proof.

THE PESO

The Council on Foreign Relations in a task force report, *Lessons of the Mexican Peso Crisis,*[1] attempts to deal with one of the central questions of the Salinas debate: whether it was he or his successor who led the economy into its present collapse by playing poker with the exchange rate of the peso. The task force members, who represent a broad spectrum of the United States financial establishment, record their disagreement on this question. Salinas, one opinion goes, should have devalued drastically in 1993 or 1994, after it became clear that an overvalued peso was promoting excessive imports and undermining domestic savings. But others feel that Salinas's 11 percent devaluation in March 1994 would have been sufficient "if the government had implemented stricter monetary and fiscal policies." In any event, the argument can be made that the political imperatives of the moment—the need to get the North American Free Trade Agreement approved in the U.S. Congress by the end of 1993, the need to face down the Zapatista rebellion from a position of strength in January of the following year and to move forward and elect a new president after the disaster of Colosio's assassination in March of 1994—made any notion of a radical but stable devaluation almost impossible, because in Mexico devaluation and instability are knitted together in the public mind.

Salinas left Ernesto Zedillo to cope with the decision to devalue

1. Report of an Independent Task Force, U.S. Council on Foreign Relations, 1996.

and with its predictable complications, despite the fact that out-going Mexican presidents traditionally take on this burden to ease the way for their successors. But the Council on Foreign Relations task force agrees that the measure was ineptly handled by the in-coming Zedillo. As a result of the various crises mentioned above, the nation's foreign reserves had sunk from $28 billion in December 1993 to $12.5 billion when Zedillo was sworn in on December 1, 1994, and then to barely $10.5 billion by December 20. On that date, the task force reports, Zedillo broadened the band in which the Mexican peso was allowed to float against the U.S. dollar, in effect permitting a peso devaluation of 15 percent. The market reacted by intensifying speculative attacks on Mexican currency. Hard-currency reserves fell precipitously. Two days later the peso was allowed to float freely against the dollar, triggering a further flight of capital, which in turn precipitated a currency crisis.

In six weeks of panicked trading by the holders of Mexican short-term debt bonds, and by savers who wanted to buy dollars with the pesos in their accounts, the peso sank from 3.9 to 6.3 to the dollar, and reserves dwindled to under $4 billion. To make matters worse, the report continues, investor confidence was shattered by contradictory signals from the Mexican government before and immediately after the devaluation, the government's failure to propose credible measures to rein in domestic demand and tighten monetary policy, and the conspicuous absence of measures to stabilize the value of the peso.

The consequences of these various errors were dire not only for Mexico. Markets and currencies throughout Latin America tumbled, and President Clinton, among others, concluded that the peso crisis could lead to a worldwide economic meltdown. He bypassed Congress and stepped in with an emergency loan package that included $20 billion from the U.S. Exchange Stabilization Fund. That loan, plus the commitment of $27.8 billion from the IMF and the Bank for International Settlements and a belated emergency program drafted by Zedillo's economic cabinet, stabilized the peso; but the measures did nothing to ease the pain inflicted on 90 million Mexicans. Mexican GNP dropped by nearly 7 percent in 1995, and although the devaluation boosted exports, and second-quarter figures for 1996 show that the economy is beginning to grow again, the basic conditions persist that have made the Mexican economy vulnerable to three serious depressions in twenty years.

The Council task force comes closest to a historic judgment on Salinas when it several times restates its predominant conclusion: that poor governments trying to finance development through foreign investment in their financial markets should not consider portfolio investment a stable source of foreign income. As the peso crisis conclusively demonstrated, short-term investors can deplete a country's reserves virtually overnight. Although Mexico received nearly $5 billion in direct foreign investment in 1993, which went to everything from automobile plants to major shares in breweries, it also issued $28 billion in stocks and *tesobonos,* or dollar-pegged treasury bonds. It is largely the fixed investment that remains.

For the short time that the foreign speculative investment boom lasted, Mexican consumer demand—or at least certain sectors of it—also experienced euphoric growth. Restaurants and cellular phones multiplied, as did the import of dozens of brands of breakfast cereals, bottled water, and power mowers. Per capita income grew hardly at all in that same period. Even before the 1994 economic collapse, Mexico's entry into GATT had begun to have serious negative effects on backward local industry, which could not compete with the sudden flow of cheap imports. Private domestic savings moved in "the wrong direction," as the Council task force puts it, from 21 percent of the gross domestic product in 1989 to 11 percent in 1994, and meanwhile the gap grew wider between the extremely poor and the tiny percentage of the population who build jet landing strips at their country houses.

Under the circumstances, it is not entirely clear how so many previously unknown businessmen accumulated the capital that allowed them to bid for banks and buy out transnationals and make the *Forbes* list of the world's richest men. One can ponder, for example, the fortunes and fortune of Carlos Cabal Peniche (currently on the lam, and probably somewhere in Europe), who emerged from some degree of obscurity in his home state of Tabasco to bid successfully first for a bank, Banco Unión, and then for Fresh Del Monte Produce, the worldwide distributor that provides agricultural products for Del Monte Foods. Although it is now known that Cabal Peniche was using the Banco Unión to write himself large loans, the original sources of his fortune and of his fantastically generous donations to the ruling party's coffers in his home state were only questioned when it became apparent that Banco Unión, a small bank, was entangled in a huge case of fraud. In late-twentieth-century Mexico, "inexplicable enrichment" is a very useful term. It is a term generally associated with drug wealth. Raúl Salinas de Gortari, brother of the former president, is at pains to deny that association—disclaimers such as "this is not money or investments which came from or are destined to the drug trade or money laundering" recur throughout a deposition[2] he filed in the course of an ongoing government investigation into the origins of his sizable fortune—but the doubt arises nevertheless.

Drugs—particularly cocaine—became a distinct presence on the Mexican scene during the years when Carlos Salinas was in power. Marijuana had been a significant illegal Mexican export to the United States until bootleg farmers in the U.S. became adept at growing their own. Heroin has been produced for medicinal purposes in some parts of Mexico since the 1940s, and is now being smuggled across the border in much larger amounts. None of this makes much news, but cocaine is different; the amount of money cocaine generates has destabilizing and addictive effects on any society.

By the late 1980s profits from the cocaine trade had grown so enormous that the money was a burden to Colombia's drug exporters. They had already bought most of the available prime real estate and agricultural land in Colombia, made Colombian artists among the most highly paid in the world, and regularly

2. Deposition of Raúl Salinas de Gortari, published in *Época,* July 5, 1996.

flew planeloads of contraband cigarettes home from Miami simply in order to sell them at cost and get the money in circulation. Feeling the weight of what the Reagan and Bush administrations termed a "war on drugs," the Colombian drug barons searched for places outside Colombia from which to operate. Mexico, just this side of its border with the United States, has great stretches of barely populated pastureland, punctuated by the occasional landing field. The various police forces are, by the attorney general's own admission, pervasively corrupt. The military is by tradition a lumbering institution, unleashed during internal security crises—such as the present outbreak of guerrilla activity throughout the country—but otherwise used mainly to incorporate the poorest young Mexicans into society by teaching them to read and giving them a trade. The economy is large, and at the time the traffickers were looking for a place to go, Salinas was selling off the state-owned banks to anyone—like Carlos Cabal Peniche—who was willing to pay two to three times their book value.

There is no question that the Colombians took advantage of all these conditions to transfer a major portion of their transshipping and money-laundering operations to Mexico, or that their easy money contributed to the nineties spending spree. But in *The Mexican Shock*,[3] a series of essays on the events of the last three years, Jorge G. Castañeda goes further; he speculates that the traffickers were actually invited in by Carlos Salinas. A political analyst and columnist, and a long-time opponent of the PRI, Castañeda is the son of a former foreign minister. He grew up in politics and tends to be well informed. He writes:

It is not inconceivable that the regime of Carlos Salinas should have reached an agreement with Mexico's drug traffickers at the beginning of his term, assuring three goals indispensable to both sides and of benefit both to them and (why not say it?) the country as a whole. The first goal of this speculative agreement

3. *The Mexican Shock: Its Meaning for the United States* (New York: New Press, 1996).

was to encourage the drug lords to bring at least part of their money to Mexico, so as to ease the balance of payments. . . .

The second goal would have consisted in ensuring that drug-related activities stop interfering with U.S.–Mexico relations. The profile of the trafficking . . . would not expose or embarrass either the Mexican government (as did, for instance, the murder of DEA agent Enrique Camarena in 1985) or that of the United States. . . .

The third objective of this hypothetical tacit (or perhaps not even tacit) agreement would have been to allow the traffickers— or at least their most modern factions—to proceed with their activities if the first two objectives were met.

As signs of such a possible agreement between Salinas and the drug traffickers, Castañeda cites Salinas's appointment of an attorney general, Enrique Álvarez del Castillo, and of a drug czar, Javier Coello Trejo, both, he writes, "well known to the drug lords." And as possible evidence of the breakdown of that agreement—partly the result of U.S. pressure and NAFTA negotiations—he points to a famous incident in the state of Veracruz in 1991, in which a U.S. customs plane filmed a shoot-out between Mexican troops, drug traffickers, and members of the much-feared Judiciales, or crime-investigating police, which are under the control of the attorney general's office.

Violence involving drugs was no longer simply a matter of settling internal accounts. The state itself came under attack, and even the Church was affected in May 1993, when Juan Jesús Cardinal Posadas was gunned down at the entrance to the Guadalajara city airport. According to the official version, his death was the accidental by-product of a shoot-out between rival drug lords. This version has never found many takers, and Castañeda seems to agree with the widespread belief that the cardinal was, in fact, the intended target of the hit. As one of those who find it difficult to believe that Salinas plotted to murder his political associates, he wonders if the cardinal's assassination, along with those of Luis Donaldo Colosio and José Francisco Ruiz Massieu, were the traffickers' way of conveying their anger to the Salinas administration about an agreement that had broken down and of issuing "warnings that the government, for various reasons, chose not to heed."

The other main path of speculation that does not point to Carlos Salinas as responsible for the Colosio and Ruiz Massieu murders leads to the Institutional Revolutionary Party itself. In the days when Carlos Salinas was popular with the press, it was an article of faith that he and his team of young, cocksure technocrats were despised by the traditional leadership of the PRI. It was said that Salinas, always with an eye to his possible reelection in the year 2000, was gradually abandoning the party structure and setting up his own preparty organization through Solidaridad, the social works program headed by Luis Donaldo Colosio, whom Salinas then designated as his presidential successor. It was also said that some PRI leaders were so enraged by Salinas's decision to let opposition parties take over governorships in three states that they arranged for Colosio's murder. (As head of the PRI, Colosio had been in charge of smoothing the anger of party officials over the opposition's gubernatorial victory in Baja California, the state in which he was later killed.)

There is, of course, no more evidence for these theories than for Castañeda's or any of the others, but even the speculation points to the fact that the PRI is no longer what it was. In the last ten years it has suffered enormous internal divisions (the largest of which produced the presidential candidacy of Salinas's archrival, Cuauhtémoc Cárdenas, in 1988). It has lost power in four states; it has seen its candidate and its secretary-general murdered; it has lost its umbilical link to the presidency; and thanks to a series of reforms in the electoral code, it will not long have such easy access to the kind of money that used to purchase guaranteed victories in previous elections.

In *Bordering on Chaos,*[4] Andrés Oppenheimer, a veteran Latin American correspondent for the *Miami Herald,* reports in intricate

4. *Bordering on Chaos: Guerrillas, Stockbrokers, Politicians, and Mexico's Road to Prosperity* (Boston: Little, Brown, 1996).

detail on how the old PRI used to work, how much money it needs, and how, despite internal hatreds, Salinas looked after the party's interests.

Here, for example, is Oppenheimer's account of a famous dinner in February 1993, in which Carlos Salinas determined to enrich the PRI's coffers. The dinner, attended by Salinas, Genaro Borrego, president of the PRI, and the thirty richest men in Mexico, takes place at the home of the international banker Antonio Ortiz Mena. During the meal, the millionaires josh with the PRI's Genaro Borrego:

> "Well, how much are we supposed to collect?"
> "*Mucho* [a lot]," Borrego responded, smiling.
> "But how much?" the business tycoon insisted.
> "*Muchísimo* [a whole lot]," Borrego responded, drawing laughter from around the table.

An hour later, after pep talks by Borrego, Ortiz Mena, and Salinas himself, the president's great friend, the banker Roberto Hernández, gets the donations going:

> "Mr. President, I commit myself to making my best effort to collect twenty-five million," Hernández said.
> There was an awkward silence in the room.
> "Mexican pesos or dollars?" one of the billionaire guests asked.
> "Dollars," responded Hernández and Borrego, almost in chorus.

Despite some initial balking, by the end of the evening the other guests had agreed to pay up in kind.

Oppenheimer could have paid more attention to the contradictions he has unearthed during his muckraking, for they are central to any judgment about Salinas. This is what he observes in passing about that dinner:

The PRI needed the money badly, and not just because it wanted to avoid an embarrassment during the electoral race over the massive financial help it had long received from the government. After decades of functioning like a de facto government agency that got its money directly from the Finance ministry, the PRI was discovering that the flow of government funds was running dry. A few months earlier, Finance Secretary Pedro Aspe had sent a memo to party president Borrego informing him that the central government would no longer finance the party's needs.

So this was Carlos Salinas de Gortari's contribution to the modernization of his country's politics: to make the party financially independent of the government, and then to extract money from the men who multiplied their wealth through cozy deals with that same government, so that the PRI's candidates could campaign with more funds than ever.

Conditions in Mexico at present seem so awful that it is hard to keep in mind how many changes for the better there have been in Mexican public life. It is the case, for example, that beginning in the Salinas years the press was allowed to do its work with greater freedom than ever before, and that, as a result, newspaper editors and reporters can now begin to see themselves as something other than either paid-off hacks or righteous adversaries. It is also true that whereas in 1988 there was only one party that mattered—the PRI—there are now two hardworking opposition parties attempting to organize the left- and right-of-center votes. In 1989, only 2 million people paid income tax. Halfway into the Salinas administration, 3 million did so.

Taxpayers may see themselves as passive victims of a state, but they tend to respond differently from nontaxpayers; they quarrel, and protest, and demand their rights, and so Mexicans have done, increasingly, over the last few years. A variety of civic organizations represent the newly active citizens: human-rights watch groups, ecology lobbies, election-monitoring associations, consumer defense groups. Alianza Cívica, a citizens' rights group that monitored the 1994 elections, has now set up a program called Adopt an Official to monitor corruption among public servants. It is to a large extent to these new activists—and to the international audience on whose stage he hoped to become a star—that Salinas addressed many of his showier reforms.

Castañeda, and Oppenheimer particularly, do their best to take the positive changes into account, but the overall balance of both authors is pessimistic: there are, they find, no political forces to guarantee that even the best reforms do not go awry. Legislative and administrative reforms have made it much easier for the opposition to control the PRI's spending, for example, but the obvious and urgent concern is whether the PRI is turning to the drug trade as an alternate source of funds. Castañeda writes:

> The string of assassinations under Carlos Salinas suggests that the stagnation of Mexican living standards beginning in 1981 . . . combined with the collapse of traditional ways of settling disputes among the elites had finally brought about the breakdown of the system. . . . For various reasons, [Salinas's] government dismantled or discarded many of the traditional means of settling disputes among elites. Corruption did not abate, of course; it was merely rechanneled toward a few privileged beneficiaries. In PRI jargon, it stopped splashing the way it did before. The distribution of privileges, posts, sinecures, jobs, seats in the Chamber of Deputies, governorships, scholarships, and embassy posts and all the Mexican system's scaffolding of cooptation, corruption, and consolation started shrinking. There are fewer state-owned companies, and those still there are handed over to groups that are ever more closed.

Salinas set about destroying the old system, but the chaos of the last three years is evidence of how little there is to replace it. Violence, so long dormant under the old authoritarianism, is on the rise. Murder is the new way in which disputes get settled among the various factions in power, but it is also the increasingly frequent tool of robbers and kidnappers. And violence is once again in vogue among certain sectors of the left. Last month a new guerrilla organization, the People's Revolutionary Army, made its debut—an agglomeration of various militant groups left over from the 1970s whose name and rhetoric might seem drearily familiar to everyone except the enraged peasants who suffered most under the Salinas regime.

Salinas, Castañeda writes, badly distorted the economy by carrying out his reforms in a way that pleased international bankers but was unsuited to the needs of a weak and poor nation; and the painful difference between Mexico's outward growth signs in the last decade and the life of poverty led by 45 million Mexicans—half the population—would seem to support his claim. Unfortunately, no one has yet come up with a model of development suitable to a poor country with a weak industrial base and scarce agricultural potential, whose population has doubled in the last thirty years, and which is situated next to the world's most powerful economy and most voracious market for illegal drugs. Nor, despite the progress made, do the scaffoldings of a truly representative democracy with which to replace the current system spring up overnight, or even in the six years a Mexican presidency lasts. It may be unrealistic to expect that Ernesto Zedillo will fare better than his talented and deeply flawed predecessor in these respects. But at least one can hope that he will not do worse.

—September 5, 1996

One hardly knew what to stare at: the pointy boots the president-elect of Mexico, Vicente Fox Quesada, has not given up wearing; the anxious minions of President Ernesto Zedillo Ponce de León adjusting the microphone so that the president-elect could address the nation from the official residence; or the Styrofoam panel placed just behind Fox, which had the words LOS PINOS lettered on it, just in case anyone might find it impossible to believe that this scene was taking place—that the first member of the opposition to win a presidential election in seventy-one years was actually standing in the very center of power, the presidential residence of Los Pinos, giving a press conference, assuring reporters that his first meeting with Zedillo had gone swimmingly and that, just two days after the historic presidential elections of July 2, 2000, the process leading to an orderly transition of power next December from one party to another (the first in Mexico's history) was already under way.

Beyond Los Pinos's lovely wrought-iron gates, down in the noisy heart of Mexico City, the party that was once all-powerful, the Partido Revolucionario Institutional, or PRI, was threatening mutiny against its leadership. In another part of town, militants of the leftist Partido de la Revolución Democrática, or PRD, were vowing to stand in opposition to the president-elect no matter how he might try to woo them and their leader, Cuauhtémoc Cárdenas, to his side. Even some of Vicente Fox's former rivals in his own party, the Partido Acción Nacional, or PAN, were barely suppressing their rage at this upstart who had dared to outrun them all. Despite all the background distractions, however, it was, if not the end of the political cynicism that Mexico's long and often dismal history has imposed on its citizens, at least the most cheerful hiatus anyone can remember.

"Politicians are all crooks—in the end, everyone betrays." Mexicans would repeat these words to one another every six years, when the time came to elect a president, a congressman, or a mayor, and then they would either stay home on election day or, with due resignation, take themselves off to the polling station to cast yet another vote for the PRI—which was often enough the only party in the electoral contest. They reenacted this ritual in thirteen consecutive presidential elections, and thirteen times the PRI renewed its grasp on power. Familiarity with the wily old party might have bred disgust, apathy, and corruption beyond compare, but the system offered its own rewards: stability; relative peace; an all-important sense of ritual; undeniable, if insufficient, progress; order; and, above all, no disappointments for a population that had disciplined itself always to expect the worst.

On July 2, that changed. Ten days after the final polls to be made public established that the winner of the election—by a very narrow margin—would be Francisco Labastida Ochoa, the candidate of the ruling party, the people casting the ballots drummed the PRI out of the presidency, out of the majority position in Congress, out of any number of mayoralties, and, for good measure, out of the governorship of the state of Morelos. In Mexico City, a bastion of left-wing opposition to the regime, they even kicked the PRI out of the local legislature entirely.

Standing amid the rubble, all six feet six inches of him, was Vicente Fox, the unlikeliest, least *típico* president Mexicans could have chosen. His grandfather was an American immigrant of Irish background, his mother hails from the Basque country in Spain, one of his favorite holidays is Thanksgiving, his four children are all adopted, he is divorced and, by his own confession, not disposed to womanizing, and his skin is rather pale. He was, before entering politics, the general manager of Coca-Cola in Mexico. And yet, in a country that is overwhelmingly poor, nationalist, distrustful of big business to the point of paranoia, much inclined to the rituals of machismo, and obsessively concerned with its Indian heritage and its revolutionary past, Fox comes across as a kind of latter-day Pedro Infante, the still-mourned matinee idol of countless *nacionalista* musical comedies of the 1940s: hearty, friendly, macho on the outside but with a cream-puff center, and, above all, a man of the people. By contrast with the gestureless politicians in cast-iron suits whom the PRI turns out, almost any other candidate would look lively, but Fox stands out much more. Other Mexican leaders let on that they have read Kundera and love Mozart. Fox states in his published autobiography-by-interview that in his youth—he is now fifty-eight—his favorite cultural activity was watching Olga Breeskin, a violinist known for her skill at playing Hungarian czardas while wearing a bikini. On election morning, waiting for his daughter to vote, he took himself to the nearest *taquería* and wolfed down a couple of tamales and several tacos. Arriving at Los Pinos for his first photo op with President Zedillo, the president-elect sprawled in a formal armchair and showed off his trademark rancher boots, which have the words "Vicente Fox Quesada" embossed on them. "We'll see each other soon, King," he signed off to Juan Carlos I of Spain, after receiving the monarch's congratulations. Who could resist?

But how will he govern? Both the PRI and the leftist PRD, in their attempt to halt the Fox juggernaut, did their best to identify Vicente Fox with the sixty-year-old PAN. The PAN currently has governors in six of Mexico's thirty-one states, all of them in the northern half of the country—where they have ruled, it appears, with somewhat greater efficiency and less corruption than their PRI counterparts. As governor of the state of Guanajuato from 1995 until last year, Fox concentrated on upgrading education and promoting exports to the United States. Administratively, the outstanding characteristic of PAN governments appears to be don't-rock-the-boatism, but when its opponents vilify it, and warn of the hellish future in store for Mexico under Fox, they are referring to the attempts of local PAN governments to intervene in matters generally regarded as private or aesthetic. In Jalisco, the PAN governor has tried to enforce a conservative dress code for women in the bureaucracy; in Coahuila, theater performances featuring nudity were banned.

The PAN has a complicated history: it was the first strictly political organization to defy the authoritarian regime born of the Mexican Revolution, and to defend religious—or, specifically, Catholic—freedom. (The descendants of the revolutionaries who drafted the 1917 Constitution forbade religious education, deported foreign-born priests, and denied others the right to wear cassocks, vote, or speak in public.) The PAN has often taken brave stands against the regime's ingrained corruption and not infrequent brutality—in 1968, for example, it was the only party in Congress to speak out against the massacre of hundreds of students during a peaceful protest demonstration. But the PAN has also been identified for many years with the more probusiness and intensely conservative crusaders in a certain sector of the middle class that prefers to think of itself as white, rather than mestizo, and with the more extremist tendencies in the Catholic Church, like the Opus Dei. Last September, when Vicente Fox waved about a standard with the image of the Virgin of Guadalupe, liberals shuddered. (The gesture didn't seem to affect Fox's popularity one way or the other: Mexicans are known for their devotion to the Virgin, but they are less partial to the Church and to churchy politicians.)

Vicente Fox is probably as unlike his fellow PAN politicians as he is unlike his predecessors in Los Pinos. He is neither self-effacing nor an ideological scold, and, whereas other PAN candidates have given the impression that running hard for office strikes them as vulgar, Fox loves to win. He is nominally opposed to abortion, though he appears to hold no strong views on the issue. He is, however, extremely keen on microloan programs, which target women, primarily, for low-interest loans of amounts as small as $50 to start up a business (dressmaking, shoeshining), and which have been very successful in poor countries like Bolivia and Bangladesh, where the idea started. Fox seems to like women.

He has no particular need to insist that he will strive for equal gender representation in his Cabinet, and yet he has. Mostly, Fox seems either unpredictable or infinitely pragmatic; he is capable of offering contradictory views on a given subject in the course of a single interview, and this quality is both his weakness and, one hopes, his strength.

Three years ago, Fox, having decided that the PAN party structure would not necessarily name him its presidential candidate, or have the energy to push him toward the finish line, started his own campaign organization and put it on the Internet; he called it the Amigos de Fox. He recruited two former members of the militant left, Jorge Castañeda and Adolfo Aguilar Zinzer, to be his political Henry Higginses, and to help him build a broad-based coalition with the left that would insure him a majority vote. (Castañeda and Aguilar Zinzer, intellectuals with many years of experience in political parties and in Congress, did rather well on the first count and less so on the second.)

Fox also hired three prominent Mexican political consultants and Dick Morris, the former adviser to Bill Clinton. With their advice, Fox made a key decision: to start campaigning two years ago not only for his party's nomination but for the presidency, running television ads about himself while the field was clear— "Before all the election clutter started," as Morris put it. It meant stepping ahead of all the other PAN party hopefuls, and raising serious money, but Fox never questioned the gamble.

The consultants' canniest decision, according to Morris, was to leave Fox's image alone. Nothing in Fox's speeches allows one to think that he has dazzling proposals to make about globalization, say, or the North American Free Trade Agreement, or Mexico's macroeconomic program or its agricultural development. But, by unleashing Fox's outlandish personality on the television screen— warts and boots and all—his advisers conveyed the idea that Fox was not only almost compulsively honest but also an original.

I asked Morris about what was generally considered Fox's worst moment in the campaign—one Tuesday in May when he refused, on live television, to accept Cárdenas's and Labastida's decision to hold a postponed debate among the three candidates the following Friday. *"Hoy!"* Fox insisted for about twenty minutes, while Labastida and Cárdenas tried to explain to him why "today" wasn't practical. *"Hoy!"* he repeated, stabbing the table with his finger for emphasis while his opponents smirked. To some of us, he came across as more than stubborn—slightly mad, and something of a fibber. (He claimed, inaccurately, to have a letter from the head of Mexico's largest television network guaranteeing him live coverage if the debate were held immediately.) The following day, Fox's campaign team was in despair, but Morris asked to see a copy of the tape. "I loved it," Morris told me. "I thought it was neat, this guy going *'Hoy! hoy! hoy!'* " Less than a week later, the campaign was running spots of Fox at meetings in which the candidate asked, "When is change going to come to Mexico?" and the crowd roared back, *"Hoy!"*

The decision to take advantage of the *"Hoy!"* moment might have been his American adviser's, but Morris, a man not known for modesty, stressed to me that the campaign was not "run by consultants." It was run by Fox. "He was present at all our meetings, and he took the lead." Later, Morris put it another way: "It was sort of like writing a script where all you have to put in is 'Enter Harpo' and then 'Exit Harpo.' You couldn't script a guy like Fox to save your life. You just had to get out of the way and let Fox be Fox."

The answer to the question of whether Vicente Fox really belongs to the PAN came less than a week after the election. In a long interview with the leftist daily *La Jornada*—Fox is still courting the left—he declared, "In the end, the one who governs is Vicente Fox, not the PAN! The one who screws up or makes mistakes is Vicente Fox, not the PAN!" And then, displaying a fondness for American-style self-help literature, he finished up, "It's like that book *Hold Them Close, Then Let Them Go.* [The Party] gives us values, principles, ideology. . . . Then it has to let us go." (Prudently, the chairman of the PAN replied the next day that "the Party must not invade . . . the areas . . . that legally and politically correspond to the chief executive. . . . In turn, the government . . . must not invade the spaces that belong . . . to the Party.")

What Vicente Fox represents remains a mystery. The bad Vicente Fox—who gets most of the attention—is, conceivably, the one that poor, frustrated, and humiliated Mexicans were happy to vote for: the ignoramus who makes faces at his opponents in the course of a simulscreen confrontation, the zealot, the Angry Man. He is also the waffler who sang the praises of bankers at a national bank convention, calling them *colegas,* and then, four days later, accused bankers of "serving themselves with the biggest spoon."

The bad news is that although the good Vicente Fox is reassuringly calmer, more tolerant, and more pragmatic than his evil twin, he is still not a very interesting political thinker. One can comb through his speeches and his autobiography, probe in interviews, and find little more than nostrums. "Real democracy is achieved through transparency, honesty, and government accountability," he says. And "Congress is obliged to exercise a severe and timely vigilance on the executive branch." The point is that because these principles are straightforward, old-fashioned, and democratic, and because they are stated simply, in the seven-step managerial language Fox acquired in his earlier career, in Mexico they sound fresh and wonderfully practical.

When I interviewed Fox a few days before the elections, I found him understandably tense, tired, and harassed but remarkably articulate and unguarded. And also punctual: as he keeps informing us, Fox is a manager, and he manages his time well, delegating tasks, making important decisions quickly, and sticking to a schedule. His adversaries accuse him always of an excessive fondness for the United States—the term used, by Cárdenas and others, is *vendepatria* (fatherland-seller)—and it is true that in his career path, his can-do spirit, his love of inspirational literature, and that peculiar approach to public speaking that consists of making simple, forceful pantomime gestures, as if addressing the slow, Fox seems very American. But I found his views on relations with the United States similar to those of his opponents, and, if anything, more forthrightly expressed.

I asked him, given all his denunciations of Mexico's most recent rulers, including Carlos Salinas de Gortari, what he would change about the North American Free Trade Agreement, which Salinas negotiated, and he said that, in fact, he saw it as a good starting point. "But as an instrument it is too limited for the kind of neighbor relations we can build. . . . In the future the central element has to involve narrowing the gap in income between Mexico and the countries to the north. Here a worker earns five dollars a day; there, he earns sixty. That would be a measurable goal which would bring with it the solution to our current problems of migration and unstable frontiers. Because for the United States the problem of continuous middle- and long-term growth has to do with migration; the United States needs immigrants in order to continue growing at its current rates. So if we face this problem jointly, in forty years I can see us enjoying a truly equal relationship."

I asked him how he thought the two countries could collaborate on the drug question, and he answered that, since no single country can solve the drug problem, what was needed was multinational agreements with precise and shared goals among all concerned countries, rather than the current system, in which the United States grants itself the role of certifying progress by others as a condition to aid. "The United States could, for example, meet certain goals in terms of detecting and detaining drugs at its borders," he said. "Because I can't understand how tons and tons get through every day and they can't find them. They could make a commitment to reducing consumption and the size of their market by a certain amount each year, and show results in terms of the detection and punishment of major drug distributors within their borders. Of course, the drug-producing countries would have to meet obligations as well: Mexico would have to reduce the amount of drugs produced or transshipped here, and all of this could be supervised and certified by a multinational group; we could invite the OAS [the Organization of American States] for example, for this task."

Repeatedly, his answers to an assortment of questions about national politics came back to the need for building coalitions, not only in order to win the elections but to govern effectively. "No single party in Mexico can govern, represent, or lead the entire country today," he said. "The PRI is already a minority in Congress. The PRD has an electoral ceiling of twenty percent, as the left does in general all over the world. With that scenario, 'us' has to be a consensus, as it is in Chile, Italy, or Spain. We need alliances." And later: "I know what a phenomenal challenge it is to govern Mexico, with the amount of backed-up needs it has accumulated. . . . I want to share power and responsibility in solving them. I don't want to face all these problems alone!"

In the days since the election, Fox has embarked on a headhunter search for candidates. He has also presented a project to modernize the country's dysfunctional legal system, and proposed meetings with the other contenders for the presidency. Neither Labastida nor Cárdenas has accepted thus far.

Fox's obsession with coalition building and agreements comes out of a keen awareness that the PAN too is a minority in Congress, and that he himself got only 15 million votes—considerably less than half of the 35 million votes that were cast, and only 2.5 million more than the PRI got. (Mexico has a total population of 96 million, of whom about two-thirds are of voting age.) In the good old days, the PRI could have made up the 7 percent difference easily. Indeed, on election day, I visited towns and villages with significant numbers of Otomí and Mazahua Indian inhabitants—most of them poor and many illiterate—and watched the PRI try to work its magic at the polls as usual. PRI operatives stood in groups a few feet from the polling booths and glared at the voters, or, conversely, shook their hands and greeted them familiarly by name. But the real change in the country had actually taken place long before election day, because this time around the PRIistas could not perform some of their best-known acts of prestidigitation: the *ratón loco,* or crazy mouse, in which a group of hired voters was sent to one polling station after another to cast ballots for the PRI; the *urna embarazada,* or pregnant urn, in which a ballot box lost its way on the road to the counting station and was found again, mysteriously fuller of PRI votes than when it started out; and the *voto comprometido,* in which even before voting day the Party was able to tally millions of votes that had been promised—sometimes in writing—by labor and peasant unions, small businesses, street vendors, and the garbage pickers of every town.

Some of the credit, at least, for the new rules of the game must go to Carlos Salinas de Gortari, who became president in 1988, in elections that were probably the most crooked in Mexico's history, and who, once in power, undertook the constitutional and electoral reforms that allowed Vicente Fox to win. He granted the children of immigrants equal rights with second-generation Mexicans, which allowed Fox to run for president. He normalized relations with the Church, which helped remove the stigma from the PAN. And his administration created something called the Instituto Federal Electoral, which by the time Ernesto Zedillo was elected, in 1994, produced reasonably unfraudulent results. The first task of the IFE, as it is known, was to eliminate the *ratón loco:* in the months before the 1994 elections, would-be voters were encouraged to register with their local IFE committee and obtain a credential with their photograph on it. On election day, card carriers had their names checked against a computer printout of local voters before being allowed into a private, curtained polling booth. Afterward, they had their thumbs smeared with indelible ink. In Mexico, these simple measures were revolutionary. As president, Zedillo separated the IFE from the Ministry of the Interior, making it autonomous.

This year the IFE spent almost a billion dollars not only to guarantee fair elections but to convince voters that they were so. The IFE also supervises the amount of campaign money each party receives (it is directly proportional to the number of votes won in the previous election), the amount of media coverage candidates get, and its tone.

José Woldenberg, the cigar-smoking head of the IFE's multi-party governing body, can't help sounding a little mournful at the immense outlay, even though he knows it is the best investment the country could make. "There was such a level of mistrust that we couldn't ask for volunteer poll supervisors," he told me when I talked to him just before the elections. "We had to have a draft; we sent letters to everyone born in April, and out of those 5.8 million people we drew four hundred and sixty thousand booth presidents, secretaries, and supervisors." Woldenberg, a remarkably sanguine intellectual, began as the left's representative in the IFE council. In recognition of his unflagging levelheadedness, he emerged two years ago as the consensus candidate for the top job.

The change in the country's electoral politics had actually begun long before the creation of the IFE, however. It was easy to forget in the glow of election day, for example, that whereas in 1988 the opposition had barely thirty-nine small mayoralties to its name, twelve years later half the population was governed at the local level—mayoralties and governorships—by the PAN and the PRD. Honor for much of this sea change was due to Cuauhté-moc Cárdenas, who in 1987 abandoned the PRI after he realized that he was not going to be its presidential candidate. (His father, Lázaro, is revered as the PRI's principal creator.) Running against Salinas, and then again, in 1994, against Ernesto Zedillo, Cárde-nas carried on a long, brave campaign against the PRI's corruption and its new neoliberal policies, and in favor of the nationalist, sta-tist, *mexicanista* beliefs of the original PRI.

But there were many others. There was Luis Álvarez, a veteran leader of the PAN, who in 1986 went on a hunger strike that lasted forty-one days after the PRI blithely stole his party's victory in the gubernatorial elections in Chihuahua. There was Dr. Sal-vador Nava, from the central state of San Luis Potosí, who, in 1991, already mortally ill, embarked on a long protest march toward Mexico City after President Salinas tried to impose a PRI governor on his state. And there was the group that coalesced around Octavio Paz and his magazine, *Vuelta,* which led the cam-paign among non-leftist intellectuals for representative, electoral democracy.

Perhaps no party or group fought as hard, though, and on so many levels, or paid as high a price, as the candidates and leaders of the once-militant left. Sergio Aguayo, a youthful-looking, square-shouldered, dark-skinned congressional candidate of fifty-three, started fighting many years ago. He is a survivor of a 1960s street gang known and feared in the city of Guadalajara as *los Vikingos,* and one of the central acts of his campaign this year was to return to his neighborhood of San Andrés to meet with other survivors, whom he had not seen since he left, thirty-one years earlier. Aguayo had not known what kind of a reception to expect. In the group of paunchy, graying men, there was one with a thick gold chain around his wrist, several in suits, and one in a Zapatista T-shirt and a beret. Most were members of Cárdenas's PRD, some of the PRI. But in the sixties, when they were young and waging war on PRI-sponsored thugs who controlled the local high schools and, above all, the local university, they were all radicals. "Anyone who wanted to participate in student politics had to become a vassal of the Federación de Estudiantes de Guadalajara," Aguayo recalled before his fellow ex-Vikingos. "And our tragedy was that we refused to be vassals, or to ask permission." The sixties were a rebellious time anyway, and, in Aguayo's words, all over the country poor working-class kids like him, who were expected always to say yes, decided to start saying no. With his chums, Aguayo got into fights on a regular basis, before going home to feed the cows and chickens his mother kept on the outskirts of San Andrés. When she asked, he told her the black eyes and bloody head wounds were the result of a fall. In reality, there were times when the Vikingos' rivals in the Federación tied Aguayo to a pole and took turns beating him on the head.

In Aguayo's telling, this was a happy time: practicing the twist and the cha-cha-cha with the local girls at the corner hang-out, studying, emerging victorious from phenomenal street wars, gradually acquiring blurry notions of politics and class struggle and facing down the PRI student thugs with increasing success. Then came the student rebellion of 1968, the student massacre in Mexico City, and the beginning of organized government repression against the Vikingos. One day, Chucho, the Vikingo Aguayo loved best, took him aside. "There's a rifle waiting for you," he said. It was Aguayo's first contact with the numerous guerrilla

movements that had sprung up in the wake of the student massacre, and which had now established a foothold in San Andrés. "I
don't remember if I hesitated two days or two months," he said
now. "But I knew the weapon wasn't for me. I knew I wasn't a
coward, but I wasn't convinced by the idea of guerrilla struggle."
By then, local death squads were circulating a list with his name
on it. Aguayo felt lonely, vulnerable, confused, and guilty. At the
age of twenty-two, he left San Andrés for good.

Dozens of Vikingos who chose to join the guerrillas were killed
in the years that followed, while Aguayo got a degree in international relations in Mexico City and tried not to think about his
former friends. (He was, however, picked up at one point by the
police and interrogated, as he says, "in the fashion of the day.")
After his friend Chucho was arrested in the seventies and forced to
sleep upright in his cell, because his interrogators had broken all
his ribs and he could neither sit nor lie down, Aguayo became
involved with the Mexico chapter of Amnesty International and
helped set up one of the country's first human-rights commis-
sions. Like much of the left, he felt during that time that electoral
politics was a corrupt and corrupting activity, and, like much of
the left, he changed his mind when Cárdenas ran against Salinas
de Gortari, in 1988. (Many believe that without the PRI's scan-
dalous manipulations, which included shutting down the computerized vote-tallying system for forty-eight hours, Cárdenas
would have won.) Three years later, in preparation for the 1994
elections, Aguayo and a group of fellow activists founded a citizens' volunteer organization, Alianza Cívica, to insure that Cárdenas, who was running this time against Ernesto Zedillo, would
get a fair vote.

Running for office himself seemed a logical next step to Aguayo:
once the right of the opposition to obtain the presidency had been
guaranteed, it was time to stir up Congress with some citizen
activism. If elected, Aguayo told his listeners, he would try to join
the congressional human-rights oversight commission, which had
languished in recent years, and give it some teeth. But on this July
evening in San Andrés, as in every meeting I attended during

Aguayo's shoestring campaign, his friends, collaborators, and admirers were not completely convinced. Politics, they said in so many words, is for politicians, and politicians are all crooks. Aguayo's leftist audiences were obsessed with purity, and still saw militancy—which seeks to vanquish adversaries—as far superior to politics, which seeks to compromise with them. "We'll be with you even if you win," one of his former Alianza Cívica collaborators told Aguayo at the end of a campaign meeting. And in San Andrés a former Vikingo shouted out, "Just don't do anything with *la reacción*! Anything is better than their winning."

If the left is small in terms of numbers, it is influential in public opinion, and many of the most skilled and dedicated people now in academia, public office, or nongovernmental organizations—people Fox would like to count on—are leftists. They can either provide greater scope, experience, and variety for Fox's administration or hobble it. Now the left is in disarray, but its various warring factions agree on one thing: they will not help Fox rule.

The PRD's announcement of this decision provided a spot of cheer for PRIistas during the worst week in their history. They have been kicked out of power, mocked, called corrupt and decadent, and humiliated by their president, Ernesto Zedillo, who, determined to insure that the election stayed fair to the very end, preempted any possible mutiny by the PRI by going on national television to acknowledge his party's defeat even before the IFE had given its definitive statement. The PRIistas are out of work, many of them—at least for the next six years (or could it be forever?)—in debt, and scared. They are the descendants of a triumphant revolution—or, at least, of a triumphant faction of it—and their unswerving loyalty was always sustained by the vital link between the state and the Party, with the president as the kingly leader of both. In the days since the election, they have cast off the armature of silence that once guaranteed the PRI's "monolithic discipline," and have vented their rage at Zedillo. In their newfound loquaciousness, PRIistas are denouncing all the recent presidents—Miguel de la Madrid, Salinas de Gortari,

Zedillo—and also their cohort of *perfumado* technocrats for their obsession with number crunching and the foreign debt.

When I heard these denunciations, I decided it was time to call on Manuel Garza, affectionately known to all as El Meme. I last talked to Meme Garza before the 1994 elections, when he was, against all conventional wisdom, predicting a landslide victory for his party's lackluster candidate, Ernesto Zedillo. He had explained then the PRI's deep roots in traditional Mexican ways of organizing power and revering authority, and he had helped me understand in a new way the old system of *acarreados*—members of the poorest sectors of the population, such as *campesinos* or garbage pickers, who were traditionally trucked in to voting centers on election day, or to public demonstrations of support for PRI hierarchs. They were, Garza argued, a means of making manifest local PRI leaders' organizing ability and strength.

It has been a long time since Garza has held any kind of government job (he tends to act as a consultant, and will take a seat in Congress for the second time this September), but he is a busy man. His secretary called twice to postpone our meeting—he was in an emergency session of the PRI's Central Committee, then he was called off to a meeting with Zedillo's closest adviser—and when we finally chatted, in his comfortable office, not far from PRI headquarters, vice ministers and business leaders interrupted on the phone. I could see how anyone suffering from postelection doldrums might want to talk to El Meme, or just say hi. He is by temperament so bubbly and by long training so wise that anyone would leave his company feeling that victory for the PRI was not only possible again but imminent. Nevertheless, Garza was clearly struggling to overcome his anger and suffering. In the past, he had always reminded me of a sleek, well-fed beaver, but on this recent morning he looked ruffled, and definitely older.

The causes of his party's defeat were clear to him. "Politics was replaced by ad-mi-nis-tra-tion"—he rolled out the syllables contemptuously—"and administration is something technocrats know how to do. Dinosaurs"—he applied the mocking term others use for traditional PRIistas to himself—"do the spadework of politics. That is why we are thought despicable."

He turned to a folder full of charts with voting trends and statistics, and explained how he had outlined the campaign strategy to his party. "I said, 'First, we go after our own. Then we go after the ones who don't belong to anyone. And lastly we go for the ones who are going to vote against us.' And, instead"—he bounced back and forth to emphasize the magnitude of the *tecnócratas'* incompetence—"they decided that the thing to do was to go chasing after *civil society!*" By this, he presumably meant a useless bunch of electoral do-gooders.

When I asked El Meme about Zedillo's decision to preempt Labastida's concession speech, he looked tired for a moment. "I don't doubt Zedillo's honesty," he said. And then, for the first time since I've known him, he looked defeated. "At the age of sixty-seven, I'm going to have to struggle to learn how one uses liberty. I'm a politician who was brought up on discipline as the binding element for all the forces who coalesce around an ideal, or an objective . . . just like a soldier! Orders are obeyed. At the most, one had the right to ask for an explanation to an order one couldn't understand." He shook his head.

But Meme Garza would not be Meme Garza if he were capable of more than a few seconds' despondency, and soon he had picked up his didactic, optimistic narrative thread again, this time with a little parable. "I come from cyclone country—Tamaulipas, on the Gulf Coast," he told me. "And every so often a cyclone wipes us out, and the next morning the ranch hand comes rushing over to say, 'What do we do? We've lost everything!' And we say, 'Let the waters subside.' Then, when the land has dried out a little bit, we take a reconnoiter and see if the cattle have drowned, if the fences are down, if the ditches are silted up. If we suffered a lot of damage, we start fixing it. But maybe we didn't come out so badly! In that case, we go look up our neighbor and see if he needs a little help."

I felt I had learned enough from Manuel Garza to take his meaning: if the PRI was suffering, Cárdenas's PRD was much worse off. It had lost congressmen, city council members, and also, as a result, significant federal budget allocations. But perhaps it could now be persuaded to give up its enmity toward the PRI—

the two parties have much more ideologically in common, after all, than either one does with the PAN or Vicente Fox. Perhaps the PRD could learn to wield its 52 votes in the lower house in concert with the PRI's 209, preventing the PAN, which has just one less seat in the lower house than the PRI, from ever having a majority. Perhaps, together, they could make the PAN cry uncle.

There is something endearing about Vicente Fox's by now legendary stubbornness, even when it reaches nutty extremes. (*"Hoy!"*) He will need all the doggedness at his command to get through the four and a half months remaining until his inauguration, and then even more for the following six years. It is hard to know which of this country's problems requires a more urgent solution—the impoverished, backward, and overextended educational system, the desertification of more than a third of the agricultural land, the violence and corruption generated by the United States's inexhaustible preference for illegal intoxicants, the lack of employment opportunities for a population that almost doubled in size in the last thirty years—but there are no easy fixes for any of them. The way things stand now, the new president of Mexico will not be able to rely on a loyal opposition to help approach these issues, and even in the most optimistic scenario he will not get much assistance from his party either, simply because it is still too small for the country it has now been elected to govern. Nor does the citizenry have much reason to trust the odd mustachioed fellow they have just elected. He first came to their notice twelve years ago—the year the PRI shut down the voting system—when, as a congressman, he stepped to the podium, took a couple of paper voting ballots, tore holes in them, looped them over his ears, and strutted about protesting Salinas's victory. His learning curve since then has been phenomenal, but, even at his conciliatory, statesmanlike, postelectoral best, he remains very much an unknown, untested leader.

But at least there is one problem the country now doesn't have, and that is how to persuade a party that had remained in power for a few decades too many to take a break. When I called the human-rights activist Sergio Aguayo the night after the elections to find out how he'd fared in his congressional race, he greeted me enthusiastically. "Isn't it wonderful?" he asked, and, assuming he'd won, I answered that I was delighted to congratulate him on his victory. "What, me?" he said. "Oh, no, I lost. But the PRI lost, too, and that's just marvelous."

—July 24, 2000

ALSO BY ALMA GUILLERMOPRIETO

*"[Guillermoprieto] burrows unerringly beneath the skin of
complex societies."* —The Boston Globe

THE HEART THAT BLEEDS
Latin America Now

In this transcendent work of vivid reportage, Alma Guillermoprieto
gives us indelible snapshots of contemporary Latin America, offering
insightful variations on the region's recurring themes: violence and
inequality, the faithlessness of leaders and the stubborn faith of those
they lead. With profound sympathy and a novelist's eye for detail,
Guillermoprieto talks with earnest assassins in Colombia and enterprising garbage pickers in Mexico; reveals the eerie logic behind the
fanaticism of Peru's Shining Path guerrillas; and unravels the web of
scandal surrounding the presidential elections in Argentina. *The
Heart That Bleeds* is journalism from the inside out—a work that
probes beneath the daily news to capture history both hidden and all
too real.

Current Events/0-679-75795-3

SAMBA

Samba—that sensuous song and dance marked by a driving, raptur-
ous beat—is for the people of the villages, or favelas, surrounding
Rio de Janeiro their most "intense, unambivalent joy" in the face of
poverty, violence, and racism. Every year, after months of fervent
preparation, each of the favelas sends a samba school to compete in
Rio's renowned Carnival parade. Alma Guillermoprieto lived for
one year in the favela Mangueira, joining its famed samba school.
Here is an exuberant account of her experiences, as well as a cogent,
lucid examination of the history and culture of black Brazilians, and
of the social and spiritual energies that inform the rhythms and ritual of samba.

Travel/Sociology/0-679-73256-X

VINTAGE BOOKS
Available at your local bookstore, or call toll-free to order:
1-800-793-2665 (credit cards only).